The Spe[illegible]ople

The Speckled People

HUGO HAMILTON

TED SMART

The author would like to thank Colm Tóibín and Eileen Ahearn for their generous help and encouragement with *The Speckled People*. Many thanks also to Colum McCann, Joseph O'Connor, Seán Ó Riain, Hans Christian Oeser, Gerald Dawe, Leo Lecours and John Smallwood. The author also wishes to acknowledge the financial assistance of Aosdána and The Arts Council in Dublin, as well as the financial support and hospitality of DAAD in Berlin and Künstlerhaus Schloss Wiepersdorf in Brandenburg.

This edition produced for The Book People Ltd,
Hall Wood Avenue, Haydock, St Helens WA11 9UL

This paperback edition first published in 2004
First published in Great Britain in 2003 by
Fourth Estate
A division of HarperCollins*Publishers*
77–85 Fulham Palace Road
London W6 8JB
www.4thestate.com

1 3 5 7 9 10 8 6 4 2

A catalogue record for this book is
available from the British Library

ISBN 0 00 770542 5

Typeset by Palimpsest Book Production Limited,
Polmont, Stirlingshire
Printed in Great Britain by
Clays Ltd, St Ives plc

'I wait for the command to show my tongue. I know he's going to cut it off, and I get more and more scared each time.'

Elias Canetti

One

When you're small you know nothing.

When I was small I woke up in Germany. I heard the bells and rubbed my eyes and saw the wind pushing the curtains like a big belly. Then I got up and looked out the window and saw Ireland. And after breakfast we all went out the door to Ireland and walked down to Mass. And after Mass we walked down to the big green park in front of the sea because I wanted to show my mother and father how I could stand on the ball for a count of three, until the ball squirted away from under my feet. I chased after it, but I could see nothing with the sun in my eyes and I fell over a man lying on the grass with his mouth open. He sat up suddenly and said, 'What the Jayses?' He told me to look where I was going in future. So I got up quickly and ran back to my mother and father. I told them that the man said 'Jayses', but they were both turned away, laughing at the sea. My father was laughing and blinking through his glasses and my mother had her hand over her mouth, laughing and laughing at the sea, until the tears came into her eyes and I thought, maybe she's not laughing at all but crying.

How do you know what that means when her shoulders are shaking and her eyes are red and she can't talk? How do you know if she's happy or sad? And how do you know if your father is happy or whether he's still angry at all the things that are not finished yet in Ireland. You know the sky is blue and the sea is blue and they meet somewhere, far away at the horizon. You can see the white sailing boats stuck on the water and the people walking along with ice-cream cones. You can hear a dog barking at the waves. You can see him standing in the water, barking and trying to bite the foam. You can see how long it takes for the sound of the barking to come across, as if it's coming from somewhere else and doesn't belong to the dog at all any more, as if he's barking and barking so much that he's hoarse and lost his voice.

When you're small you know nothing. You don't know where you are, or who you are, or what questions to ask.

Then one day my mother and father did a funny thing. First of all, my mother sent a letter home to Germany and asked one of her sisters to send over new trousers for my brother and me. She wanted us to wear something German – lederhosen. When the parcel arrived, we couldn't wait to put them on and run outside, all the way down the lane at the back of the houses. My mother couldn't believe her eyes. She stood back and clapped her hands together and said we were real boys now. No matter how much we climbed on walls or trees, she said, these German leather trousers were indestructible, and so they were. Then my father wanted us to wear something Irish too. He went straight out and bought hand-knit Aran sweaters. Big, white, rope patterned, woollen sweaters from the west of Ireland that were also indestructible. So my brother and I ran out wearing lederhosen and Aran sweaters, smelling of rough wool and new leather, Irish on top and German below. We were indestructible. We could slide down granite rocks. We could fall on nails and sit on glass. Nothing could sting us now and we ran down the lane faster than ever before, brushing past nettles as high as our shoulders.

When you're small you're like a piece of white paper with nothing written on it. My father writes down his name in Irish and my mother writes down her name in German and there's a blank space left over for all the people outside who speak English. We're special because we speak Irish and German and we like the smell of these new clothes. My mother says it's like being at home again and my father says your language is your home and your country is your language and your language is your flag.

But you don't want to be special. Out there in Ireland you want to be the same as everyone else, not an Irish speaker, not a German or a Kraut or a Nazi. On the way down to the shops, they call us the Nazi brothers. They say we're guilty and I go home and tell my mother I did nothing. But she shakes her head and says I can't say that. I can't deny anything and I can't fight back and I can't say I'm innocent. She says it's not important to win. Instead, she teaches us to surrender, to walk straight by and ignore them.

We're lucky to be alive, she says. We're living in the luckiest place in the world with no war and nothing to be afraid of, with the sea close by and the smell of salt in the air. There are lots of blue benches where you can sit looking out at the waves and lots of places to go swimming. Lots of rocks to climb on and pools to go fishing for crabs. Shops that sell fishing lines and hooks and buckets and plastic sunglasses. When it's hot you can get an ice pop and you can see newspapers spread out in the windows to stop the chocolate melting in the sun. Sometimes it's so hot that the sun stings you under your jumper like a needle in the back. It makes tar bubbles on the road that you can burst with the stick from the ice pop. We're living in a free country, she says, where the wind is always blowing and you can breathe in deeply, right down to the bottom of your lungs. It's like being on holiday all your life because you hear seagulls in the morning and you see sailing boats outside houses and people even have palm trees growing in their front gardens. Dublin where the palm trees grow, she says, because it looks like a paradise and the sea is never far away, like a glass of blue-green water at the bottom of every street.

But that changes nothing. *Sieg Heil*, they shout. *Achtung. Schnell schnell. Donner und Blitzen.* I know they're going to put us on trial. They have written things on the walls, at the side of the shop and in the laneways. They're going to get us one of these days and ask questions that we won't be able to answer. I see them looking at us, waiting for the day when we're alone and there's nobody around. I know they're going to execute me, because they call my older brother Hitler, and I get the name of an SS man who was found in Argentina and brought back to be put on trial for all the people he killed.

'I am Eichmann,' I said to my mother one day.

'But that's impossible,' she said. She kneeled down to look into my eyes. She took my hands and weighed them to see how heavy they were. Then she waited for a while, searching for what she wanted to say next.

'You know the dog that barks at the waves?' she said. 'You know the dog that belongs to nobody and barks at the waves all day until he is hoarse and has no voice any more. He doesn't know any better.'

'I am Eichmann,' I said. 'I am Adolf Eichmann and I'm

going to get an ice pop. Then I'm going down to the sea to look at the waves.'

'Wait,' she said. 'Wait for your brother.'

She stands at the door with her hand over her mouth. She thinks we're going out to Ireland and never coming back home again. She's afraid we might get lost in a foreign country where they don't have our language and nobody will understand us. She is crying because I'm Eichmann and there is nothing she can do to stop us going out and being Nazis. She tells us to be careful and watches us going across the street until we go around the corner and she can't see us any more.

So then we try to be Irish. In the shop we ask for the ice pop in English and let on that we don't know any German. We're afraid to be German, so we run down to the seafront as Irish as possible to make sure nobody can see us. We stand at the railings and look at the waves crashing against the rocks and the white spray going up into the air. We can taste the salt on our lips and see the foam running through the cracks like milk. We're Irish and we say 'Jaysus' every time the wave curls in and hits the rocks with a big thump.

'Jaysus, what the Jaysus,' I said.

'Jaysus, what the Jaysus of a big huge belly,' Franz said, and then we laughed and ran along the shore waving our fists.

'Big bully waves,' I shouted, because they could never catch us and they knew it. I picked up a stone and hit one of the waves right in the under-belly, right there as he stood up and rushed in towards us with his big, green saucer belly and his fringe of white hair falling down over his eyes.

'Get down, you big bully belly,' we laughed, as the stone

caught the wave with a clunk and there was nothing he could do but surrender and lie down across the sand with his arms out. Some of them tried to escape, but we were too fast for them. We picked up more and more stones and hit them one by one, because we were Irish and nobody could see us. The dog was there barking and barking, and we were there holding back the waves, because we didn't know any better.

Two

I know they don't want us here. From the window of my mother and father's bedroom I can see them walking by, going from the football field around by our street and down to the shops again. They carry sticks and smoke cigarette butts and spit on the ground. I hear them laughing and it's only a matter of time before we have to go out there and they'll be waiting. They'll find out who we are. They'll tell us to go back to where we come from.

My father says we have nothing to worry about because we are the new Irish. Partly from Ireland and partly from somewhere else, half-Irish and half-German. We're the speckled people, he says, the 'brack' people, which is a word that comes from the Irish language, from the Gaelic as they sometimes call it. My father was a schoolteacher once before he became an engineer and *breac* is a word, he explains, that the Irish people brought with them when they were crossing over into the English language. It means speckled, dappled, flecked, spotted, coloured. A trout is brack and so is a speckled horse. A barm brack is a loaf of bread with raisins in it and was borrowed from the Irish words *bairín breac*. So we are the speckled-Irish, the brack-Irish. Brack home-made Irish bread with German raisins.

But I know it also means we're marked. It means we're aliens and we'll never be Irish enough, even though we speak the Irish language and my father says we're more Irish than the Irish themselves. We have speckled faces, so it's best to stay inside where they can't get us. Inside we can be ourselves.

I look out the window and see the light changing on the red-bricked terrace across the street. I see the railings and the striped canvas sun-curtains hanging out over the front doors. There's a gardener clipping a hedge and I hear the sound of his shears in English, because everything out there is spoken in English. Out there is a different country, far away. There's a cloud moving over the street and I can see the gardener looking up. I hear my mother behind me saying that there's something strange about the light this afternoon. She says the sun is eclipsed by the cloud and throws a kind of low, lantern light across the red-bricked walls and it feels like the end of the day.

'*Falsches Licht*,' she calls it, because everything inside our house is spoken in German, or in Irish. Never in English. She comes to the window to look for herself and says it again, false light. She takes in a deep breath through her teeth and that means it's going to rain. It means the seagulls will soon come in from the sea and start screeching and settling on the chimneys. It's a sign for people to run out and bring in their washing. A sign for the gardener to go inside, because large drops are already appearing on the pavement. And when all the drops are joined together and the pavement is fully wet, then my mother goes downstairs to the kitchen.

She lets us play with some of her things. My older brother Franz, my younger sister Maria and me examine everything on her dressing table – lipstick, scissors, nail clippers, rosary beads. There's a brush lying on its back with a white comb stuck into it like a saw. A bowl of hair clips and a box of powder and a gold and blue bottle with the big number 4711 written on it. We empty out a box of jewellery and find the emerald snake which my mother calls the Smaragd. Maria keeps calling out the big number 4711 as she blesses herself around the ears and on the wrists and behind the knees, again and again, just like my mother does, and the whole room fills up with scent of cologne. I look at the print that the hairbrush makes on my arm. Franz finds the crocodile-skin purse with lots of heavy silver coins inside and we're rich. The smell of rain and leather are mixed together all in one with the smell of cologne. In the drawers on each side of the dressing table we find letters, scarves and stockings. Passports and photographs, rail tickets, sleeper accommodation on night trains.

And then we came across the medals. I knew immediately that they were German medals because everything that belongs to my mother is German. She tells us lots of stories about Kempen where she grew up, so I knew that my grandfather Franz Kaiser was in the First World War and that my mother was in the Second World War. I knew that my grandmother Berta was an opera singer and that my grandfather Franz once went to listen to her sing at the state opera house in Krefeld, and because everyone else was sending her flowers, he decided to send her a bouquet of bananas instead, and that's how they fell in love and got married. Sometimes my mother puts on the radio to see if she can hear some of the songs that her own mother sang. I know how far away Germany is by the way my mother sometimes has shadows around her eyes. By the way she stays silent. Or by the way she sometimes throws her head back and laughs out loud at some of the things that her father used to do. Like the time he once asked to borrow the postman's cap and said thank you very politely and then climbed up the monument in the middle of the square to put it on top of St George's head.

We didn't have to be told that these were military medals which belonged to Franz Kaiser. When he was on duty during the First World War, his wife Berta brought him his dinner once a day by train in a straw basket. Sometimes she just put the straw basket on the train by itself and it came back empty in the evening. Then he had to go to the front one day and came back with a disease in his lungs that killed him. He was not well even before the war started and my mother says he should never have been taken into the army because he died when she was only nine years old. She says she still remembers the smell of flowers in the room around his coffin and the shadows around her mother's eyes. So I put on Franz Kaiser's medal with the cross and march up and down the bare floorboards of my mother and father's bedroom, looking at myself in the mirror of the dressing table and saluting, while my brother salutes behind me with his own medal and my sister behind him with the emerald snake.

Then the sun lit up the street outside and I thought somebody had switched on a light in the room. The cloud had already passed over and gone somewhere else and there was steam rising from the pavement. The gardener was back out, clipping the hedge, and there was no other sound anywhere except my sister Maria breathing through her mouth and sometimes the sound of a train in the station. The smell of baking was coming all the way up the stairs from the kitchen and we should have rushed down to get the leftovers in the bowl. We should have been running up to collect my father from the train. But we were too busy looking for all these old things.

At first there was nothing much in my father's wardrobe,

only cufflinks, ties and socks. But then we found a big black and white picture of a sailor. He was dressed in a sailor's uniform with square, white lapels over his tunic and a rope lanyard hanging down over his chest. He had soft eyes and I liked the look of him. I wanted to be a sailor, even though I had no idea what this sailor was doing in my father's wardrobe.

I know that my father comes from Cork and works as an engineer in Dublin and writes his name in Irish. When he was small, Ireland was still under the British. His father's family were all fishermen. His father fell on deck one day and lost his memory and died not long after that in a hospital in Cork city. But we never talk about that. I knew there would be trouble when my father came home, but I didn't think about it, not even when I saw the shape of his good Sunday suit swinging on the hanger in front of me. Not even when I heard the trains coming into the station, one by one. We continued to inspect everything quickly, pulling out drawers full of handkerchiefs and gloves and mothballs and socks rolled up.

There were boxes at the bottom of the wardrobe, full of letters and postcards, certificates and holy pictures. And at last we came across more medals. Heavy bronze medals this time, one for each of us. The medal I put on hung from a striped ribbon that was just like the faded sun-curtains across the street. We didn't know where these new bronze medals came from, except that they must have belonged to the sailor hiding at the back of the wardrobe. Whoever he was, he must have owned the waterproof identity papers, too, and the photographs of HMS *Nemesis* with sailors lined up in a human chain along the deck. And he must have got all the postcards from King George wishing him a happy and victorious Christmas.

Some things are not good to know in Ireland. I had no idea that I had an Irish grandfather who couldn't even speak Irish. His name was John Hamilton and he belonged to the navy, the British navy, the Royal Navy. He joined up as a boy of fifteen and served on all kinds of ships – *Defiance*, *Magnificent*, *Katoomba*, *Repulse*. He fell on a British naval vessel called HMS *Vivid* when he was only 28 years of age. He died because he was homesick and lost his memory. But I didn't know any of that. There's a picture in the front room of Franz Kaiser and Berta Kaiser with her head leaning on his shoulder, both of them laughing with a big glass of wine on the table in front of them. There's no picture of John Hamilton or his wife Mary Frances, alone or together, hanging anywhere in our house. Our German grandparents are dead, but our Irish grandparents are dead and forgotten. I didn't know that the bronze medal I was wearing beside the Iron Cross belonging to my German grandfather came from the British navy and was given to my Irish grandmother, Mary Frances, along with a small British war widow's pension which she had to fight for. I didn't know that my Irish grandfather, John Hamilton, and my German grandfather, Franz Kaiser, must have stood facing each other in the Great War. Or that my mother and father were both orphaned by that same war. Or that I was wearing the medals of two different empires side by side.

I didn't know what questions to ask. I heard the trains coming home one by one and I knew that we were not allowed to speak the language of the sailor. It's forbidden to speak in English in our house. My father wants all the Irish people to cross back over into the Irish language so he made a rule that we can't speak English, because your home is your language and he wants us to be Irish and not British. My mother doesn't know how to make rules like that, because she's German and has nothing against the British. She has her own language and came to Ireland to learn English in the first place. So we're allowed to speak the language of Franz Kaiser, but not the language of John Hamilton. We can speak Irish or German, but English is like a foreign country outside the door. The sailor in the wardrobe, with his short haircut and his soft eyes looking away, was not able to talk to us. Even if he was still alive and came to visit us and was ready to tell us all about his travels around the world on those ships, about all the cities and ports he had been to, I could not have asked him any questions.

There were so many boxes at the bottom of the wardrobe that we could sit on them and pretend we were on a bus. We called it the number eight bus, and Franz was the driver holding a hat for a steering wheel. I was the conductor bedecked in medals, and Maria was the only passenger apart from my father's Sunday suit hanging on the rail and the quiet sailor in the back seat looking away out the window.

'Hold the bar please,' I called and Maria got on. She was carrying her crocodile-skin purse and paid the fare with the precious coins.

'Fares please,' I kept demanding, until she had no money left and I had to let her on without paying. I rang the bell with my fist against the handle of the drawer. Then I closed the door and the wardrobe drove off in the complete darkness. Maria cried and said she wanted to get off, but it was already too late for that, because the bus was going so fast that it started leaning over. Before we knew it, the whole wardrobe was lying on its side. The only thing stopping it from crashing all the way down to the floor was my mother and father's bed. We didn't even know what happened. All we knew was that we were now trapped inside and unable to open the door. We knew there would be trouble. We were silent for a while, waiting to see what would happen next. Maria kept crying and then Franz started calling for help.

'Mutti, Ma Ma . . .' he said.

I started calling as well. My mother was far away downstairs in the kitchen baking the cake. We called and called and waited for a long time. But nobody could hear us, not even the gardener or the neighbours or anyone out on the street, because they could only hear things that were said in English. Nobody even knew that we were calling for help, because we had the wrong words. We were the children in the wardrobe and no matter how loud we shouted and knocked, they could hear nothing.

Some time later I heard my mother's voice outside saying that she could not believe her eyes. She said she had seen a lot of strange things in Germany during the war, and in Ireland, too, after she came over, but never before had she seen a wardrobe on its side, crying. She was not able to lift the wardrobe by herself, or to open the door because it was jammed shut against the bed. But everything was going to be all right in the end, she said, because even if we had to stay in the dark for a while longer, she would tell us a story until help came. We listened to her and almost fell asleep with the fog of 4711 and mothballs and the cake downstairs, until my father came home and the wardrobe suddenly stood up and the door opened. It was daytime again. I rubbed my eyes and saw my father blinking through his glasses and saying everything with a frown on his forehead.

'Who gave you the right to look at my things?' he said, because he didn't want any of us to know that he had a father in the navy who could not speak Irish and once stood with the British in a war against the Germans, when his own country was still not free.

Maria was huddled in my mother's arms, crying even more after she was rescued than before when she was trapped. She said Franz was the driver and I was the conductor and she was only a passenger, like the sailor in the back seat. My father's voice filled the room and I felt the sting of his hand, but it was nothing because soon we were all safe again and my mother was talking about the cake for after dinner. The medals were taken off and put away. The picture of the sailor with the soft eyes disappeared and we never saw him again after that. Nobody mentioned him. I had no way of keeping him in my head because he was gone, back into the wardrobe where nobody could rescue him. We didn't know how to remember him, and like him, we lost our memory.

Three

My mother's name is Irmgard and she was in a big film once with lots of war and killing and trains on fire. It's a black and white picture that happened long ago in Germany. A man trapped her in a place called Venlo where she was working and she couldn't escape. She says it was just like us being in the wardrobe because she was far away from home and couldn't call for help. She couldn't write home or tell any of her sisters what was happening. She didn't know who to talk to. The man's name was Stiegler and he would not listen to her when she spoke to him and would not let her go. Instead he told her to smile. And even though she was too afraid to smile, he just put his hand up to her lips and made her show her teeth like a big unhappy grin. She can't talk about it any more than that. She has told nobody else, not even her sisters, not even my father. One day, when we get older we'll hear the whole story. But now we're too small, and some things about Germany are not good to think about. 'That's a film you can see when you grow up,' she says.

All we need to know is that at the end of the film, when the war is over, my mother runs away to Ireland to go on a pilgrimage. She meets my father in Dublin and they talk about everything except the time she was trapped once by the man in Venlo. They go back to Germany to get married with the snow all around. They travel through the white landscape and go to a mountain along the River Rhine called the Drachenfelz, and after that my father brings her back to Ireland to another mountain close to the Atlantic called Croagh Patrick.

'And that's how the film ends,' she says, because it's time to sleep and she doesn't want us to keep calling her and asking more questions about Germany that she can't answer. 'The End. Film over.' She says the same thing sometimes when we start fighting over the leftovers of the cake bowl. Or the time we went to the strand and stayed there all day until it started raining and she said it was a pity it had to end like that. Or when something breaks, like the time the blue vase that came from her father and mother's house in Kempen smashed in the hallway and she said it was a very nice film but now it was over.

In my mother's film, she was in a building where there was nobody else living. At night when everybody was gone, she was afraid and locked the door of her room. She knew that there was no point in shouting for help, because nobody would hear her. Then she heard the man coming in and there was nothing she could do except pray and hope that it would be all over some day. She could hear him coming up the stairs as if he was counting them on the way up. She could hear him breathing outside the door. She could see the doorknob turning and she could smell cognac.

During the day, the man was always very nice to everybody. He looked very well, dressed in a suit and a clean shirt every morning, and he wore good shoes. He spoke kindly and shook hands with everyone when they arrived to work. He smiled and even remembered everybody's birthday. He brought flowers to work when somebody had bad news. Everybody said he was a good man during the day and full of compliments. He had read a lot of books and he was very generous, giving presents of theatre tickets and opera tickets.

But you can't always trust nice people. My mother says that sometimes there is no defence against kindness. It's easy to be taken in by compliments, by smiles, by nice words. But you can't let yourself be stung by things like flowers and theatre tickets and invitations to the opera. Everybody can make mistakes but there are some mistakes you can't even talk about, because you feel so stupid that you can only blame yourself. My mother wants us never to be fooled by nice words. She wants us never to have things that we regret, because everybody in Germany has things in their heads that they keep to themselves. Everybody has things they wish had never happened.

When you're small you can inherit a secret without even knowing what it is. You can be trapped in the same film as your mother, because certain things are passed on to you that you're not even aware of, not just a smile or a voice, but unspoken things, too, that you can't understand until later when you grow up. Maybe it's there in my eyes for all to see, the same as it is in my mother's eyes. Maybe it's hidden in my voice, or in the shape of my hands. Maybe it's something you carry with you like a precious object you're told not to lose.

'That film will still be running when we grow up,' she says.

All we need to know for now is that she ran away to Ireland to become a pilgrim in a holy country with priests and donkeys that had crosses on their backs. She picked Ireland because she heard there were lots of monastic ruins. She didn't expect so much poverty. But the Irish people knew how to deal with poverty, through celebration, with smoke and stories and singing. A man with a packet of cigarettes was a millionaire in Ireland. And the Irish people had never tried to hurt anyone. So maybe they would not pass judgement on a German woman. In the days before she left Germany, it was so exciting, she says, because nobody in her family had ever been that far away before. Everybody was talking about Ireland, even the neighbours, asking what the weather was like and what the houses were like inside. What she should bring and what she didn't need. She said she packed and unpacked all over again so often that it was hard to believe she was going away at all in the end.

At the station, she embraced her aunt Ta Maria and her Onkel Gerd and her youngest sister Minne, but it was hard to feel she was leaving. They all had tears in their eyes and would not let her get on the train because they thought she would never come back. They made her promise to write home every week. Even when she was sitting down in her seat, even when the train carriages jerked and the train moved out of the station, it was still hard to feel anything except fear. Everybody in Germany was used to being afraid. She waved her hand slowly. She saw the houses and the fences and the fields passing by, but she still had the feeling that she was trapped. But then, my mother says, there comes a moment when you don't care about anything, when all fear and doubt disappear. It's a moment of weakness and strength at the same time, when nothing matters and you're not afraid any more.

Sometimes she still thinks about it as though it just happened yesterday, as though the film is never over and she'll never escape. Maybe the reason why people are good at stories is that they sometimes have things they can't tell, things they must keep secret at all costs and make up for in other ways. So she tells us the story of the pilgrimage instead. She tells us how Ireland was a place where you could trust everyone, where people prayed every day, where you could go and say the rosary and make up for all the things that happened in the war.

It was a great way for a film to come to an end, cycling along the small roads with the sun slanting through the clouds like in holy pictures, lighting up the mountains like a stage in the opera house. It was flickering through the stone walls. Everywhere these stone walls and everywhere the grass combed in one direction by the wind. Trees bent like old men and everywhere so empty except for the haystacks in the fields and the monastic ruins. Once or twice along the way there were cows on the road that made her stop completely. Big cow faces looking at her, as if they were amazed to see a German woman in Ireland after the war.

Then it started raining and getting dark and she had to find a place to stay quickly. It was raining so much that the water was jumping away from her eyes when she blinked and her shoulders were shivering. She got off the bicycle because it was impossible to go any further. A man pointed to a house that didn't even look like a guest house, but it was better to stay there because you couldn't see a thing any more. There was a light on inside and the woman of the house came to the door with lots of children behind her. One girl had her dress in her mouth, all of them staring as if my mother had come in with the rain.

'It's not often we see a German woman cycling around these parts on her own,' the woman said.

My mother says you can't be sure in Ireland if people say things with admiration or not. Irish people are good at saying things in between admiration and accusation, between envy and disdain. She says the woman looked her up and down as if she liked German clothes but didn't completely trust her.

'I have come from Lough Derg,' my mother explained.

That made everything right. She was a pilgrim. A pilgrim coming to Ireland to pray for all the bad things that happened in Europe.

In the kitchen, they made her sit and eat a meal while they all watched and the man of the house kept asking questions about Germany. Was it in ruins like they said in the papers? She had to describe the cities after the war – Nuremberg, Hamburg, Dresden. The woman of the house kept saying 'You're not serious', but people in Germany wouldn't make up something like that. The children kept staring. They were so shy that they were afraid to move closer to her. It was like being a film actress. They spoke about her as if she was still in a film. She'll have some more bread, the man of the house said. She'll be needing a glass of whiskey, he said after she was finished eating, as if they had to celebrate the guest who came in with the rain.

The man of the house raised his glass with all the children looking up.

'Heil Hitler,' he said.

There was a big smile on his face, my mother says, and she didn't know what to say. Of course, he was only being friendly. It was part of the Irish welcome.

'Fair play to the Germans,' he said.

He said the Germans were great people altogether. He kept saying it was a pity they lost because they were a mighty nation. He winked at her with admiration, then left a long silence, waiting to see how she would respond.

'Fair play to the Germans, for the almighty thrashing you gave the British. Fair play to Hitler for that, at least.'

He was only being hospitable, my mother says, to make her feel at home. She could not argue with him. She was trapped inside German history and couldn't get out of it. Instead she smiled and said it had been a long journey back from Lough Derg. She thanked them for such a lovely welcome, but said she could no longer keep her eyes open.

She was given a room with a small fire going. Her clothes were still steaming. There was a smell of cabbage and damp walls. The bed sank down in the middle, but she was so tired that nothing mattered any more and it didn't take long to fall asleep to the sound of the rain. She heard the voices of children on the far side of the wall and sometimes the man of the house, too, speaking in a deep voice. But the rain was whispering and bouncing into an enamel basin outside and rushing away into a drain like the sound of the rosary being said all night.

Sometime later she woke up and saw the woman of the house standing beside the bed, holding a lamp, gently shaking her arm. The woman explained that there was an emergency. Would she mind giving up the bed and spending the night in another room? There were three men soaked to the skin outside on the doorstep needing accommodation for the night.

'I can't turn them away,' the woman said. 'Poor creatures.'

My mother says she had to get up and take her things to the family room where the woman pointed to the marriage bed. The children were all fast asleep in another bed. And the room was in such a mess, with clothes and newspapers on the floor, bits of food, too, even a harness for a horse and a hay-fork and wellington boots. She stood there looking around as if she couldn't believe her eyes.

'It's only topsy dirty,' the woman said.

'But where is your husband?'

'You have nothing to be afraid of, love. He'll stay by the fire.'

My mother says you can't complain if you're a pilgrim escaping from Germany. She says you have to offer things up. For people who are less fortunate and for all the awful things that happened. So she just got into bed with the woman of the house. She felt the warmth left behind by the man of the house. She could hear the whole room breathing, until the woman started speaking in the dark. She listened to the woman talking for a while, and then she began to talk as well, as if there were things that could only be said in the dark.

She says she never saw the men. She heard them coming in and muttering for a while to each other in the room. She never saw the man of the house again either, but she heard him in the kitchen, tapping his pipe against the fireplace. She heard the children dreaming sometimes and the cows elbowing each other in the barn outside. She smelled the rain and heard it drumming on the roof, like somebody still saying the rosary. They whispered so as not to wake up the children. They talked for a long time as if they were sisters.

Four

On the front door of our house there is the number two. I know how to say this number in German: *Zwei*. My mother teaches us how to count up the stairs: *Eins, Zwei, Drei* . . . And when you get to ten you can start again, so many steps all the way up that you can call them any number you like. And when we're in our pyjamas, we say goodnight birds and goodnight trees, until my mother counts again very quickly and we jump into bed as fast as possible: *Eins, Zwei, Drei*.

There are workers in the house and they know how to smoke. They made a mountain in the back garden and sit on it, drinking tea and eating sandwiches. They smoke cigarettes and mix sand and cement with a shovel. They whistle and make a hole in the middle where they pour in the water to make a lake, and sometimes the water from the lake spills over the side before the shovel can catch it. We do the same with spoons. The workers have different words, not the same as my mother, and they teach us how to count in English: one, two, three . . . But my father says that's not allowed. He says he'll speak to them later.

One day there was a fox in the kitchen, just like the fox in the story book. The workers were gone, so my mother closed the door and called the police. Then a Garda came to our house and went into the kitchen on his own and started banging. There was a smell of smoke and we waited on the stairs for a long time, until the Garda came out again with the fox lying dead on a shovel with his tail hanging down and blood around his mouth and nose.

'You'll have no more strangers in your house, please God,' he said.

The Garda showed his teeth to my mother and called her 'Madam'. The workers called her 'Maam'. We called her 'Mutti' or 'Ma Ma' and my father is called 'Vati' even though he's from Cork. The Garda had a moustache and said it was no fox we had in the kitchen but a rat the size of a fox. And the rat was very *glic*, he said, because he hid behind the boiler and would not come out until he was chased out with fire and smoke.

There are other people living at the top of our house, all the way up the stairs, further than you can count. They're called the O'Neills and they never take their hats off, because they think the hallway is like the street, my mother says. They are very noisy and my father makes a face. He goes up to speak to them and when he comes down again he says he wants the O'Neills out of the house. There will be no more chopping wood under this roof.

Áine came to look after us when my mother had to go away to the hospital. She's from Connemara and has different words, not the same as the workers, or the O'Neills, or the Garda, or my mother. She teaches us to count the stairs again in Irish: *a haon, a dó, a trí* . . . She doesn't lay out the clothes at night or tell stories. She doesn't call me Hanni or Johannes, she calls me Seán instead, or sometimes Jack, but my father says that's wrong. I should never let anyone call me Jack or John, because that's not who I am. My father changed his name to Irish. So when I grow up I'll change my name, too.

Áine can't speak my mother's words, but she can speak the words of the Garda. She brings us for a walk along the seafront and shows us the crabs running sideways and the dog barking for nothing all day. She says she wants to go to London, but it's very far away. And Connemara is far away, too. I said London was far away one, and Connemara was far away two, and she said: 'Yes.' She sits for a long time looking out across the sea to London. Then she takes us up to the shops to buy sweets and I get more than Franz because I'm very *glic*. She teaches us how to walk on the wall, all the way back along the seafront, and Franz makes up a song about it: 'Walk on the wall, walk on the wall . . .'

My mother came back with a baby called Maria, so that's Franz, Johannes and Maria: *Eins, Zwei, Drei*. We speak German again and my mother shows us how to feed the baby with her breast. Maria opens her mouth and shakes her head and then my mother has to change her nappy because the baby did 'A A'. After that, my mother puts Maria out in the garden with a net across the pram to stop the birds from stealing her dreams.

Áine took us down to the sea again because Franz had a fishing net and he was going to catch one of the crabs, but they were too fast. I said they were all 'two fast and three fast', and Áine said: 'Yes.' She took out a box with a small mirror and put lipstick on her lips. She took off her shoes to put her feet into one of the pools with the crabs. I started throwing stones into the pools. Franz got all wet and Áine said 'A A' in Irish. Then I threw a stone in Áine's pool. She chased after me and on the way home she would not let me walk on the wall, so I tried to walk sideways, like the crabs.

My mother knows everything. She knows that I was

throwing stones, but Áine said it wasn't 'half as bad as that', which is the same as what my mother says only in different words: *Halb so schlimm*. My mother wagged her finger and said: *Junge, Junge*, which is the same as what Áine says in English: 'Boy, oh boy', and in Irish '*a mhac ó*'.

That evening, my mother brought us up to the station to collect my father from the train. She picked us up to look over the wall at the tracks. We waved and shouted at the train rushing through under the bridge and then we started running towards my father coming out of the station. My father is different to other men. He has no moustache, but he has glasses and he has a limp, too. He swings his briefcase and his leg goes down on one side as if the ground is soft under one foot. It's the same as when you walk with one foot on and one foot off the pavement. My mother kisses him and puts her arm around him. He looks into the pram at Maria to see if she has her eyes open. Franz tries to carry the briefcase and I try to walk like my father, but that's not allowed. He hits me on the back of my head and my mother kneels down to say it's not right to imitate people. You always have to walk like yourself, not like your father or the crabs, just like yourself. At home, my father was still angry. He wanted to know why I was throwing stones at the pools so I told him that Áine said 'A A' in Irish. I mixed up the words like sand and cement and water. I used Áine's words and told my father that she said 'A A', what the baby did, in my mother's words.

'What did you throw?' my father asked.

'Stones.'

I saw myself twice in his glasses and he made a face, just like when the O'Neills were chopping wood upstairs.

'Stones,' he said again, very loud. Then he stood up.

My mother was laughing and laughing until the tears

came into her eyes. She said it was so funny to hear so many words and so many countries being mixed up.

'Stones,' my father said again. 'I won't have this.'

'It's not half as bad as that,' my mother said, still wiping her eyes.

'She's here to speak Irish to them,' my father shouted, and then my mother tried to stop him going up to speak to Áine. She was holding on to his arm and saying: 'Leave it till the morning. Let me talk to her.'

My father says there will be no more chopping wood and no more speaking English under his roof. I stay awake and look at the light under the door. At night, I hear my mother and father talking for a long time. I hear the O'Neills coming up the stairs and I hear my father coming out on the landing to see if they will start chopping wood. Then the light goes out. I hear water whispering. I hear a fox laughing. I hear stones dropping into the pools and I hear sand and cement being mixed with a shovel. Then it's silent and nobody is listening, only me.

My mother spoke to Áine the next day. She's not able to speak Áine's words. So in the words of the Garda and the workers, my mother tells her never to speak the words of the Garda and the workers to us again.

'You must try to speak to them in Irish,' my mother said.

'What good is that to them?' Áine said.

'Please. It's my husband's wish.'

So we have to be careful in our house and think before we speak. We can't speak the words of the Garda or the workers, that's English. We speak Áine's words from Connemara, that's Irish, or my mother's words, that's German. I can't talk to Áine in German and I can't talk to my mother in Irish, because she'll only laugh and tickle me. I can talk to my father in German or Irish and he can speak to the Garda and the workers for us. Outside, you have to be careful, too, because you can't buy an ice pop in German or in Irish, and lots of people only know the words of the Garda and the workers. My father says they better hurry up and learn Irish fast because we won't buy anything more in English.

Sometimes Áine speaks to herself in the mirror. Sometimes when the O'Neills go through the hall on their way out the front door, my mother says good morning to them, but they say nothing at all and just walk out as if they don't understand their own language. Sometimes the man in the fish shop says *guten Morgen* as if he's forgotten his own language. Sometimes people whisper. Sometimes they spell out the letters of a word. And sometimes people try to forget their own language altogether and Áine continues to say 'stones' as if there's no word in her own language for it.

'*Stone mór*' and '*stone beag*,' she says. Big stone and little stone.

On Saturday, Áine goes into the city on the bus to speak English. The O'Neills were gone away, too, and my father was in the garden digging. He said he was going to get rid of the mountain the workers left behind and grow flowers and radishes, so I watched him as he jabbed the spade into the soil and then pushed it down with his foot. The worms living in the mountain had to go away in the wheelbarrow. My father emptied it and spread out the soil in another part of the garden. Then he let me hold the wheelbarrow while it was filling up again.

Franz made a wall with a line of bricks and he was walking on it singing: 'Walk on the wall, walk on the wall . . .' My father stopped digging and told him to stop. He made the O'Neill face again. But Franz kept on saying 'walk on the wall' because that was his song and he couldn't forget it. Then my father jabbed the spade into the mountain and it stayed there, standing up on its own while he went over to Franz and hit him. He hit him on the back of the head so that Franz fell off the wall and his face went down on the bricks. When he got up, there was blood all around his nose and mouth, like the fox. He opened his mouth and said nothing for a long time, as if he had forgotten how to use his voice and I thought he was going to be dead. Then he started crying at last and my father took him by the hand very quickly and brought him inside.

'*Mein armer Schatz*,' my mother kept saying as she sat him up beside the sink and started cleaning the blood away from his face. Franz kept crying and trying to say something but he didn't know what words to use. Then my mother turned around to my father and looked at him as if she could not believe her eyes.

'His nose is broken,' she said.

There were drops of blood on the kitchen floor. They made a trail all the way out into the garden. My father said he was very sorry, but the rules had to be obeyed. He said Franz was speaking English again and that had to stop. Then my mother and father had no language at all. My father went outside again and my mother brought Franz upstairs. Even when the blood stopped, he was still crying for a long time and my mother was afraid that he would never start talking again. She sat down on the bed and put her arm around the two of us and told us what happened when she was in Germany in a very bad film. She held us both very hard and I thought my bones would crack. She was crying and her shoulders were shaking. She said she was going to go back to Germany. She would take us with her. She started packing her suitcase, wondering what she should bring and what she should leave behind in Ireland.

I looked out the window and watched my father fill the wheelbarrow and bring it to another part of the garden, empty it and bring it back to start again. I watched him digging and digging, until the mountain was gone. I wanted to go down and tell him that my mother fixed Franz's nose with a story. I wanted to tell him that I would never say 'walk on the wall' as long as I lived. I wanted to tell him that my mother was going home and she was going to take us with her. But he never looked up and he didn't see me waving. Instead, he made a big fire in the garden and the smoke went across the walls, away over the other gardens, all around the houses and out on to the street. He kept stacking on more and more weeds and leaves with a big fork, as if he wanted to send a message around the whole world with smoke. The fire crackled and whistled, and it smelled like cigarettes. My father was standing with the fork in his hand and sometimes he disappeared. Sometimes the whole house disappeared and people must have thought we were never coming back.

My mother carried Maria in one arm and the suitcase in the other. In the hallway, she put the suitcase down so that she could open the front door and escape on to the street. I knew that my father would be searching for us all over the place in the smoke. But my mother said we were not going to be trapped again. She picked up the suitcase and told us to follow her, but then I heard my father coming in from the garden. His footsteps came all the way as if he was counting the drops of blood on the ground. We tried to run away fast, but it was too late because he was already standing right behind us. I could smell the smoke on his clothes. He asked my mother where she was thinking of going to without any money. He said there was nothing left in Germany and she had nowhere to go home to with three children. He closed the front door and said she was married now, so she sat down on the suitcase and cried.

'She's just a bit homesick, that's all,' my father said. He smiled and said he would put on some German music. He kissed my mother's hand and carried the suitcase back up the stairs.

Then the big music filled the whole house. It went into every room and all the way up the stairs. Outside, the fire kept going until it got dark and I stood at the window of the bedroom again with my mother, saying goodbye smoke, goodbye birds, goodbye trees. But we didn't go anywhere. We stayed in Ireland and my mother told us to get into bed: *Eins, Zwei, Drei*.

Five

My father's name is Jack and he's in a song, a long ballad with lots of verses about leaving Ireland and emigrating. The song is so long that you couldn't even sing it all in one day. It has more than a thousand verses, all about freedom and dying of hunger and going away to some other land at the end of it all. My father is not much good at singing, but he keeps repeating the chorus about how we should live in Ireland and be Irish.

'No more shall we roam from our own native home,' is what he says when we're standing at the seafront, holding on to the blue railings, looking out at the white sailing boats. He doesn't want us to live in England or America where they speak only English and keep dreaming about going back home. So we stay in Ireland where we were born, with the sea between us and all the other countries, with the church bell ringing and the mailboat going out across the water. Instead of always going away, my father had a new idea. Why not bring people from somewhere else over to Ireland? So that's why he married my mother and now she's the one who does all the dreaming and singing about being far away from home. It's my mother who left her own native shores, and that means we still end up living in a foreign country because we're the children from somewhere else.

My father comes from a small town in west Cork called Leap and he had lots of uncles and cousins who had to emigrate. One of his uncles only sent his first letter back from America after twenty years, just to tell everybody that the rumours still going around in Ireland about a girl he left behind with a baby were not true. It was easy to say what you liked about people who went away. And it was easy for those who left to deny Ireland, to look back and say it was full of poverty and failure. Maybe they made a lot of money abroad, my father says, but they were lonely and they wanted everybody who was left in Ireland to come and join them over there. My father and his younger brother Ted were going to emigrate, too. They lived in a house at the end of the town with their mother and a picture of a sailor over the mantelpiece. They had plans to go to America to work with their uncle, but then they got a scholarship and went to school instead.

The town is called Leap after a famous Irishman by the name of O'Donovan who once got away from the British by leaping across a nearby gorge. *Léim Uí Dhonabháin:* O'Donovan's Leap, they call it. The peelers chased him all over the countryside, but he escaped over the impossible gorge and they were afraid to follow him. 'Beyond the Leap, beyond the law' is what the people of the town said. There was no freedom at that time. The whole town could hardly jump across the gorge after him, so they stayed behind where they were, under the British. They talked about it and went up there for a walk on summer days to look across to the far side. But nobody could do it. So the town was called after something that might as well not have happened at all. It was called Leap because that's what the people in the town wished they had done, what they dreamed about and sang songs about.

Lots of them emigrated after that, my father says. The people who stayed told their children that unless they wanted to jump after the famous O'Donovan and spend the rest of their lives running away, they might as well speak English, because that's all they spoke in places like America and Canada and Australia and South Africa. It was English they spoke on ships and English they spoke in films. The Irish language was bad for business, they said, so why should anyone have to risk his life across a deadly gorge for being Irish? It was madness even to think of it. Everybody in Cork started speaking English and calling each other 'boy' at the end of every sentence whether you were young or old. You'd only kill yourself, boy, they said. They started saying they could make the leap across the gorge any time they liked, no problem at all, boy. They said everything twice to make sure you believed them. They claimed they were living beyond the law and there was no need to prove it, boy.

There was lots of killing and dying and big houses on fire in my father's song, too. He tells us bits of the song, like the time the fighting started around west Cork when they tried to take down the British flag. About children hiding sweets in bullet holes along the wall of the creamery, and about a man named Terence MacSwiney, the Cork lord mayor who died on hunger strike in a London jail. He puts on the record with the song about another man named Kevin Barry who was hanged one Monday morning in Dublin. He tells us about the time when the British soldiers came to their house in Leap, threatening to burn it down because they thought the rebels were shooting from the upstairs window. They had to run away in the middle of the night to Skibbereen and on the way down the hill the cart overturned with their belongings, so the donkey ended up on his back like a beetle with his legs in the air. And then the very same thing happened again after the British had gone and the Irish started fighting among themselves, because that's what they had learned from the British. Then one day they had to leave the house a second time when Irish Free State soldiers said they would burn it down, because they were sure they saw IRA snipers in the upstairs window.

'There will be no more fighting and dying,' my father says. He wants no more people put out of their houses, because it's time to live for Ireland and stop arguing among ourselves over stupid things. He says there are too many things to do and too many places to see in Ireland like the round tower in Glendalough and the new IMCO building that looks like a white ship when you pass it by on the bus. My father pays the fare in Irish and sometimes when the bus turns around the corner you think you're going straight into a shop window. We go to the zoo and have a picnic in the Phoenix Park with a big spire in the distance called the Wellington Monument. We run across the grass, but we're not allowed to play on the monument because it's something the British left behind and forgot to take with them. Wait till we get our own monuments, my father says.

There are parts of the song, too, that my father will not tell us anything about. Some of the verses are to do with the town of Leap and things he doesn't want to remember. Like the picture of the sailor over the mantelpiece. Or the people in the town who used to laugh at him for having a father who fell and lost his memory in the navy. It was a bad thing to have a mother who was still getting money from the King of England. So they called him names and said he would never be able to jump across the gorge.

'Every curse falls back on its author,' my father says.

He promises to bring us to see his own home town, but he never does. Instead, he would rather show us the future, so that's why there are verses of the song he leaves out altogether. He lost his memory when he was small and vowed instead that he would be the first person who really leaped over the gorge since O'Donovan did it. He said they were not beyond British law as long as they were still depending on Britain for their jobs and still speaking English. So when the time came, my father jumped. He didn't emigrate or drink whiskey or start making up stories either. Instead he changed his name and decided never to be homesick again. He put on a pioneer pin and changed his name from Jack to Seán and studied engineering and spoke Irish as if his home town didn't exist, as if his own father didn't exist, as if all those who emigrated didn't exist.

There are things you inherit from your father, too, not just a forehead or a smile or a limp, but other things like sadness and hunger and hurt. You can inherit memories you'd rather forget. Things can be passed on to you as a child, like helpless anger. It's all there in your voice, like it is in your father's voice, as if you were born with a stone in your hand. When I grow up I'll run away from my story, too. I have things I want to forget, so I'll change my name and never come back.

My father pretends that England doesn't exist. It's like a country he's never even heard of before and is not even on the map. Instead, he's more interested in other countries. Why shouldn't we dance with other partners as well, he says, like Germany? So while he was still at university he started learning German and listening to German music – Bach and Beethoven. Every week he went to classes in Dublin that were packed out because they were given by

Doctor Becker, a real German. He knew Germany was a place full of great music and great inventions, and one day, he said to himself, Ireland would be like that too, with its own language and its own inventions. Until then, he said, Ireland didn't really exist at all. It only existed in the minds of emigrants looking back, or in the minds of idealists looking forward. Far back in the past or far away in the future, Ireland only existed in songs.

Then he started making speeches. Not everybody had a radio and not everybody could read the newspapers at that time, so they went to hear people making speeches on O'Connell Street instead. The way you knew that people agreed with what you were saying is that they suddenly threw their hats and caps up in the air and cheered. The biggest crowd with the most amount of hats going up was always outside the GPO for de Valera. Some people had loudspeakers, but the good speakers needed nothing, only their own voices, and my uncle Ted says the best of them all was further up the street, a man named James Larkin who had a great way of stretching his arms out over the crowd.

My father wouldn't throw his hat up for anyone, so he started making his own speeches at the other end of the street with his friends. They had their own newspaper and their own leaflets and a party pin in the shape of a small 'e' for Éire: Ireland. He said it was time for Ireland to stand up on its own two feet and become a real country, not a place you dreamed about. The Irish people spent long enough building stone walls and saying the opposite. There were no rules about starting a new country and he wasn't interested in saying what everybody agreed with either. He had his own way of bringing his fist down at the end of a sentence, like he was banging the table. Hats went up for him all right. He had the crowd in his pocket when he put his hand on his heart, and he could have stolen all the flying hats from de Valera and Larkin and Cosgrave, but he started speaking in Irish and not everybody understood what he was saying.

One day he bought a motorbike, a BSA, so he could drive all around the country making speeches in small towns. Up and down the narrow roads he went, with his goggles on and his scarf flying in the wind behind him and the music of Schubert songs in his ear. He said Ireland would soon be like Germany with its own great culture and its own great inventions. He told them Ireland could never fight with the British in a war against Germany. Sometimes he stopped to say a prayer if there was a shrine by the roadside. Or to speak to somebody in Irish. And sometimes he had to stop because of cattle on the road, until the farmer cut a passage for him through the middle and the big cow faces got a fright and started jumping to escape in all directions from the noisy new sound of the motorbike driving through.

And then my father had the big idea of bringing people from other countries over to Ireland. After the war was over he met my mother in Dublin and decided to start a German-Irish family. He was still making speeches and writing articles for the newspaper and going around on his motorbike wearing goggles. But what better way to start a new country than marrying somebody and having children? Because that's what a new country is, he says, children. In the end of it all, we are the new country, the new Irish.

So that's how the film ends and the song goes on. My mother never imagined meeting someone, least of all an Irishman who could speak German and loved German music. She never imagined staying in Ireland for good, talking about Irish schools or making jam in Ireland and picking out children's shoes. My father asked her if she was willing to accompany him on a walk and correct his pronunciation. And because Germany had such great music, he wanted to tell her something great about Ireland, about St Patrick and about Irish history and Irish freedom. He told her he was not afraid to make sacrifices. He spoke quickly, as if he was still making a speech and people were throwing their hats up in the air by the thousands and didn't care if they ever came back down again.

My mother said she had to go home to Germany because that was a country that had just got its freedom, too, and had to be started from the beginning. He would not emigrate or leave his own native shores. He said he had bought a house that was not far away from the seafront. There were no pictures on the walls yet. There was no furniture, only a table and two chairs in the kitchen and a statue of the Virgin Mary. At night, you could be lonely and you'd miss your people because it was so quiet and so empty, just listening to the radio with a naked light bulb in the room and the wallpaper peeling on the walls. But in the end of it all, you would be starting a new republic with speckled Irish-German children.

They got married in Germany at Christmas. It all happened very quickly, because you had to do things immediately, without thinking too much. She didn't get a white dress but she got snow instead, thick silent snow. They went on the train together along the Rhine. They talked about the future and he said she would always be able to speak German in her own home. She said she would try and learn Irish, too. The children would be dressed for Ireland and for Germany. She said she was good at baking and telling stories. He said he was good with his hands. He said he would buy a camera so he could take lots of photographs, and she said she would keep them in a diary along with their first locks of hair. She said she would write everything down, all the first words and the first tears and everything that was happening in the news around the world.

There were things they didn't talk about. She kept her secret and he buried his past as well. He hid the picture of his own father in the wardrobe. He didn't want to offend her, having photographs of a British sailor hanging in the house. But she had nothing against England. It was not a marriage against anything, but for something new, she said. My mother even invented a new signal so that we would never get lost. A whistle made up of three notes, two short notes dropping down to one long note, like a secret code that no other family in the world would recognise.

They went to a mountain in each country. And no two mountains could be any more different. First they went to the famous Drachenfelz, right beside the River Rhine. They stayed in the hotel at the top and had breakfast looking out across the river below them, at the barges going up and down without a sound, like toy boats. She collected the train tickets and hotel receipts, even the thin decorated doilies under the coffee cups. Everything was important and would never be forgotten. She would not forget the smell of the sea either, or the smell of diesel fuel, or the faces of Irish people on the boat coming across to Ireland. They went up to a famous mountain in Ireland called Croagh Patrick to pray. It was a much harder mountain to climb and some people were even going up in their bare feet, with sharp rocks all along the path. At one point the wind came up so quickly they had to hold on to the rocks with their hands. There was no cable car. There was no hotel at the top either, where you could have coffee and cake. But when they reached the small church at the top and heard the voices of people praying the rosary together, there was a great view. They looked back down at the land all around them, with tiny houses and tiny fields and islands going out into the Atlantic.

Six

Inside our house is a warm country with a cake in the oven.

My mother makes everything better with cakes and stories and hugs that crack your bones. When everybody is good, my father buys pencil cases with six coloured pencils inside, all sharpened to a point. I draw a picture of the fox with blood around his nose. And Franz draws a picture of the house, with everybody in separate rooms – Vati, Mutti, Franz, Hanni and Maria, all standing at different windows and waving. Áine is gone away to London. The O'Neills are gone away, too, so there's no chopping wood and no English and everybody in our house is in the same country, saying the same words again.

It's Sunday and there's a smell of polish on the floor. There is a smell of baking and ironing and polish all over the house, because Onkel Ted is coming for tea. Onkel Ted is my father's brother, a Jesuit priest, and he comes to visit us after his swim at the Forty Foot. His hair is still wet and combed in lines. He once saved my father's life, long before he was a priest, when they were still at school and used to go swimming down in Glandore, not far from where they lived. My father started drowning one day so his younger brother had to jump in in his shirt to rescue him. Afterwards my father couldn't speak because he was shivering for a long time. But we don't talk about that now. Onkel Ted can speak German, too, but he doesn't say very much and my mother says he's not afraid of silence. So he listens instead and nods his head. I tell him that Franz has shadows around his eyes because he fell off the wall and broke his nose, but my mother says we won't talk about that now. My mother is trying to prove how decent and polite the Germans are and Onkel Ted is trying to prove how decent and polite the Irish are. And then it's time to reach into his jacket pocket for the bag of sweets and we can have two each and no more.

Outside our house is a different place.

One day my mother let us go down to the shop on our own, but she gave us a piece of rope and told us all to hold on to it so we would not get separated. An old woman stopped and said that was a great way of making sure we didn't get lost. My mother says we're surrounded by old women. Miss Tarleton, Miss Tomlinson, Miss Leonard, Miss Browne, Miss Russell, Miss Hosford, two Miss Ryans, two Miss Doyles, two Miss Lanes, Mrs Robinson, Mrs McSweeney and us in between them all. Some of them are friendly and others hate us. Some of them are Protestant and others are Catholic. The difference is that the Protestant bells make a song and the Catholic bells only make the same gong all the time.

You have to be careful where you kick the ball, because if it goes into Miss Tarleton's garden next door you'll never get it back. She told us not to dare put a foot inside her garden. Mrs McSweeney is nice and calls you in for a Yorkshire Toffee. The two Miss Lanes across the road have a gardener who wanted to give you back the ball one day but he couldn't. He came to the gate, ready to hand it back, but then one of the Miss Lanes appeared at the window and shook her head. The gardener stood there, not knowing what to do. We begged him please to give it back quickly before she came out, but he couldn't because he was working for Miss Lane, not for us, and she was already at the door saying, 'Give that ball here.' She said she was going to 'confiscate' it. We stood at the railings until Miss Lane said: 'Clear off. Away from the railings. Go on about your business, now.'

My mother laughs and says 'confiscate' doesn't mean kill or stab with a knife. It just means taking control of something that belongs to somebody else. One day I confiscated my brother's cars and threw them over the back wall into Miss Leonard's garden, but we got them back. One day Miss Tarleton declared a football amnesty and we got nine balls back, some of which never even belonged to us in the first place and most of which were confiscated all over again very shortly after that. Miss Tarleton might as well have handed them straight over to the Miss Lanes. My mother wants to know if the Miss Lanes play football in the kitchen at night. And she wants to know what the Miss Lanes have against her, because they just slammed the door in her face.

My mother says maybe they still hate Germany, but my father says they hate their own country even more. He says they still think they're living in Britain and they can't bear the sound of children speaking German on the street and, even worse, Irish. My mother says that means we have to be extra-nice to them, so they don't feel left out. You have to try not to throw the rockets up so high because the bang frightens old women and makes them think the Easter Rising is coming back again. You have to make sure the ball doesn't go into their garden. My father says it's your own fault if you lose the ball, because their garden is their country and you can't go in there. He says our country is divided into two parts, north and south, like two gardens. He says six counties in the north have been confiscated and are still controlled by Britain. The difference between one country and another is the song they sing at the end of the night in the cinema and the flag they have on the post office and the stamps you lick. When my father was working in the north of Ireland once, in a town called Coleraine, he refused to stand up in the cinema because they were playing the wrong song. Some people wanted to put him against the wall and shoot him. And then he left his job and came back to his own country where he could speak Irish any time he liked.

So, you have to be careful what country you kick your ball into and what song you stand up for in the cinema. You can't wave the wrong flag or wear the wrong badges, like the red poppies with the black dot in the middle. You have to be careful who to be sad for and not commemorate people who died on the wrong side.

My father also likes to slam the front door from time to time. And he's the best at slamming doors because he makes the whole house shake. Lots of things rattle. Clocks and glasses and cups shiver all the way down to the end of the street when my father answers the door. He sends a message out all over the world, depending on who knocked. If it's the old woman with the blanket who says 'God bless you, Mister', and promises to pray for him and all his family, if it's the man who sharpens the garden shears on the big wheel or if it's somebody collecting for the missions, then he gives them money and closes the door gently. If it's people selling carpets he shakes his head and closes the door firmly. If it's the two men in suits with Bibles then he slams it shut to make sure not even one of their words enters into the hall. And if it's one of the people selling poppies, then he slams it shut so fast that the whole street shakes. Sometimes the door slams shut in great anger of its own accord, but that's only because the back door has been left open and there's a draught going through the house.

One day Mr Cullen across the street asked us to help him wash his car. Afterwards he gave us a whole chocolate bar each, because he works for Cadbury's and has boxes and boxes of chocolate bars and Trigger bars in the boot of his car all the time. A woman came along the street selling the red badges with the black dot in the middle, so, as well as the chocolate, he bought us each a badge and pinned them to our jumpers. Lots of people on the street were wearing them – Miss Tarleton, Mrs Robinson, Miss Hosford, and the two Miss Lanes.

We didn't know they were wrong. We didn't know that wearing the wrong badge was like singing the wrong song in the cinema. So when my father saw us coming into the house wearing poppies, he slammed the door and all the clocks and cups and saucers shivered. Franz shivered too. My father ripped the poppies off so fast that he stabbed his own finger with the pin and I thought the badge was bleeding. He ran into the kitchen and opened the door of the boiler and threw the badges into the fire. Then he ran his finger under the tap and looked for a plaster while the badges burned to nothing and I thought it was a big waste because Mr Cullen had paid money for them.

'Who gave you those damn things?' my father wanted to know.

'Not like that,' my mother said. 'They don't understand.'

'Who gave you those poppies?' I could see that my father

hated even saying the word. 'They're British army poppies. Who gave them to you?'

'Mr Cullen.'

'Mr Cullen has no right. I'm going over to have a word with him.'

But my mother pulled on his elbow again. She told him that Mr Cullen's father died in the First World War and we didn't want to offend him. My father said Mr Cullen was trying hard to offend us. Lots of good people died on the German side, too, as well as all the Irish people who died fighting against the British army instead of joining in with them. And what about all the people who died in the famine and there are no badges you can get for them. Mr Cullen was mocking us, he said, giving us the poppies on purpose because the Germans lost the war and the Irish lost the six counties. My mother says she's not offended and Mr Cullen is too nice a man to even think of something like that. Its time to be big-hearted, she says. It's not important to win. And one day they'll commemorate all the people who died in those wars, not just their own.

'They have no children,' she said.

I was afraid that my father would find out we got chocolate and that would go in the fire, too. One day when we were coming home from the shop with Smarties, Franz dropped one of them on the street and my mother told him to leave it there because it was dirty. Then he threw the rest of the Smarties on the ground as well. If one was dirty then they must all be dirty. So I thought this was the same, that we had brought home something from outside on the street that was dirty.

'Never let me see those things again,' my father warned.

'Explain it to them, for God's sake,' my mother said. She doesn't like things being taken away from us without something else put in its place. She wants everything to be explained in a calm way, sitting down.

So my father sits at the table and we sit opposite him and he tells us why we can't accept poppies from anyone. First of all, he says, there was the British empire. He takes out a map of the world and points to all the pink bits that were owned by the British. Then he says the Germans wanted to have an empire, too, but the British didn't like the idea, so that was the First World War. He says millions of men died when two empires fought against each other and not even one person was killed on their own soil. It was big countries squabbling over little countries. Then right in the middle of it all the Irish decided to declare their own free state. We serve neither king nor kaiser, is what the Irish were saying to themselves and to all the other small countries around the world. But after that it's hard to understand what my father is saying any more because my mother's name was Kaiser and I don't know what the difference is between the First World War and the Second World War, and who the Nazis are and what they have to do with us. My mother says the Germans hardly behaved any better than the British, that instead of just having an empire and keeping slaves, the Nazis made slaves of their own people. The Germans turned themselves into slaves and started killing all the other people who were not German enough and my father says it's all the same thing.

'That's the end of the road,' he says, and I think there are people being killed at the end of the road and I don't want to go down there any more. My father says all we need to know is that poppies are not allowed in the house and that's the end of the story. We'll get our own badges and flags and songs. On St Patrick's day, we get shamrock and green badges and tricoloured jelly and ice cream.

At night in bed I'm afraid of silence. I can see the light coming under the door and I think my father still wants to go over to Mr Cullen, only that my mother is holding him back telling him to leave it. It's all in the past. We're in the future and we have to behave like the future. Then I hear the music coming up from the front room. Big German music spreading all over the house again, all the way up the stairs and in under the door with the light.

On Sunday, Onkel Ted comes to tea again with his wet hair combed in lines. I tell him about all the balls that Miss Tarleton gave back but the Miss Lanes took away again. I tell him that we were allowed to wash Mr Cullen's car and that we got chocolate. I tell him about the poppies and all the people being killed at the end of the road, but my mother says we won't talk about that now. I tell him that a man on the bus said Nazi to my mother under his breath, but we won't talk about that either. Then it's time to reach into Onkel Ted's pocket for the sweets and I don't know what to tell or not to talk about any more.

After that it's hard to know what's right and wrong. My mother says we've started doing a lot of things that make no sense. One day Franz put stones in his ears and he couldn't hear anything any more. Maria put a marrow-fat pea in her nose and it swelled up so much that the doctor had to come and take it out. Franz hit his thumb with a hammer and his finger went blue. Then I started burying all the silver spoons in the garden with my grandfather's initials FK written on them and my mother had to find the treasure. She laughs and says she hopes we won't do any more stupid things for a while. But then one day I started throwing the toy cars in the fire. I carried the box with all my cars into the kitchen and opened the door of the boiler by myself. I could see them lying on top of the orange coals. I watched them lighting up blue and green for a moment, until the flames disappeared and they went black and silver. One by one, I threw my cars on top of the coals until my mother came and asked me if I was out of my mind. She pulled me away and slammed the door of the boiler shut. She kneeled down and looked straight into my eyes. She makes everything better with hugs that break your bones. She tells me a story and says it's all forgotten now and we won't talk about it any more.

Seven

One day the boiler burst. It started hissing and clicking because of all the bad things that had been thrown into it. It got so hot that you could hear it cracking inside. Then there was a bang and it burst open with hot brown water gushing out all over the kitchen floor like tea with milk. My mother told my father to call the fire brigade. He frowned and sucked in air through his teeth. But then he put out the fire by himself. He carried the red coal out on a shovel and rolled up his sleeves to sweep the tea out the back door.

Then it's winter and our house starts filling up with mice. The pipes are cold and there are mice in every room because they get in under the back door. More and more of them are coming in every day until all the mice from the whole city are living in our house, my mother says. They're in the hall and on the stairs, everywhere you go. Any time you open the door and go into a room you see them running away. But mostly they're under the stairs where things are kept, like jam jars and pots and old shoes. There are so many of them that you have to watch where you walk, because one day when Franz was running down the three steps from the hallway into the kitchen, a baby mouse ran out from under the stairs and got squashed. We all crouched down to examine the flattened corpse until my mother told us not to be so interested in blood and took it away on the shovel.

It's so cold, we stay in one room by the fire where it's nice and warm, but if you go from that room up to the bedroom, it's like going out on the street and you need your coat on. My mother shows me her hands and says they will never get warm again. They've gone blue and green with the cold, like mackerel. She wants me to take pity on her hands and please let them in under my jumper to get warm. Be a good boy and give shelter to my poor fish-blue hands, she says. Just let them in for a little second or two to get warm. Then I scream and laugh and my mother screams and laughs, because the mackerel are fast swimmers and they go up under my jumper and down around my neck into my shirt and my mother says: '*Wie schön, wie schön warm*', oh lovely and cosy and warm.

Áine came back from London, but she's so sad that she only talks to herself in the mirror now. She can't even say 'walk on the wall' in Irish or English or go down to the seafront because her legs won't carry her. She's never going back to London, but she doesn't want to go back to Connemara either, so she lives with us. Sometimes you hear her upstairs crying and my mother says something happened to her, something that can't be explained or forgotten about either, so we just had to wait for her to get her words back. Onkel Ted has to come and make the sign of the cross over her, but still she won't come out and nobody knows what to do. My mother says it's the worst thing of all to be sad for yourself. You can help other people but often you can't help yourself.

At night you can hear the mice scratching and chasing each other around. For a while we counted the number of mice we saw every day, but then we didn't know if we were counting the same mouse twice in different rooms. My father bought two traps to catch them but that wasn't enough, so he bought another one that would catch three of them at the same time. It made no difference. Even if you caught three mice each day, my mother said it would still take a hundred years to catch them all because they could have families faster than we could kill them. The only thing was to stop talking about them and then they would go away. One day, there was a dead mouse in the trap that was half eaten by his own friends, and my mother said it was time to stop talking about it. Mice have no feelings, she said, and some people have no feelings either.

Áine spent all her day sitting up in bed smoking cigarettes. My mother said the best thing was for her to find a new job, then she could buy new clothes and go out and meet new people. Áine's legs wouldn't even carry her to the front door, so my mother went around to all the neighbours to ask if anyone knew of any jobs. She spoke to people who owned a man's shop and people in two grocery shops. After a long time she found a job in a gift shop, but Áine burst into tears on the first day and the owner told my mother that a gift shop is meant to be a happy place and nobody was going to buy anything from a person with tears in their eyes. He said he would prefer it if my mother came to work for him instead. My mother said she would love to work in the gift shop, but her hands were like mackerel and nobody was going to buy anything from fish-cold hands.

My mother said she knew what the problem was. If Áine had nice shoes then she would feel better and her legs would carry her down the street with no shame. My father said it was a waste and that everyone else in our house needed shoes, too, but my mother said it would all be paid back in other ways. So Áine got new shoes, but it made no difference. At night she left the light on in her room and my father said that was a waste, too, because she was not even reading a book, only sitting there smoking cigarettes. He said he gave up smoking when he wanted to buy German records and the only way of paying for them was to take the money from the cigarettes instead. If he had a mouse for every cigarette that Áine smoked and a penny for every mouse that he caught, he would be able to buy every opera and every symphony that ever existed on Deutsche Grammophon. He said it was the cigarettes that were making Áine sad. And one morning, my mother found a black hole in one of the pillow cases and she was afraid the house would burn down.

Every day my mother sits down with Áine and tries to make her smile. She says nobody can make you smile if you don't want to. Every day my father goes to work on the train. Every day we catch three mice and every day new ones come. Every day I scream and laugh when my mother's mackerel hands go under my jumper. Every Sunday Onkel Ted comes to tea after his swim at the Forty Foot because he doesn't feel the cold. We tell him things that happened, but not about mice and not about Áine or the black holes burned in her dresses. My sister Maria pulls up her dress to show Onkel Ted her tummy and then we reach into the pocket of his jacket for the sweets. He goes upstairs to make the sign of the cross over Áine and when he comes down again, he says my mother should take her out dancing.

'Irish dancing,' my father said. 'It would have to be Irish dancing.'

Then everybody is silent for a while looking at each other. Until my mother suddenly bursts out laughing and says she's forgotten how to dance. Two silent brothers looking at my mother laughing and laughing at the idea of coming all the way over from Germany to bring an Irish woman out to Irish dancing. Onkel Ted smiles and waits for my mother to finish. He's very serious and says there are things you never forget like cycling and swimming and helping other people. So one evening, my mother and Áine got dressed up and went dancing in the city. She put on her blue dress with the white spots and Áine put on her new shoes and a dress without holes in it. My father stayed at home reading his book and we sat on the carpet playing cars and listening to mice.

My mother said Irish dancing was not like waltzing or any kind of dancing that she had ever seen before. She said in Ireland your feet never even touch the ground. Everyone was floating, except for a man who sometimes slapped his heel down with a bang to the music as if he were trying to make holes in the floor. The dance hall smelled of smoke and perfume and sweat and it was filled with people of all ages. There was a priest and some nuns as well, sitting down in the seats. An old woman with long hair was dancing as if she were only sixteen. All the men were on one side of the hall and all the women on the other. The women danced as if the men didn't exist, and at the refreshments counter there were people talking over tea and sandwiches as if the dancing didn't exist. My mother watched three boys sharing a bottle of fizzy lemonade. Each time one of them drank through the straw, the other two kept watch to make sure he didn't go past a certain mark before he passed it on to the next boy. They had tears in their eyes from drinking so fast.

All the time, men came walking across from the other side of the hall to ask my mother to dance, but she smiled and shook her head. She thanked them and asked them to dance with Áine instead. My mother says you can see a man's face drop. But once they had come all the way over, they could not just turn around and go away again empty-handed. Áine didn't want to dance either. She said her legs were gone soft. So the man had to pull her out by the hand, with my mother pushing her from behind. Then Áine tried to hold on to her seat with her foot and the chair went scraping out on the dance floor behind her, until my mother finally got it off. Even then the man had a hard job trying to make Áine dance, because her feet stayed on the floor and would not move. My mother said Áine had cement in her shoes and all the men soon stopped coming over.

She says it was funny, a German woman pushing an Irish woman out to dance against her will. She says it's hard to understand what's going on in people's heads in Ireland. She says Irish people dance with their heads and speak with their feet. Everybody knows what's inside everybody else's head, but nobody ever says it out loud. They like to keep everything inside. She says German people say what they think and Irish people keep it to themselves and maybe the Irish way is sometimes better. In Germany, she says, people think before they speak so that they mean what they say, while in Ireland, people think after they speak so as to find out what they mean. In Ireland the words never touch the ground.

After the dancing, Áine lost her words altogether. There was something inside her head that was making her sick and my mother said if she didn't speak about it, she would die. She was not eating any more either, only smoking cigarettes. Dr Sheehan had to come one day, because Áine started burning holes in her legs and arms. He said she would have to go to hospital, but then Onkel Ted came to make the sign of the cross over her once more. He spent a long time in her room talking to her very quietly and nodding his head. He gave her lots of time to remember everything that happened, until she finally spoke in her own language. She told Onkel Ted something in Irish and he came downstairs with the answer. He said if Áine was to stop burning holes in her arms and legs, if she was ever to smile again and stop being sad, then she would have to get her baby back. So one day my mother and Áine went out and they came back with a new baby. She was going back home again because she was happy now. She didn't need to smoke cigarettes and talk to herself any more because she had the baby to talk to. My mother helped her to pack her suitcase with lots of German baby clothes and they laughed because Áine said it was nearly like a German baby going home to Connemara. And the day she was leaving, it was my mother who was crying because Áine was smiling.

Men came to fix the boiler. There was some more brown tea with milk on the floor of the kitchen, but then it was all over and the pipes started heating up again. My father put lots of coal into the boiler so the house got warm. Then there was a delivery of coal. A truck stopped on the street outside and because they couldn't go around the back, the men with black faces and black hands had to come through the house. My mother was afraid the wind would slam the doors shut in anger, so we had to hold them open, Franz at the front door, me at the in-between door, and Maria at the back door. She told us to count the bags as they came in. In Ireland people count in their heads, she said, but in Germany people count out loud. Out loud we counted – *Eins, Zwei, Drei, Vier, Fünf* . . . all the way up to fifteen. The men walked in stooped over with the heavy sacks, leaving long black marks where the sacks scraped against the wall on their way through. And where they went down the three steps towards the kitchen and out the back door, they put a black hand up every time to hold on to the door frame. One of the men winked and made me forget what number I was on. I didn't know if I should be counting the sack that was coming or the sack gone by. But then I heard Franz counting the next number at the front door and I was able to catch up.

When the shed outside was full and the coal was spilling out across the path, the men got back into the truck. One of them counted the empty sacks as if he could not trust us to count right. He came back inside with a pink piece of paper covered with black fingerprints and asked my mother to sign her name. That was to make sure she agreed that there was no mistake in the counting and that nobody ran away with one of the empty sacks. But there could be no mistake because we counted out loud in German and the man counted the empty sacks in English, and it was the same number no matter what language.

Eight

My mother has to go home to Kempen and we can't go with her. She's on the phone in the front room crying and speaking in a loud voice to Germany and we're outside the door listening until she comes out with shadows around her eyes. She says she has to go away for a while. So then we have to stay in the house with the yellow door where they speak no Irish and no German, only English. My mother lays everything out on the bed for us and packs it into a bag. We get up very early in the morning when it's still dark outside and the light in the bedroom is so bright that you can't look at it. It's cold, too, and Franz is standing on the bed in his underpants, shivering and singing a long note with his teeth clacking. I'm able to put my shirt on by myself but I can't do the buttons because my fingers are soft. My mother is in a hurry and she pinched my neck when she was doing up the top button, but she said sorry and then it's time to go. It's still dark outside on the street and you can blow your breath out like smoke. It's still dark when we get on the bus and still dark when we come up to the yellow door and then I can't walk because my legs are soft. I have a limp in both legs and I hold on to my mother's coat because I don't want to emigrate and live in a different country from her.

I don't know where Germany is. I know it's far away

from Ireland because you can't go there on the bus, you can only look at it on the map. I know there was the First World War and the Second World War and the second would not have happened without the first. I know the Germans wanted to have an empire and that wasn't allowed. The goat wanted to have a long tail but only got a short one, my mother says, whenever we want something that we can't have.

I don't like the house with the yellow door. I don't like the room with the toilet and ten potties hanging on the wall. I don't like the smell of the brown rubber sheet on the bed and I don't like the smell of custard. The house with the yellow door and the yellow custard is a place where you wait for your mother to come back and sometimes you hear other children crying on the stairs because they're waiting too. Franz would not eat the custard or go to the toilet. He closed his mouth and said he would never open it again for the rest of his life. The nurse tried to pretend that the spoon was a train going into his mouth, but he shook his head and turned away. He could only eat and go to the toilet in German. So my father had to come and bring him to the toilet. I closed my mouth and refused to speak because the nurse would not say goodbye to the moon. I said she was from a different country and then my father had to come another time and give the nurse the word for moon in Irish.

I know that my mother's father, Franz Kaiser, owned a stationery shop in the town of Kempen and nobody had any money to buy anything, so he had to close it down. But that didn't stop him making jokes and playing tricks on people just to see the look on their faces. My mother says he was famous for all the funny things he did because he always made up for it afterwards. One day in the Kranz

Café he stuck his finger into a doughnut and held it up in the air to ask how much it cost, just to see the look on their faces when he said it was too expensive. But then he bought all of them, one each for my mother and her four sisters and one each for all the other children he could find on the market square.

One day he played a trick on the commanding officer of the Belgian army. I know that my mother's town was in the Rhineland but that was occupied by the Belgians and the French as punishment for the First World War. It was confiscated from the Germans by the Treaty of Versailles. So one night Franz Kaiser and his cousin Fritz planned a new trick. They filled a porcelain potty full of ink from the shop. They spread out a sheet of paper on the table and took down the big quill from over the door outside the shop. Then they invited the commanding officer of the Belgian army to come to the house for a drink, just to see the look on his face when they brought him over to the table and asked him to sign a new treaty. The officer was very angry, but then they gave him a cigar and the best wine in the house. My mother says everybody liked Franz Kaiser's jokes, even the people who were joked about, and maybe the Second World War would not have happened if there were more people like him. Then the Nazis took over and there was no more time for joking in Germany.

Then he was ill and my mother had to tell him what was happening outside on the square. He sat up in a bed in the living room upstairs over the shop, with the big alcove and the piano at the window. She had to look out and tell him who was going by. And every day, her mother played for him to make him better. She sang the *Freischutz* and all the Schubert songs she had performed at the opera house in Krefeld, when he sent her a bouquet of bananas instead of flowers. Every day, she shaved his face and played the piano, but he didn't get better. My mother was nine years old and one day he asked her to bring him a mirror so he could say goodbye to himself. He didn't want to know who was passing by the house any more. All he did was look into the mirror for a long time in silence. Then he smiled at himself and said: *'Tschüss, Franz . . .'*

My mother says she will never forget the smell of flowers all around his bed and she will never forget the people of the town all standing outside on the market square. She remembers the shadows around her mother's eyes when the coffin came out of the house. She says that maybe it's not such a good thing to be the child of two people who loved each other so much, because it's like being in a novel or a song or a big film that you might never get out of.

After that her mother was always dressed in black. Every evening she gathered all the five girls together in the living room over the shop. Marianne, Elfriede, Irmgard, Lisalotte and Minne all listening to Schubert songs and looking out at the people crossing the Buttermarkt square to go to the cinema. My mother says she can remember the soft, sad rain that blurred the sign above the cinema saying 'Kempener Lichtspiele' and made the tree trunks black. There was no money left in Germany, so her mother then had to teach the piano and put a candle in the fire to make the house look warm. They had to sell things like candlesticks and vases. The furniture began to disappear and the rooms began to look empty. Then Germany was so poor that they decided to emigrate to Brazil.

Things were happening in the town of Kempen that made people afraid. Everyone was afraid of the Communists and one night two men in brown shirts were beaten up with sticks in the street near the old school. Then it was all turned around and the Communist men were beaten up with sticks and fists by the men in brown shirts. People stayed inside their houses because of things like that. They didn't want to go outside and my mother says Germany belonged to the fist people and it was better to start again somewhere else like Brazil.

First of all it was the oldest sisters Marianne and Elfriede who were to go and marry two German boys already out there. There was a Catholic organisation in the Rhineland which matched up German girls with German boys to go and start a new life planting coffee and tobacco and looking for rubber trees. They would arrange the passage first to San Francisco and on to Brazil through missionary routes. Marianne and Elfriede went to special courses at the weekend to learn about agriculture. My mother and her sisters started laying out their things on the bed, getting ready to pack their bags, and reading books about the rainforest. They knew it would be very hot, so they bought straw hats and fans. There would be lots of insects, too, so they had to learn how to smoke to keep them away.

'Can we do the pipes now,' Lisalotte kept asking.

But first of all they had to sit by the piano and learn all the Schubert songs. In Brazil, it would be just as important to keep singing the German songs and telling German stories as it was to smoke and keep the insects away. And maybe the music would even help to bring back the good times. Maybe it was not too late and the music would help the word people to take over again from the fist people in Germany. They even sang one or two pop songs as well, swing songs that everybody whistled and sang on the Buttermarkt square.

They sang and laughed until the tears came into her

mother's eyes and nobody knew if she was crying or laughing any more. And then, at last, they took out the pipes and filled them up with tobacco from a tweed pouch. They got out the flint lighter with the initials FK that Franz Kaiser used for cigars. All the things still there from the time he invited men from the town to come over to the house and smoke until you couldn't even see the wallpaper. Now it was time for the girls to do the same. They lit up the pipes and passed them around. Each one of them had to practise puffing and coughing and spitting and holding the pipe in the side of her mouth. The smell of tobacco filled the room and it was like her father was back again.

'At last the room smells like men again,' my mother said, and they had to laugh and cough so much that they couldn't speak. They practised singing and smoking every night until they were ready to go away. But then my mother's mother Berta got ill. She was not able to live without Franz Kaiser, either in Germany or in Brazil. She died and there was another big funeral with lots of people standing outside on the Buttermarkt square waiting for the coffin to come out of the house. Then my mother and her sisters had to go to live with their Onkel Gerd and aunt Ta Maria. Then it was the end of smoking pipes and talking about Brazil, because Onkel Gerd was the lord mayor and he said he couldn't let them emigrate until they were eighteen. He said they would be homesick. They would be able to make German cakes and sing German songs but they would miss their own country. He didn't say they were not allowed to go. Instead, he gathered them all in the living room and turned the question over to them.

'What would you do if you were in my shoes?' he asked them. 'What if you suddenly had five lovely daughters, would you send them away to Brazil to be eaten by insects?'

After that there was lots of trouble for Onkel Gerd because he would not join the Nazi party. He said there was no place left in Germany for the word people to go. He said the fist people had robbed all the words, from the church, from all the old songs, from books and films. They had broken into the theatre and taken the drama out on to the streets. Everybody was excited by the new colours and the new words. But if you were not one of the fist people, you had to learn silence. You could only speak in the privacy of your own house, Onkel Gerd said. You could make jokes inside, but that's where they had to stay because it was not safe to speak outside any more. There were jokes you could not make on the Buttermarkt square any more because the fist people had taken over Germany. My mother says that if there were more people like Onkel Gerd then lots of things would not have happened.

One day my father came to the house with the yellow door and took us home on the bus. He was smiling and said we would never have to eat custard again. I know that Germany is a place full of cakes and nice things that you can't get in Ireland, because my mother came back with four large suitcases, full of chocolate and toys and clothes. There were new games, too, like the game where you throw all the coloured sticks on the floor in a big mess and then you have to pick them out one by one. My mother looked new because she had new clothes. She was smiling all the time and had new perfume on. She brought home a pewter plate and candlestick that was left over from her father and mother's house. She had pictures of the house and said we would all go there one day. My father and mother drank wine and there was big German music all around the house, maybe outside the house, too, and all the way down to the end of the street.

Sometimes my mother turns around suddenly to take us all into her arms so that my face is squashed up against Franz and Maria. Sometimes she wants to take a bite out of Maria's arm, just a little bite. Sometimes she still has tears in her eyes, either because she's so happy or because she is still sad for Onkel Gerd. He was a good man who spoke very little, only when he had something to say. It was the biggest funeral she had ever seen in Kempen, because he was a lord mayor once and he would not join the fist people. He was not afraid to resist. She hung a photograph of him in the living room so that we could see him and be like him.

My mother also brought back a typewriter and some days later she opened it up and allowed me to type my name. Johannes. The letters fly out and hit the page. *Lettetet. Lettetet.* Sometimes two letters get stuck in mid-air and my mother says we have to be more gentle, only one at a time. She holds my finger and helps me to pick out the letter. I press down on the key and the letter shoots out so fast that you can hardly see it. It slaps against the paper like magic. I want to write 'Johannes is the best boy in the world', but it would take too long. Then I ask her if I can write 'Johannes is the boldest boy in the world' instead and my mother laughs out loud. She says I'm the best boy and the boldest boy at the same time, because I get the most amount of slaps from my father and the most amount of hugs from her to make up for it. Then Franz wants to write down that he will never have to emigrate and go to the yellow house again but it's too late and we have to go to bed now.

At night, I can hear my mother downstairs in the kitchen

with the typewriter. She's *lettetetting* on her own, while my father is in the front room reading. The letters fly out and hit the page faster than you can speak. She's *lettetetting* and *lettetetting* because there's a story that she can't tell anyone, not even my father. You can't be afraid of silence, she says. And stories that you have to write down are different to stories that you tell people out loud, because they're harder to explain and you have to wait for the right moment. The only thing she can do is to write them down on paper for us to read later on.

'To my children,' she writes. 'One day, when you're old enough, you will understand what happened to me, how I got trapped in Germany and couldn't help myself. I want to tell you about the time when I was afraid, when I stood in my room and couldn't shout for help and heard the footsteps of a man named Stiegler coming up the stairs.'

Nine

On the first day of school I slapped the teacher in the face. I knew there would be lots of trouble. I thought Onkel Ted would have to come and make the sign of the cross over me, but when my mother came to collect me she said nothing, just smiled. The teacher said she had never been hit by a child before and that I was the boldest boy she had ever met in her entire life. My mother was so proud of me that she smiled and kneeled down to look into my eyes for a long time. Outside she told all the other mothers that I slapped the teacher in the face and they shook their heads. On the way home the bus conductor threw his eyes up and said I would go far. She even told the man with one arm in the vegetable shop.

'You'll have trouble with him,' they all said, but my mother shook her head.

'Oh no,' she said. 'He's going to be like his uncle, Onkel Gerd.'

The teacher's name is Bean Uí Chadhain and the school is called Scoil Lorcáin. You go down the steps into the classroom at the bottom and there is lots of noise from all the other children and a sweet smell, like a school bag with a banana sandwich left inside. There are toys in boxes to play with, but some of them are broken and the cars have bits of plasticine stuck to the wheels. There's a map of the world on the wall and you learn to sing and go to the toilet in Irish, to the *leithreas*. And after that you get into another line to go to the yard, where the older girls are chasing and screaming, and across the wall the older boys are chasing and fighting. Then it's time to sing the song about the little red fox. Everybody who is good gets a *milseán*, a sweet, and anyone who is bold has to stand on the table to show how bold you are.

'*Maidirín a rua, 'tá dána*,' we all sing together. The little red fox is bold. Except that bold doesn't just mean bold, it also means cute and cheeky and brave and not afraid of people. The little red fox who is not afraid of anyone at all, we sing. But then Bean Uí Chadhain lifted me up on the table and said I was not going to get a sweet.

'Bold, bold, bold,' she said. '*Dána, dána, dána.*'

So then I slapped her in the face and my mother was proud of me. She's so happy that she puts her hand on my shoulder and tells everybody in Ireland what I did. They shake their heads but they should be nodding. Only Onkel Ted nods his head slowly on Sunday when he comes, but then you don't know sometimes what's right and wrong because he nods slowly even when you tell him bad things that happened. He says there are some things you can only do once in your life and most people never do at all. My father says Bean Uí Chadhain is the wife of a famous Irish writer called Máirtín Ó Cadhain who wrote a book about dead people talking. It's about a graveyard in Connemara where all the dead people talk to each other and anyone who dies brings new stories from the living world over the ground. I slapped the writer's wife, my father says, and he's proud, too, because the book was written in Irish. And dead people have the best conversations of all. Lots of people don't really speak until they're dead, because only then can they say all of the things to each other in the graveyard that they have been keeping secret all their lives.

My mother says you can't be afraid of anyone. You can't let anyone make you small, because that's what they tried to do with Onkel Gerd. He had to keep quiet and say nothing while he was alive, but now he's talking in the grave. He's talking to my mother's father and mother in Kempen, telling them that my mother didn't go to Brazil after all, but went to live in Ireland instead. Now they're having a great talk about how things were in the old days, all the jokes that Franz Kaiser made and why nobody had a sense of humour any more except for the people who were already in the grave and had nothing to lose. Now Franz Kaiser is playing all the tricks he didn't get to finish before he died. And now Onkel Gerd is telling everybody down there that Hitler is dead. There were stories brought down with the war, when the planes were all going back home to England and they dropped the bombs on the bakery in Kempen very early one morning when everybody was queuing up for bread. There were stories going down of people killed all over Europe when nobody was able to stop the fist people from taking over.

My mother says you can't keep people from talking in the grave. And you can't keep them quiet by making them stay at home or locking them up or stopping them from writing in newspapers. That's why you should never be afraid to speak. My father says that all the people who died in the Irish famine are still talking. They're whispering with dry lips and staring out with empty eyes. He says you can't go anywhere in Ireland without hearing them. You go out into the fields around west Cork, he says, and it's never silent, not even for a moment. He says a lot of the people born after the famine could not talk because they had lost their language and that's why they speak English and have to listen to the words first before they can be sure of what they're saying. But all that will be put right now that we're speaking Irish again.

You're better off dead than not being able to speak, my mother says. That's what they tried to do to Onkel Gerd. He was the Bürgermeister, the lord mayor, and they came to him every day and asked him to do things he didn't want. Ta Maria was the sister of my mother's mother Berta and she was called Frau Bürgermeister, Mrs Lord Mayor. Then they suddenly had five daughters to look after and send to school every day on the train to the convent in Mühlhausen. So when people came to the house and said the lord mayor should belong to the Nazi party, he said he was the father of five girls and shook his head every time. They were friendly and polite and spoke to Ta Maria, too, on the way across the Buttermarkt square, hoping that she would change his mind. They liked Onkel Gerd and said he was a good lord mayor, so they didn't want him to be made small like the other man Lamprecht who had to be taken away to a camp in Dachau because he kept on writing in the newspaper. They said they were hoping that would not happen to a man with five lovely new daughters.

Onkel Gerd sat in silence for a long time every evening, my mother says, because it was not easy to know what was right and wrong sometimes. My mother and her sisters kept on going to school and every Sunday they went to the graveyard to visit their father and mother. They passed by the old house on the Buttermarkt square but never went inside again because there were other people living there now. The town had changed. Everyone was poor and it was all right to beg and have a leg missing. People who had never dreamed of asking for things before were coming up to the house looking for help. So then there was an election and the Nazi party promised there would be no beggars in Germany ever again. At night, people said there were groups of men gathering around fires outside the town. People didn't know whether it was exciting or frightening or both, because on the day of the election the town was full of cars and people drinking beer in their best clothes, and when Onkel Gerd went up to vote, there was trouble.

My mother says they were very sly. They wanted to see what side Onkel Gerd was on, so they gave him a ballot paper with a special mark on it. He looked at the names of the parties and the boxes beside them to make an X in, with the Nazi party at the top and all the other parties like the SPD and the Central party below. When he held the ballot paper up to the light he found a small watermark in the corner that should not have been there. He knew they could check afterwards to see where he put the X.

'This is still a secret vote,' Onkel Gerd said and handed back the paper.

Everybody had their eyes on him and the hall was silent. He knew there would be trouble because he asked what the watermark was doing on his ballot paper, but the official just smiled and said he was making too much of it. In any case, they said, if he had a clear conscience and had nothing to hide, then the watermark wouldn't bother him because everyone else was voting for the Nazi party, too.

'What about the secret ballot?' Onkel Gerd demanded. If everyone was going to vote for the Nazi party, then wasn't it better if they did so by choice? He refused to leave. He knew it was the only way that he could be honest and not take the easy way out like everyone else. He didn't say he was against anyone or for anyone else.

He just stood and waited while the officials all whispered among themselves and wondered what to do. Until they gave him a clean ballot paper at last, because they couldn't bear to look at his face any more and they didn't want the lord mayor standing around in the polling station all day with his arms folded for everyone to see.

My mother says it's important to make a stand. Onkel Gerd won his fight in the polling station, but he went home and knew that everything was lost. Within days they heard from the other towns in the Rhineland that the lord mayors who had not spotted the watermark on the ballot paper were not so lucky. They were put out of office immediately the following day and replaced by people on the side of the Nazi party. Many of them were beaten up, my mother says. The fist people came to their houses and some of them were sick for a long time and couldn't hear properly afterwards or had trouble with their kidneys and never went to work again.

Onkel Gerd stayed on as lord mayor because nobody knew where he put his X. But that didn't last long either because they came to his office every day and asked him to do things he didn't want. And one day, when it was suddenly against the law to be a lord mayor without belonging to the Nazi party, he had to go. They gave him a last chance, but he still shook his head. Another man was waiting to take over and sit down as soon as Onkel Gerd cleared his desk. There was some handshaking and polite conversation, but then it was over quite suddenly and it was hard to walk home that day. It was hard to walk past people on the street because everybody knew he was nothing any more. And it was even harder to explain to Ta Maria and their five new daughters. She had her apron up to her eyes as they gathered together in the living room.

He stood there to tell them that even though he was not the lord mayor any more and nobody knew where the money was going to come from, he would still do everything he could to look after them. He had been made small, but he would not let them down. Some of the women still called Ta Maria Frau Bürgermeister on the street, but that was just a habit and it didn't really matter. Anyone who was not with the Nazis had nothing more to say.

After that, Onkel Gerd would sit at home for a long time without saying a word. Sometimes he played the lute in the evening and sometimes he lit a cigar and let the smoke fill the room until nobody could see him any more and it looked like he had disappeared. It looked like the Bürgermeister had vanished from the town altogether because that's what the Nazi people wanted, and even when he went for the short walk to Mass or to the library, nobody saw him. Mostly he stayed at home reading books, because there were very few people he could talk to and reading was the best kind of conversation you could have. With no secrets held back. It was as good as any conversation you could have in the graveyard.

I am the boy who slapped his teacher in the face. I'm the boy who's not afraid of anything, my mother says. One day she didn't come to collect me. I ran up to the gate of the school but she wasn't there. She was late because the bus driver didn't see her, even though she had her hand out. She says bus drivers in Ireland are blind because they don't know what it's like to be a passenger. So she didn't come and I ran all the way home in the rain. She was waiting at the door when I got back. She took off my shoes and stuffed them with newspapers. She put them beside the boiler and started rubbing my head with the towel and laughing because my hair was standing up like a hedgehog. And then it was time to make a cake. I stood beside her in the kitchen and tried to teach her Irish. She was holding the bowl in one arm and stirring with the other. I looked at her mouth as she repeated the word in Irish for milk. But it was all wrong. Her lips were still trying to speak German and it was funny to hear her say it as if she didn't know what milk was. I tried other words like the Irish for water, bread, butter, but she didn't know what they were either. Every time she tried to get it right, she had to smile and surrender, because she knew that Irish was my language.

'*Ceol*,' I said. 'That's music.'

'*Ceol*,' she repeated, but it was still not right.

She kneeled down and watched me say it again. She held her hands up in the air as if she was counting to ten with cake mixture all over her fingers. She followed my lips with her eyes but she could see no difference. Then she continued making the cake and trying the word out by herself.

'*Ceol, ceol, ceol*.'

She thought it was funny that I was teaching her how to speak. I was the teacher now and she was the schoolgirl learning to say the words and trying to grow up. Sometimes in the evening after dinner, she went back to the school on the bus to learn Irish and then we had to help her with her homework. But she can't be Irish. It's too hard.

Then I made a rule about Irish in the kitchen. I drew a line and said that anyone crossing the border into my land was not allowed to speak German, only Irish. If my mother or Franz or Maria wanted to come in, they had to stop and say something in Irish first. And if they spoke German, I expelled them. Even my mother has to cross over to Irish if she wants to get into my country. But she laughs. She says there will be no yellow cake with chocolate on top if I stop her. She says you can't make rules like that in the kitchen. It's like something the Nazis would do. I keep saying that nobody can break my rules but she keeps laughing at me. She says she's going to cross over and tickle me. She puts the cake in the oven and then says the word in Irish for music again. And even though she doesn't say it right, even though she's still saying it with German lips, I can't stop her coming across the line and I can't stop her laughing and tickling me to death.

Ten

First of all you have to mix the butter with the sugar. You have to do it hard, my mother says, but after that, everything has to be done very gently because you don't want to make an unhappy cake. If you bake in anger it will taste of nothing. You have to treat the ingredients with respect and affection. You lift the mixture and slip the beaten egg inside, the way you would slip a love letter into an envelope, she says and laughs out loud. You fold in the flour with air-kisses and you stir in one direction only, otherwise people will get the taste of doubt. And when you lay the mixture into the baking tin, you place a piece of brown paper all around the edge and another flat piece across the top to create a dome that will keep it from burning. And once the letter is posted and the cake is in the oven, you have to be very quiet and wait. You don't trudge around the house shouting and slamming doors. You don't argue and you don't say a bad word about anyone. You whisper, you nod, you tiptoe around the kitchen.

My mother likes the radio. She likes the song 'Roses Are Red, My Love, Violets Are Blue', but she's not allowed to sing it and she can only listen to it when my father is at work. When he comes home he switches on the news. The light comes on and you see all the names of the different cities like Budapest and Prague, but it takes a while for the radio to warm up and the voices to come out. After the news the radio should be speaking Irish. If you sing a song, sing an Irish song, the man says, and my father nods his head. If there's a pop song in English my father suddenly pushes back the chair with a big yelp on the floor and rushes over to switch it off. The voice doesn't take time to go away again, it disappears immediately. But even in the few seconds it takes my father to switch it off, before it gets a chance to go as far as 'Sugar is sweet, my love . . .', enough of the song has escaped and the words are floating around the breakfast room. We all sit around the table in silence, but you can still hear the song echoing along the walls. It gets stuck to the ceiling. Stuck to the inside of your head. And even though my mother is not allowed to sing it, she can't stop humming to herself in the kitchen afterwards.

In Germany, my mother says, there was good music on the radio. You had great singers like Richard Tauber and you heard some good stories and theatre if you were lucky. But it wasn't long before you got the speeches. Onkel Gerd said people thought Goebbels and Hitler had rabies because they were always foaming at the mouth. He said that having the radio on was like letting somebody into the house, somebody you thought you could trust, somebody who would pretend to be your friend and then start saying things in your ear. And once you invited them in for afternoon coffee and cake, you would be slow to argue back. Sometimes Onkel Gerd talked back at the radio, standing in the middle of the room and waving his finger, but there was no point because the radio never listens. Ta Maria said you could always tell a decent person by their shoes and their hands, but Onkel Gerd said the radio would sit there all polite and decent in your front room and, before you knew it, you found yourself agreeing with the most outrageous gossip and resentment. The radio made you feel that you belonged to a great country. It made you feel safe and hurt and proud, all at the same time. Some people had no friends at all and no mind of their own, only the radio and the voice of Hitler foaming at the mouth. The radio was a scoundrel who never listens, a scoundrel with nice hands and nice shoes and nice music.

'You can't switch off what's happening,' Ta Maria said.

But Onkel Gerd preferred the silence. Sometimes they huddled together and listened to jazz music from London in secret, like my mother does when my father is out at work. But that's dangerous, too. In our house, it's dangerous to sing a song or say what's inside your head. You have to be careful or else my father will get up and switch you off like the radio.

In Kempen, the man on the radio could just walk in the front door of any house and invite himself in for coffee and cake. People threw their arms out. Sometimes they brought out their best linen tablecloth and lit a candle. Some of them got dressed up to listen to the radio. If it was a Strauss concert they clapped along with the audience at the state concert hall in Vienna as if they were there themselves. They believed what they heard. And before they knew it, they were clapping after some speech, too, because they had no idea who they were letting into their home. The town hall on the Buttermarkt square was then called the 'brown house' because it was full of men in brown uniforms. The newspaper man Lamprecht was taken away to the KZ in Dachau where he could not say another word and that's what was going to happen to Uncle Gerd, too, if he opened his mouth. They had switched him off. He had no name any more and no voice. He had no face and no hair and no eyes. Nobody saw him, even when he walked over to Mass on Sunday morning. And then one day they made a rule that the Jewish people had no names and no faces either. Everybody had to pretend they had disappeared, too. When they came to the market square you could not buy their pickled gherkins, you could not even say 'good morning' to them. They still walked around the streets but nobody could see them. It was easy enough, because once the lord mayor was gone and the newspaper man was gone, anyone else could disappear, too.

'*Unverschämt*,' Ta Maria said. It was a rule that nobody would be able to obey. Onkel Gerd said it was un-German and wouldn't last long. He said they would continue to greet Jews in the street as always. No matter what rule they made in the brown house, they would carry on recognising Jewish names and faces. But it didn't matter any more because it was like the people with no faces saying hello to other people with no faces. They might as well be like the people in the graveyard talking to each other. Nobody in the brown house cared very much whether Onkel Gerd was still saying hello to the Jews or not because he didn't exist anyway. What they did care about was my mother and her sisters. They didn't want them to disappear, so they made another rule which forced them to join the Bund deutscher Mädels – the League of German Girls. It was another rule that could not be obeyed. So they ignored it and continued to attend their own Catholic youth meetings until people came around to the house and asked questions. Three hundred other girls from Kempen and the surrounding district had all joined in the BDM rallies without question, so why not the Kaiser girls.

Ta Maria heard things at the Café Kranz on the Burgring. She went around there for coffee every afternoon because it was the place to hear what people were saying around the town, what they whispered, what you did not hear on the radio. Everybody said it was best to go along with things for the moment, see what happened. It wasn't all that serious anyway, because they were joking and giving the BDM funny new names in secret. Instead of calling it the League of German Girls, everybody was now calling it Bund deutscher Matratzen – the League of German Mattresses. My mother says her father would have laughed at that.

Onkel Gerd called them all into the living room and asked them to sit down. He waited for a long time, quietly picking out his words before he slowly looked around at each of them individually and told them they had to decide for themselves. He was always calm. He didn't trust things that were said with emotion, the way they spoke on the radio. Instead, he spoke slowly in clear sentences, breathing quietly and hardly moving his head, like a father. He said it was all right for him to make a sacrifice, but he would not force it on them. He said you have an instinct and you have an intellect and if you had to join the BDM meetings by law, then maybe there was another way out. Sometimes it's good to tiptoe around things to avoid trouble.

'The silent negative,' he said. 'We will use the silent negative.'

On Sunday the Buttermarkt square was full of colour. There were flags everywhere, flying above the trees and hanging from all the windows around the square. There were standing columns, too, with eagle wings. Loudspeakers had been broadcasting speeches and marching music all morning, and a massive portrait of the Führer had been put up outside the brown house. My mother says she looked up and saw a long red flag with the black swastika on a white circle hanging from the window where her mother once played the piano and where her father said goodbye to himself in the mirror. Sometimes, she says, you have to bite your lip and not allow yourself to be hurt.

Onkel Gerd said it was only a matter of time before somebody took it into his head to play God. The BDM meeting had been arranged to coincide with Mass, so that the girls in Kempen would turn away from the church, so they would belong to the state instead, like a big family. My mother insisted on getting up for early Mass. She could hear the loudspeakers on the square as if they wanted to drown out the prayers inside. And when she arrived late on the square with her missal under her arm, the BDM leader was already foaming at the mouth. She told the Kempen girls they would never need Mass or missals, or candles or head scarves or Corpus Christi processions any more, because now they would be devoted to the Führer. One day, the men in brown broke into the convent school in Mühlhausen smashing everything up and painting swastikas on the walls of the classrooms. And not long after that, they closed the convent down altogether so the nuns had to disappear, too.

The leaves of the missal are not like any other book, they are soft and thin, easy to bend and easy to turn without the slightest bit of noise in church. But outside at the big BDM assembly on the square, my mother says they made a big noise that nobody could ignore. All the girls had to raise their right arms in salute. So when my mother raised her arm, the missal fell down on the cobbles with a clack. It opened up and the breeze rustled the pages so they could be heard all around the square, maybe even all around the town. She bent down and picked it up. She dusted off the covers and then finally raised her arm in the air towards the portrait of the Führer over the Rathaus. The entire square was suddenly tilted at an angle, like a tilted painting, like the dizzy way you can see things when you bend down to look back through your legs. It was time to be obedient, time to swear an oath of allegiance to the Führer, time for the silent negative.

'I swear under oath that I will – NOT – serve the Führer as long as I live.'

After that it was like any other Sunday. Apart from the flags and the loudspeakers left behind on the Buttermarkt square, everything was normal. The shops stayed closed, but you could buy cake and you could see people coming out of the Café Kranz with precious parcels wrapped in coloured paper, holding them flat as they walked. Like every other Sunday, they went to the graveyard to put flowers on the graves. And then it was time to prepare for visitors in the afternoon.

You have to open the doors to be sure that the smell of soup is not lingering in the hallway when the visitors arrive. A sensitive nose can detect a hint of fat in the air, my mother says. Then you let the smell of baking take over. You would commit a mortal sin any time for a decent cup of coffee, my mother says, and then she laughs out loud, because that's what her aunt Ta Maria always said. The smell of coffee and cake is like a hearty welcome, like an embrace. Your visitor will want to jump right into bed and snuggle up with the cake. And when you're serving, you have to cut the slices without touching the cake. You have to serve with the same affection that has gone into the baking, using the silver trowel that has been in the family for generations. The cake has to appear on the plate as though it had never been touched by human hands.

On Sunday we went for a walk in the afternoon. We had to put on our coats and hats and gloves because it was windy and cold outside. My father criss-crossed his scarf over his chest and we did the same. Maria's gloves were attached to an elastic band inside the sleeves of her coat so they wouldn't get lost. We walked past the station where my father gets the train every day. We came to a place where we could kick through the brown leaves with a hissing noise. Sometimes my trousers rubbed against the inside of my leg and it was sore. And sometimes when we walked around the corner, the wind was so strong that we couldn't even breathe or speak any more. We had to push hard against it until we started laughing.

Then we came to the shop and everyone got pocket money. Franz wanted a toffee pop and I wanted a bag of sherbet with a lollipop inside. We waited outside while my father and mother were still inside trying to help Maria decide what to buy. There were boys standing by the wall of the shop and they started calling us Nazis. There were lots of things like that written on the wall in paint, including a big swastika sign in red. They kept saying we were Nazis, until my mother came out and heard them.

'Heil Hitler,' they shouted.

They were not allowed to say that kind of thing and I looked at my mother to see what she would do. They said it again and laughed out loud, so there was no way that she might not have heard it. She even stopped and looked at them for a moment. But she said nothing. I knew she was biting her lip. I knew by her eyes that she was sad this was happening, but she could do nothing about it.

'Come on, let's walk ahead,' she said. She didn't wait for my father and Maria to come out, she just turned us around and walked away. Behind us we could hear them laughing and clicking their heels. I was sure my father would do something, but he said nothing either and we all walked quickly down to the seafront.

We could smell the sea and hear it because it was very rough. The waves were crashing in against the rocks, all white and brown. The seagulls were balancing in the air over the waves and we were standing in a line, holding on to the railings with brown rust marks growing through the blue paint. The dog was there, too, the dog that belongs to nobody and barks at the sea until he is hoarse and can't speak. From behind the railings you could look the waves right in the eye as they came rushing in and my mother said: 'God help anyone who is out at sea.' The waves were so strong that when they threw themselves on to the rocks, the foam sprang up like a white tree. Bits of black seaweed were flung in the air with no mercy. We had to move back so as not to get wet. Only a tiny shower covered our faces and we could taste the salt. We shouted back at the waves but it was hard to talk because of the wind. Here's a big one, my father said, but there was so much noise that you could hear nothing anyway, as if the sea was so loud, it was actually silent. My mother said nothing and just looked far away out into the waves. Bigger and bigger waves all the time, hitting the rocks and bouncing up, right in front of us.

Eleven

I like giving the wrong answer. My father sits on the far side of the table in the breakfast room and says he's going to wait until I give the right answer, even if it takes all day.

'Five plus six makes . . . ?'

My father was a schoolteacher once so he knows what he's doing. He says that he and his brother Ted both got a scholarship and now he wants to make me the best boy in Ireland at tables. I can see myself twice over in his glasses, sitting with my arms folded. He waits and waits, while I search around in my head and say to myself that I will – NOT – give the right answer. I know the answer but I frown and roll my eyes up towards the ceiling and even put my hand on my chin, because that's meant to help you with thinking.

'Nine,' I answer.

'Wrong,' he says. 'Think again.'

We have all the time in the world. It's Saturday afternoon, he says, and we have better things to be doing. He could be sitting in the front room reading any one of six books about the history of Germany or the Spanish Civil War or the lives of saints or the Blasket Islands or cabinet-making or beekeeping. I could be outside running around in the garden. Franz is waiting for me to go and play football. But we're going to stay sitting there in the breakfast room all day and all night if we have to. So then I try again, squinting and frowning and humming to myself, now let me see, five and six makes . . . ? I have given every wrong answer there is so there's none left except the right one.

I look at my father's bad ear which is flattened out of shape and purple. When I asked him once what happened, he told me that a teacher in boarding school hit him with a steel ruler. Maria said she would pray for it to get better, but then he frowned and blinked and said he didn't want us looking at his ear any more or talking about it. My mother told us afterwards that he had no father and at boarding school his ear started bleeding and lost all its feeling because he was homesick and wanted his mother. It's hard not to look at his ear and think about the steel ruler coming down like a sword. I keep thinking of things like that not happening. I try to imagine stopping it with my arm. I imagine fighting off the teacher with long brush. I imagine bending my father's ear back into shape again, like plasticine.

'Concentrate.'

He slams his hand down suddenly on the table and I jump. Then my mother comes in because she doesn't want this to go on for ever either. She says it's time to give in and then I'll be free to go. Outside, I can hear the sound of Mr Richardson hammering at something and the echo coming back across the gardens. I can hear Miss Tarleton's lawnmower and I know there's hardly any grass on her lawn but she does it anyway. Then I hear the two bangs from the lifeboat, one after the other with a long gap in between, and my mother saying 'trouble on the sea'. I can hear the Corbetts' back door closing like a sneeze. Then silence again. Everyone is waiting for the right answer.

My mother is nodding. My father is staring. And Franz is standing at the door with the football.

'Nil.'

It's the only answer I could think of that I hadn't given already apart from the right one. But then there was real trouble and real silence. People passing by our house would have heard nothing at all only breathing. Now I could see my father's eyes inside his glasses, and his ear was red hot, like a piece of coal out of the boiler. He pushed the chair back with a loud howl on the floor and told me to wait while he searched in the greenhouse for a good stick that wouldn't break this time.

My mother shook her head because it was out of her hands. The person who can't hear it, must feel it, she said a few times, because that's what they say in Germany. I could see that she was sorry this was happening but she could do nothing to stop it. She took Franz and Maria away and closed the door. I could hear the 'in between door' closing, too, that separates the back of the house from the front. I could hear her going up the stairs, further and further away, closing another door behind her until she could hear nothing at all any more and didn't have to think about what was going to happen. Everybody was gone, even the sound of the hammering outside, and I could only hear the stick whipping through the air. My father was breathing hard and thinking about lots of angry things in his head like the lives of saints and beekeeping and the time he was at school in Dunmanway and couldn't go home to his mother. He was thinking about all the things that he couldn't do with his own life, that he was going to make me do instead. He said he would keep hitting me all day and all night until I gave the right answer.

'Eleven,' I cried. 'Eleven, eleven, eleven.'

Then he stopped and asked me if I was good again.

'Yes,' I said.

'Say it.'

'I'm good again.'

I could still feel the hot red lines on the back of my legs when it was time for tea. Franz and Maria wanted to look at them but I didn't want anyone talking about me, not even my mother. My father shook my hand and said it was time to put it all behind us. It was time to smile because we all have to be friends again. But I couldn't smile. So then he held my chin and pushed my lips apart with his fingers and I had to show my teeth.

'Nobody can force you to smile,' my mother said.

She had a better idea. She offered me an extra biscuit, one more than anyone else. And then she started telling a story about the time they got married and went up two mountains, one in each country. On the train going along the Rhine together, they sat in a carriage with a young boy who looked out the window and ate biscuits from a brown paper bag. All the way to Koblenz, the boy sat eating one biscuit after the other without a word, as if he would never see a biscuit in his life again, as if he was afraid the time of no biscuits would come back. Sometimes he closed the bag and put it aside, as though he told himself he was not going to have any more, but then he could not resist starting again and again until the whole lot was gone.

After that I was sick for a long time. It started after we helped to clean the windows one day, first with soap, then with crumpled newspapers that make a squeaking sound like wild dogs barking far away in the hills, my mother says. The windows were so clean that we thought we were outside and there was no glass at all. After that it was hard to breathe, because the sound of the wild dogs got into my chest. I had to stay in bed listening to them howling all day and all night. My mother came with plasticine and cars. She bought a new colouring book and new pencils, but my fingers were soft and I couldn't draw. She came in with a tray, but I could not even eat the biscuits, so she made me sit up and drink the lemon tea, at least one sip for your mother, she said.

At night she left the door wide open and the light coming up the stairs, but I was still afraid. The window rattled and there was a large piece of wallpaper hanging down on the far side of the room which looked like a man with a hat coming in sideways through the wall from next door. At first I laughed and said he was only a piece of wallpaper. But he just looked at me with one eye and kept coming with his shoulder held forward. A light from the street shone into the room and sometimes the man stepped right into the light, then moved back into the darkness again. I was very hot and shivering at the same time. I put my back against the wall and started shouting at him to stop, until my mother came running up and sat on my bed. She said I was soaked with sweat and brought in a warm towel to wipe my chest. She said I was afraid of my own imagination. My father came up and stuck a piece of folded paper in the window to stop the rattling. He put on the light for a minute to prove that there was no man coming through the wall, then he smiled and kissed the top of my head. He listened to the howling in my chest and said it didn't sound as bad as before. Then he went downstairs again and my mother stayed sitting on my bed to tell stories.

'I don't want to be a Nazi,' I told her.

'But you're not a Nazi,' she said.

She smiled and tucked the blankets in around my neck

so that only my head was out. I told her what the boys outside the shop were saying about us.

'I don't want them to call me a Nazi,' I said.

'Ignore them,' she said. She looked at me for a while and said they were the real Nazis. She said I shouldn't worry about it so much, because it was usually people who had something to hide who called other people Nazis. 'They want to make everybody believe that they're innocent. So they call other people Nazis, as often as they can. It's the same the world over.'

She stroked my forehead. She said it was not important what the boys outside the shop said. If I was a real Nazi, then I would know it myself. Maybe you can hide it from other people by pointing the finger somewhere else, but you can't hide things like that from yourself. What's inside your head is what matters.

'But that won't stop them.'

'You can't,' she said. 'You can't go around telling the whole world what you're not. That would be ridiculous. I can't send you down the road to the shop with a sign around your neck saying "I'm not a Nazi."'

It was time to concentrate on good things. Soon I would be better again, running around like before with no dogs howling in my chest. And my father has a new plan, she said, a plan to make money, so that we can take the wallpaper down. Sometimes he is very hard, she said, but he knows what's good for Ireland. He doesn't mean to be angry, but he has a lot to worry about and he's doing his best. And the next day he was busy downstairs starting a new business that would make us rich, so we could take down the old wallpaper. He bought a desk for the front room. He put the telephone on it and a desk-light so he could sit down and have his own office. He bought lots of stationery, too, and gave the business a name. Kaiser and Co., he called it, because that was my mother's name and her family had been in business for a long time in Kempen before they went bankrupt. He got a machine that printed the name on to paper, so he wouldn't have to write it out every time. And when the business was set up, he sat at his desk waiting for phone calls and saying there should be less noise in the house, because he had to try and guess what the people of Ireland needed most at that moment.

My mother said I was getting better. She let me go downstairs to the front room to see the new office. My father was out buying stamps and I lay on the sofa with all the cushions and blankets while my mother sat at the desk with her diary, writing in all the things that were happening in our family. She glued everything in, like photographs and locks of hair and tickets to the zoo. She wrote in lots of stories, like me not giving the right answer and Franz going to bed every night, laying out his socks in the shape of a crucifix. She also put in things that were happening outside in the world, like the photograph from the newspaper of the tanks in Hungary, and a photograph of the Irishman, Ronnie Delaney on his knees thanking God for winning the race at the Olympics in Melbourne, Australia. Then she went into the kitchen and it was our turn to play office. Maria started drawing a picture on the wall and Franz found a matchstick.

'Light it,' I said. But I didn't even have to say that, because the match was saying it himself with his little red head, asking to be lit. Franz struck it along the wall and it flared up. He blew it out straightaway, but my father must have heard it. His good ear can hear things from miles away. He asked if we had lit a match. He called my mother in because she has a good nose and between them they were able to prove it. She said that's why people get married, because one person has a good ear and the other has a good nose, and hopefully we would have both and that would help us not to do anything in our lives that we would regret later.

Sometimes my mother was able to talk around trouble. Sometimes you couldn't stop things happening so you tiptoed around them instead, she said. Even when there should be real trouble and my father should be much more angry than ever before, she was able to find another way out. My father proved that we had lit a match but he had other things to get angry about. He saw what Maria had done. She had taken a crayon and drawn lines all along the wall, right around the room.

'Look at that,' my mother said, and my father was frowning hard. But then she had an idea to stop him getting angry. She clapped her hands together and said it was the most beautiful drawing she had ever seen in her life and they had to take a photograph of it for the diary. It was a drawing of my mother with her arms stretching all the way around the four walls, embracing everyone who came into the room. And anyway, she said, there should be no more anger in our house, because we had a big plan for the business, Kaiser and Co. My father thought of something that the Irish people needed most. They were going to import crosses from a famous place in Germany, hand-carved wooden crosses from Oberammergau.

I was still sick. The howling dogs came back again, and something started happening to one of my legs as well. It swelled up bit by bit, until it was twice the size of the other one. Onkel Ted came to make the sign of the cross and Dr Sheehan came too, because I was still a Nazi and I knew it. He called me 'young man' and said it was serious this time. My leg was about to explode. I had to go to hospital and an ambulance came. I couldn't walk, so the men came up the stairs and wrapped me up in a red blanket, then carried me down, through the hallway and out the door, past the people on the street standing around the gate. My mother was crying and the neighbours said I would soon be better again, please God. They would all pray for me every day and every night.

Inside the ambulance I couldn't see where I was going, so I tried to follow the streets in my head, around each corner, past the church and past the people's park. But then I got lost and I was blind with my eyes wide open and I knew they were taking me to a different country again where they spoke only English. I could smell the hospital and the doctors and nurses were standing all around me looking down. They listened to my chest and heard the dogs howling. They looked at my leg and measured it. Every day, new doctors came to examine it and stick needles into it. Some of them said it was a mystery. It made them scratch their heads, because nothing like that had ever happened before in the medical books and they had no way of making it better. And then one day, the howling stopped. The swelling in my leg started going down again, and my mother came to visit me with a new toy car and said I was getting better. The nurse showed me the measurements on the chart. The doctors were amazed and said my leg would be famous and would enter into history, if only they could explain it. The nurse said I was famous already, because I was a German-Irish boy and everybody knew me. At night I begged her to let me go home. She smiled and stroked my head and said I still had to stay in hospital until the doctors said I was fully back to normal.

'I'm good again,' I said.

'You mean you're better,' she said.

'Yes, I'm better,' I said. 'I'm too better.'

'Of course you are, love,' she said. But still she could not let me go until the doctors said so. Everybody was gone and the hospital was quiet. All lights were switched off except for the small one at the door. The nurse was tidying up all around me and not saying very much. Her white shoes were making tiny squeaks on the floor.

'I'm not a Nazi,' I said.

Then she looked up and smiled.

'I'm not German,' I said. 'I promise.'

'I know that, love. I believe you.'

Twelve

It should be easier to sell a crucifix in Ireland. My mother closes the front door and stands in the hall with her coat still on, looking up at the picture of the Virgin Mary. She throws her arms up in the air and says she can't understand it. She has been to every church and every convent and every hospital in Dublin. We went with her on the bus one day and a priest gave us a sweet each, a satin cushion. He smiled and nearly said yes to the cross, but then he shook his head at the last minute. Beautiful hand-carved oak crosses from Oberammergau and nobody wants them, my mother says. It's hard to believe, when you think of everyone in Ireland praying twice a day at least and all they still have to pray for.

'Surely somebody needs a crucifix,' she says.

That's the whole idea of my father starting a business, to sell something the Irish people really need, something you believe in yourself. We believe in crosses, so we kneel down every night and pray that we will have God on our side as a partner in business. But in the end, nobody wants them and my mother sits down in the kitchen without even taking her coat off, shaking her head from side to side and breathing out slowly as if she wants to be the best at not breathing in again until you have to. Maybe they're too expensive, she says. Maybe it's too late and there are too many crosses in Ireland already. Or maybe they're the wrong kind of crosses and Irish people only like the ones where Jesus has blood on his hands and feet and there's a gash in his side and a scroll at the top saying INRI.

She doesn't understand Ireland sometimes, because they like strange things like pink cakes and soft ice cream and salt and vinegar. They spend all their money on First Holy Communion outfits. They don't like serving people and they don't like being in a queue either, because when the bus comes, they forget about the rules and just rush for the door. The bus drivers in Ireland are blind and the shopkeepers don't want to sell things to you. The butcher has a cigarette in his mouth while he's cutting the meat, and nobody knows how to say the word no. In Ireland, they nod when they mean no, and shake their heads when they're agreeing with you. She says it's like in the films, when somebody looks up with a worried face and says one thing, it means that the opposite is going to happen. When somebody says nobody is going to come out alive and that they're all going to die, then at the last minute somebody comes along to the rescue. And when everybody at the bus stop begins to say that the buses have stopped running, along comes the bus at last and they all rush forward to get on.

Sometimes Irish people don't understand my mother either. When she's trying to be helpful, they think she's interfering and being nosy. When she tries to warn some of the other mothers about their children eating too many sweets or crossing the road without looking, they say they don't want some German woman telling their kids what to do. One day, there was a woman outside the shop with a brand new pram with big wheels. It had the word Pedigree written on the side and the woman was very proud of it, because it was like a new car. My mother admired the new pram, but she warned her to be careful it didn't fall over with the baby inside. So then the woman called her a Nazi and told her to mind her own business.

Nobody knows what my mother is trying to say sometimes. And nobody has any idea where Oberammergau is either. She tells them it's a place in Bavaria, where they have the crucifixion every ten years, a bit like going up to Croagh Patrick. They nod and say yes and look very interested, so why don't they buy hand-carved oak crosses with no blood, just nails and the rest left up to your imagination?

'It's the shoes,' she says at last.

Nobody will buy anything if you don't look half-decent. You can tell a person's character by their hands and their shoes, she says, because that's what Ta Maria always said. Even though Onkel Gerd always said the opposite, that it's only what's inside your head that makes you either a scoundrel or a saint. But when you're trying to sell something, my mother says, it doesn't matter if you're a scoundrel or a saint, because what you're wearing is all they look at. You have to be honest, she says, but you can't let people know that the wallpaper is hanging off the walls at home.

Then we head off into the city so she can get a pair of decent shoes. I swing around the bus stop and climb up as far as I can until the bus comes. We fight over the window seat, and over who gets the ticket, until my mother says that's enough, it's not important to win. Everybody on the bus turns around to look at us because we're German again. Then we have to behave and sit quietly and bless ourselves whenever we pass by a church, to prove that the Germans are decent people and we did nothing wrong. I pretend to be Irish and look at the IMCO building passing by like a white ship.

My father says the Irish people can't live on their imagination for ever. They need money in their pockets now. It's time to work hard so we can be free and so that nobody will ever starve or be poor again like all the people in west Cork were. He doesn't want the song about emigration to go on for ever, so it's time to speak Irish and make Ireland a better place to live. He tells us how his mother Mary Frances spent all her money on putting him through university in Dublin while she fasted and hardly had anything to live on herself. He tells us exactly how much he had to spend each week on food and lodgings, and how he had two pennies left over, one for the Mass on Sunday and one for a razor blade. He sent his washing home by post and cycled all the way home to Leap at Christmas because he could not afford the train or the bus. He had no way of borrowing from a bank, and if it wasn't for the Jesuits who lent him the money for the final year, we wouldn't be here now but in America or Canada maybe. He paid back the money as fast as possible when he got his first job as an engineer in Dublin, making matches with Maguire and Patterson.

Even when my father started sending money home, Mary Frances was not able to spend it on herself, because Irish people didn't know how to do that yet. All she wanted in her life was to make sure that her two sons were educated, one an engineer and the other a Jesuit. And that was the happiest day of her life, when my father came home to Leap with initials after his name. Better than that, the Jesuits even allowed Onkel Ted to go home for a day to see her for the first time in seven years. So she sat looking at her two sons together in the kitchen for a few hours at least, until

Onkel Ted had to leave again very early in the morning to get back to the seminary in the Bog of Allen.

His father died in Cork and the navy refused to give them a pension at first. His mother spent all she had on getting the body home for burial in the mountain graveyard above Glandore. After that she could no longer pay the rent and the landlord wanted her out of the house. A letter went to the local police station telling them to 'proceed with eviction forthwith', so she walked up to the church and told the priest she was going to bed. She was not a political person, and some people didn't mind all too much one way or another who was in the government, because it didn't make a bit of difference to them. Some people in Ireland had no time for guns either, only education. But everybody hated landlords. So she took her two boys upstairs and got into bed. If they were going to evict her, she said, they would have to drag them out of the bed.

It was not the first time something like that happened in Ireland either. Her uncle was put out of his home and the cottage burned down because he refused to pay rent to the landlord any more. He had nowhere to go after that and if it wasn't for the local people who built him a tiny cottage to stay in, he would have become a traveller with no place to settle any more, like all the the people on the move after the famine. We would have been travellers, too, moving around from one place to another all our lives and knocking on doors to sell carpets, my father says, so that's why he gives them money when they come to the door and say 'God Bless.' In the end, her uncle went to America. But before he left Ireland he made one great speech for the Land League on a platform in Skibbereen. He stood up and said it was time to wipe landlords off the face of this earth. Then he swung his right arm over the crowd and knocked the hat off the priest sitting down behind him as he was doing it, so that everyone laughed about that story, long after he was gone. There were lots of people put out of their homes, my father says, until Michael Collins stood up for them and started the resistance.

Sometimes my mother goes over to the neighbours for coffee mornings. Mrs Corcoran invites all her friends around for sandwiches and cakes and gossip. They think my mother is very posh and unfriendly, because she has no gossip and speaks in a German accent all the time. My mother says Mrs Corcoran has a funny accent, too, because she and her friends all speak English like no other Irish people. My father says it's the famine. Even the people with money to burn and accents that hurt your mouth are still afraid of the famine. They speak like that because they're afraid of the Irish language coming back and killing everybody in the country this time. He says Irish people drink too much and talk too much and don't want to speak Irish, because it stinks of poverty and dead people left lying in the fields. That's why they speak posh English and pretend that nothing ever happened. My father talks about people dying on coffin ships going to America and my mother talks about people dying on trains going to Poland. My father talks of evictions in Leap and my mother talks of evictions in Kempen. My father says our people died in the famine and my mother says those who died under the Nazis are our people, too. Everybody has things they can't forget.

My mother likes Irish people, but she doesn't want to go to any more coffee mornings. They talk about going on holidays all the time and about new things like cars and washing machines. Mrs Corcoran talks about where she has been in the summer and shows the souvenirs she brought back, like the black bull from Spain and a big bowl with zigzags from Greece. This time, my mother says, she was in South Africa and brought back lots of wood carvings. But that's not all she brought back either, because right in the middle of the coffee morning, Mrs Corcoran started saying that black people would never be the same as white people. They would never catch up no matter how much education they got.

In the shoe shop, we sit in a line and get a liquorice shoelace each while my mother tries on shoes for a long time. She taps the heels together to hear what they sound like. She says it's as hard to buy shoes in Ireland as it is to sell a crucifix. Sometimes you have to beg people to sell you something. At first the assistant smiled and said every pair of shoes looked gorgeous. She thought people from Germany had to try on every pair in the shop before they could make up their mind. My mother started imagining shoes that didn't even exist, shoes from Italy, great shoes she had seen in the past sometime. My mother and the assistant didn't understand each other. In the end, she went for the dark blue pair that matched her blue dress with the white squiggles, the shoes that made her feet look smallest of all. She walked up along the floor one last time, turned in front of the mirror, then came back and paid.

Now my mother can sell anything. Franz carried the box with the new shoes and we walked across O'Connell Street holding hands in a chain. When you look up at Nelson's Pillar you sometimes think the white clouds are standing still and the city is moving, running fast out to the sea. If you close your eyes you can hear the sound of footsteps and buses and cars all around you. Seagulls, too. There were seagulls on the roof of the GPO and seagulls standing on the shoulders of Daniel O'Connell.

My father took a half-day and came to meet us in the restaurant. He looked at the new shoes and said they were beautiful. He said it was a great day for us because we would soon be in business, making a profit. There was a big smile on his face. He has lots of straight teeth and when he starts talking, he sometimes sounds like he's making a speech. He starts blinking and speaking fast, as if he'll never catch up with all the things he wants to say. My mother says there are lots of men who like to turn things into a joke and make people laugh. She says it's good to laugh, but my father has a different way of doing things. He can laugh too, until the tears come into his eyes. But then he's always serious again afterwards, because he is a man with ideas. A man, my mother says, who could never live for himself, only for his children and his country. That's why he frowns, even when he's not angry, because he's in a hurry to do all the things that are still left unfinished in Ireland.

My mother said we could have a cake each, but not one of the pink ones because they're too sweet and leave nothing to the imagination. My father didn't want a cake because they were nothing like hers. He said people would fight each other over my mother's cakes, and anything else that she put her hands to. Then he took her hands and held them up in the air for everyone in the restaurant to see. My mother smiled and got embarrassed. It looked like he was going to stand up and make a speech to the whole restaurant about her. My mother says you can sometimes be overcome by the smell of coffee. His eyes were soft. He said they were precious hands. He said it didn't matter that we were left with hand-carved wooden crosses from Oberammergau all over the house, because there were plenty of new ideas. He mentioned other things that the Irish people needed very badly. Like umbrellas. And Christmas-tree stands.

And German toys. We would sell things that were so well made and so beautiful that people would fight each other to buy them.

Afterwards my father bought hurling sticks, but said he would take them off us again if we used them as swords for fighting. It was dark by the time we went home and my father showed us the glass of whiskey that kept filling up again and again on the side of the building. There was a packet of cigarettes too that kept disappearing and lighting up again slowly, bit by bit. The seagulls were not there any more, but there were men shouting the names of newspapers on the street like seagulls. Herald-a-Press. Herald-a-Press. On the train, everybody was looking at us because we were the Germans with the hurling sticks. My mother told us the story about Rumpelstiltskin, who gave away his secret in the forest when he thought nobody was listening. Everybody on the train was listening to her. They all surrendered to the story, even though it was in German. One man was already asleep and Maria was trying hard to keep her eyes open. At the end of the story my mother always says the same thing: 'and if he isn't dead yet, then he must be still alive'. So I think about that for a while and look out at the lights of the city, moving along and blinking.

Thirteen

It takes a long time for things to come to Ireland. My father and mother are waiting every day for a big box to arrive from Germany. He sits at his desk in the front room and my mother is in the breakfast room typing. Then my father gets a letter to say that the box has arrived in Dublin, but the Irish government won't let it go until he pays them lots of money, nearly as much as he already paid for what's inside. Then he collects the box in a taxi. In the front room, we sit around and wait for him to open it. It's full of party hats for policemen and sailors and firemen and doctors and nurses. There are German crackers, too, and lots of caramel walking sticks in all colours. My mother says they're beautiful, but we can't play with them because they have to be sold. They put on some music and drink cognac, because a little bit of Germany has come over to Ireland at last and my mother doesn't feel so homesick. Maybe Germany is not so far away as we thought, she says. Then it's time for my father to put some of the hats and caramel canes into a suitcase, so he can take them around to the shops the next day. It won't take long before the whole box is sold. It won't be long before these party hats will be seen in every shop all over the city and people will be fighting each other to get more.

Every night, we pray for luck in business. We pray for

people in Germany and for people in Ireland, for Ta Maria and for Onkel Wilhelm and for Uncle Gerald who drinks to much in Skibbereen. Then we pray for the new baby, too. One at a time, my mother allows us to listen to her tummy, a little brother or sister kicking and playing football, she says. Then I lie awake listening to them whispering as they go into bed. Every night I can hear my mother saying that money doesn't matter, that there are far more important things in life than money, because we'll be rich once the new baby is born. Every night, I hear her washing her feet because your feet are your best friends.

Every morning, my father walks up to the station with the suitcase in one hand and his briefcase in the other. He stops halfway to swap over the briefcase and the suitcase, then he carries on. At lunchtime he leaves the office and walks around the city with the suitcase, going around to all the different toy shops and department stores. And every evening he comes home again and stops halfway to change over, because the suitcase is getting heavier all the time, not lighter, and the handle makes a mark on his hand. He has tried every shop in Dublin, but not one single hat has been sold. He starts going to all the hotels and pubs instead, even as far away as the airport on the other side of the city. And one night he came home so late on the bus that he could not even carry the suitcase up the road any more, it was so heavy. He was limping and the suitcase was left beside the bus stop, until my mother went down to collect it with the pram. Then it was my father who took off his shoes and socks one by one to wash his feet, because your feet can be your worst enemy, too.

There is nothing wrong with the party hats and crackers and caramel canes. Everybody says they're just lovely. The people in the shops and pubs and hotels say they would love to buy them but they can't. It has nothing to do with them being German or Germany losing the war or what the Nazis did. And it's got nothing to do with the Irish famine either, or the people of Ireland not having the money to spend on themselves and celebrating and having parties. The problem is not the party hats and crackers. It's the name, our family name. My father will not sell anything to anyone unless they say his name properly in Irish.

It's the name that causes all the trouble. The Irish name: Ó hUrmoltaigh.

People jump back with a strange expression and ask you to say it again. They don't really trust anything Irish yet.

'What's that in English?' they ask.

But you can't betray your family name. My father says we can't give the English version, Hamilton, no matter how often they ask for it. We can't even admit that an English version exists. If they call us Hamilton, we pretend it's not us they're talking to. Our name is proof of who we are and how Irish we are. We have to be able to make a sacrifice, even if they laugh at us. They can torture us and make martyrs of us and nail us to the cross and still we won't give in. It would be a lot easier to let them have their way, to give the English name, just to be friendly and make it simple so they'll buy things. But my father says there can be no compromise. It's hard for business, but you can't betray your own name, because if the cheque is made out to Hamilton, he will send it back and not accept it until it's paid in Irish.

Your name is important. It's like your face or your smile or your skin. There's a song at school about a man in Donegal who once wrote his name in Irish on a donkey cart. It was the time when Ireland was still under the British and it was forbidden to write your name in Irish. Every cart had to have the name of the owner written on it in English. So when a policeman saw the name in Irish, the man was arrested and brought to court. The bobby argued that he saw no name on the cart, because Irish was not a language that he could read. It was a famous court case with Patrick Pearse as the lawyer for the cart owner. And even though the law was still British and the cart owner lost the case and had to pay a big fine, it was still a big victory for the Irish, because after that, all the cart owners in Donegal started putting their names in Irish on their carts and there was nothing the police could do because there were too many of them. So that's why we have our name in Irish, too.

My mother said she would try and sell the party hats with a smaller suitcase. Every evening she went out to the local hotels and clubs, while my father stayed at home to look after us. The Royal Marine Hotel, the Royal Yacht Club, the Royal Irish Yacht Club, the Crofton Hotel, the Pierre Hotel, the Castle Hotel, the Salt Hill Hotel and the Khyber Pass Hotel. She walked so much that the new shoes were hurting. She went all the way up the hill a second time to meet the manager of the Shangri-La Hotel, the man who could not say no.

The Shangri-La was an old hotel with long blue-velvet curtains hanging in the windows, full of old smoke. The man who couldn't say no asked her to sit down in the lounge so he could look at what was in the suitcase properly. At first he shook his head from side to side and she thought she had come for nothing. But then he said they were absolutely beautiful. He praised them so much, my mother says, that she suddenly thought she had sold them all in one go, without even saying a word. She had dreams in her head of running home with an empty suitcase and ordering more and more of them to come over immediately. The problem was how fast they could get the Irish government to let go of the boxes when they arrived in future. The Shangri-La manager didn't have to be told they were German-made, because anything that was really well made had to be German, he said. He knew that she was German, too, by her accent, but then he asked for her name and all the trouble started again.

'Ó hUrmoltaigh,' she said. Irmgard Ó hUrmoltaigh.

'Good Lord, I'll never remember that,' he said.

He pulled out a packet of cigarettes and offered her one, but my mother doesn't know how to smoke yet.

'Would that be Hurley in English?' he asked.

'No,' she smiled. He picked up one of the sailor hats to admire it and she waited for him to make up his mind, to say how many of the party hats he was going to take, how many of the caramel canes and crackers. The people in all the other hotels and shops would soon be kicking their own backsides for not taking them while they had the chance.

'Hermon, Harmon? What about Harmon?'

My mother repeated her name in Irish, because you can't betray your skin. He tried again and again to get it out of her in English. And when he ran out of guesses, he finally tried to pronounce it in Irish, but it was such hard work.

'Ó Hermity, Ó Hamilty, Ó Hurmilly . . . Ó Himmel.'

My mother could not help laughing. It was her feet, she says. Her feet were tired and singing and begging to be washed and put to bed. So when the manager scratched his head and blew out smoke and called her 'Ó Himmel', she could not help laughing out loud.

Mrs O'Himmel – Mrs O'Heaven.

Nobody had come up with that one before. The party hats and caramel sticks were lying all around and she was laughing at her own name. It was the hardest name in the world. Nobody in the whole of Ireland got it right, not even those who spoke fluent Irish. Most of the neighbours and people in the shops made a complete mess of it, so that after a long time, my mother didn't mind what way they said it as long as it still proved how Irish she was and it didn't get her in trouble with my father. The postman called her Mrs O'Hummity, and the man in the fish shop called her Mrs O'Hommilty, and the man with one arm in the vegetable shop did his best and called her Mrs O'Hervulty. If only they could have agreed on one version. But it was different every time. And there was always something funny about it, too, that made people smile, or try not to smile. Some people could only manage Mrs O'Hum. The butcher with the cigarette in his mouth just called her Mrs O . . . And sometimes she came home with no name at all and wished things were still as plain and simple as they once were long ago when her name was Irmgard Kaiser.

'Ó hUrmoltaigh,' she tried once more, because you can't hate your own name. 'It's a Cork name. My husband is from County Cork.'

'That explains everything,' the manager said.

He wanted to know what brought her over to Ireland, and how she had married a man from Cork of all places. She said she loved the sea. She loved the smell of the sea and the sound of the waves crashing on the rocks. He asked her if she got homesick. He knew that she was only trying to sell these German things because she was so far away from home, because she could not go back to Germany herself and wanted instead to bring a bit of her country over here to Ireland. He asked her did she want a drink. He said she had a lovely accent and a lovely voice. He said he would love to hear her speaking a bit of German, anything at all, but then he wasn't even looking at the hats any more, only at her and her shoes. He said he would love her to come back and have a drink some other time when she was not so busy. And when she asked him finally straight out about the hats and crackers, he threw out his arms and couldn't say no. He couldn't say yes and he couldn't say no either. He said he would love to take them all, every last one of them, but he couldn't.

'I'm sorry,' he said.

It was all for nothing. It was even harder putting them back into the suitcase. It looked like there were more than she started with. Instead of any of them being sold, my mother says it looked like they were starting to reproduce. On the bus home she fell asleep and only woke up after she had gone way past her stop. She walked back and when she arrived in the door she had to sit down with her coat still on and take off her shoes first because her feet were on fire. She had to close her eyes and wash her feet until they were friends with her again. She was very quiet. She could not speak and she would not let us listen to the baby in her tummy. She had no name any more.

One day, a man with a car came to take away the box with the party hats and crackers. We were allowed to choose one hat each, but the rest were sold off all around County Cork for nearly nothing and my father said it was a mistake to try and bring things over from Germany. He said it was better to produce things at home, so then my mother started a sweet factory instead. For weeks and weeks there was a smell of caramel and chocolate all over the house. Every night she was mixing and baking. Sometimes the sweets came out too hard or too soft, but my father said that's the way any business started out, by experimenting. If they were not like shop sweets it was because they were far superior to shop sweets. My mother put them all in little jars with labels and ribbons. Soon there would be people queuing up outside our front door, my father said. But the problem was that nobody wanted home-made sweets. So the jars kept piling up, waiting and waiting on shelves under the stairs, until they eventually had to be given away or eaten by us. My mother laughed and said we were our own best customers, and when the last of the jars were gone we didn't talk about the sweet factory any more either.

My father says the only way to make money in Ireland is not to spend it in the first place. So then he started switching off lights and using as little coal as possible. He made new rules. We would make our own bread and our own jam. He found a supermarket where groceries were cheaper than anywhere else, so he went there on the bus to bring home what was needed. When my mother ran out of butter one day and had to buy it in a local shop, he wanted to know why she was breaking the rules. She explained that to get the cheap butter, she would have to spend more money on the bus fare, so if you worked it out, the local butter was cheaper and quicker. She said you couldn't save what you didn't have in the first place. Anyway, there was nothing to worry about because we would be rich when the baby was born. But he frowned and slammed the door because everybody was breaking his rules.

After that my father sat at his desk in the front room on his own every night, until at last he came up with the right idea. Then he came running out, telling us that he had found it, what Ireland needed most. He was blinking again and talking very fast, trying to catch up with all the ideas in his head. How had he not seen it before? One Sunday afternoon when we were out walking he discovered that all street names were still in English. He stood by a sign that said Royal Terrace and wondered how any Irish speaker could walk around these streets without getting lost. So then he started writing letters to the government and to the corporation. The machine printed the address at the top of the page every time and my mother typed out the letters for him. Now things were working at last. Every morning he took a stack of letters with him to the post office. He had tried so many different things like crosses and hats and crackers and sweets and savings, but now he was in business, changing the names of the streets.

De Vesci Terrace, Albert Road, Silchester Road, Neptune Terrace, Nerano Road, Sorrento Road. He had them all changed into Irish, one by one. Royal Terrace became Ascal Ríoga, because money and profit were not everything, he said. On Sundays we walked everywhere to make sure that we covered them all. He told us about the great Irish poets and scholars who once lived in Munster where he came from, among them his own grandfather who was known as Tadhg Ó Donnabháin Dall, or Ted O'Donovan Blind. When the names of people and places all over Ireland were changed into English, all those poets and Irish speakers lost their way and suddenly found themselves in a foreign land. He told us how they all went blind overnight, stumbling around in the dark with no language. And now it was time to change the names back to Irish so the people knew where they were going again.

Then my mother was sick and had to stay in bed. We were allowed to go up to her room for a while and talk to her. Maria stroked her arm and I was the doctor. Until the real Dr Sheehan arrived and we had to wait outside the door. We could hear her crying because the baby had stopped playing football. It was still inside her tummy but it would not come out alive. I knew she was crying for other things, too, because Germany was so far away, because nobody in Ireland wanted party hats, and because she had no name any more, and no face and no feet in Ireland. Onkel Ted came and made the sign of the cross. There were shadows around her eyes when we were allowed back into the room, but she was trying to smile and she put her arms around us and said she was rich because she had three children.

Downstairs in the kitchen, my father tried to bake a cake. He wanted to help and make everything better again, so he put on the apron and mixed the ingredients the way my mother told him to. Now and again he sent us back up the stairs to ask her what to do next and my mother smiled and sent us back down again to tell him to switch on the oven. He did everything he was told, step by step. He held his hands up in the air, quietly counting to ten with cake mixture on his fingers, repeating all the German instructions from above in his Cork accent. And when he was finished he put the cake in the oven and there was a smell of baking all over the house and everyone went around on tiptoes. But when it came out it was all wrong. There was a frown on his forehead and he blinked quickly when he saw the cake had sunk down in the middle. My mother didn't laugh. She said it was fine. He had done his best, but there were some things that could not be translated into Irish.

Fourteen

There's a man who comes to our house to see my father. His name is Gearóid and he's not very tall, but he smiles a lot and has a strong voice, like the radio. In the hallway, he shakes my hand with both of his and then pats me on the shoulder and looks into my eyes in a very friendly way, because he likes hearing Irish. He is my father's friend and when he comes to visit everything in the house changes. Everything is translated into Irish – the tables, the chairs, the curtains, even the teacups and saucers turn Irish. The music on the radio has to be Irish. We have to go and play and be happy and not fight in Irish. My mother has to sit down in the front room and listen, even though she doesn't understand a word. There's not much laughing either, or drinking cognac, only Gearóid and my father talking and foaming at the mouth about all the things that are not finished yet in Ireland.

Gearóid has a car, a blue Volkswagen full of newspapers on the back seat written in Irish and English. The newspaper is called *Aiséirí*, which is the Irish for resurrection, and there is a photograph of corporation men taking down an old English street sign and putting up a new bilingual one, with the Irish on top and the English below in second place. There's an article in the paper, too, about my father and a letter from Mullingar. One day at work, my father refused to answer a letter because it was addressed to John Hamilton. He kept sending it back because that was not his name. He told them there was nobody by the name of John Hamilton working at the Electricity Supply Board in Dublin. He pretended there had been a big mistake and the letter was for somebody in a different organisation, maybe even in a different country, at the electricity board in England or America or South Africa maybe. There was a lot of trouble with this letter going back and forth for weeks and weeks, because the people of Mullingar had to wait all that time for their electricity masts to be repaired. My father didn't care if the whole country was left in darkness. And in the end, the people of Mullingar got their electricity back only when they learned to respect his proper name. But then the boss at the ESB refused to give my father promotion because the Irish language was bad for business.

In the front room, Gearóid smiles and claps his hands together with a bang. He says my father is a man who does what he believes in, not just for money. He's a real fighter who wrote articles for *Aiséirí* and made great speeches on O'Connell Street once. He says people will still throw their hats up in the air these days for a good speech. Ireland is far from being finished and there is a lot of de-Anglicisation still left to be done. My father says he loves his country as much as ever, but he has a different way of fighting now, through his children. From now on he's going to use his own children as weapons, he says, because children are stronger than armies, stronger than speeches or articles or any number of letters to the government. One child is worth more than a thousand guns and bombs, he says.

'You're the lifeblood,' Gearóid says to my mother in Irish. He says the Irish language is dying, day by day. It's choking to death slowly with everybody speaking English on the radio and in the government. But he means the opposite, like in the films. He holds his fist up in the air and says the language is not dead at all, and there's a few shakes left in the animal yet, as long as there is one family like us in the country. Even if Irish is not our mother tongue and we speak German, too, we are still more Irish than many others. *Teaghlach lán-ghaelach*, he calls us, a full-Irish fireside. Then he has to leave again. He doesn't stay for tea because he has to go to visit some more families and deliver the paper to them, too. We stand at the door and watch him getting into the car. We hear the car starting with a big growl and then we wave goodbye, the full-Irish family on the doorstep.

Afterwards, my father tells us about the time he made a speech in Dublin, with thousands of people looking up at him. He can still hear the sound of them cheering every time he walks up O'Connell Street. It's something you never forget, something you carry with you, like the sound of the sea in your ears. He takes off his glasses and starts making a speech at the dinner table. His face looks very different, like a different man in the house, a man I've never seen before. There are two red marks, one on each side of his nose. His eyes look smaller and darker, and his voice gets harder and stronger, like the radio. It looks as if he has never seen us before either, as if he's surprised to be here in this house. And he talks so fast that he has a little white blob of spit on his bottom lip. Every time Gearóid comes to the house he's like this afterwards. Happy and proud one minute, sad and angry the next, because not everybody in Ireland is doing what he told them to do.

He tells us about the time he went all over the country on his motorbike, frightening the cows as he drove past. He saw cows shaking their heads to try to get rid of the noise, like a bad dream. He tells us about a time when the police tried to stop one of the articles he wrote. They came to the offices of *Aiséirí* and said they would close down the paper, but Gearóid wasn't afraid of them. They weren't afraid of going to prison for what they believed, even if the whole country was against them. So they printed the paper with the article in it, because you have to do what's right, he says. My mother nods, because she's thinking of the time when Onkel Gerd refused to be a Nazi. I want to be proud of my father, too, so I asked him what was in the article and why they tried to stop it, but he wouldn't say. My mother doesn't know either, so we all wait for him to tell us.

'Explain it to them,' she says.

It's not something he wants to talk about. I know it's all in the wardrobe upstairs, but I'm not allowed to go near anything. I know there are piles of old newspapers and things from the time he made those speeches, hidden away in boxes. So I ask him again, why the police tried to close down the newspaper. But then he slams his fist down on the table and all the cups and spoons jump in the air. Maria shivers.

'I won't be interrogated by my own family,' he said. Then he walked away to the front room and slammed the door. My mother sits with us for a long time and tells us her stories about Germany instead. She doesn't mind being interrogated. And sometimes she says things that we don't understand. She looks far away and says we will be putting our parents on trial one day and asking what they did.

'You are the fathers and mother now,' she says. 'And we are the children.'

She is starting to clear the dishes without thinking. She's not even looking at what she's doing. It doesn't make sense stacking up plates and unstacking them again. I know she's thinking right back to when she was a girl in Kempen. She says things were different when she was small in Germany and my father was small in Ireland. We will soon be adults, she says, and they will be the children. We will grow up and look back at all the things they did in their lives, like trying to sell crucifixes and party hats and sweets. We will go over the secrets, too, that are hidden in the wardrobe.

'You'll say we're children and we didn't know any better.'

Then she starts clearing the dishes all over again, stacking up the plates and collecting the knives and forks. We start asking her more questions. I want to know if she's Irish or German now.

'What country do you love?' Franz asks.

'Ireland,' she says, because that's where she's living now and that's where the postman brings her letters and where her children are going to school. But what about Germany? And then she says she loves Germany, too, very much, because that's where she was born and went to school herself and where she remembers the postman coming to the door.

'You can't love two countries,' I said. 'That's impossible.'

'Why not?'

'What if they start fighting against each other?'

'I don't just love one of my children,' she says. 'I still love all my children, even when they start fighting.'

In school, they teach us to love our own country. They sing a song about the British going home. The *máistir* takes out a tuning fork and taps it on his desk. It rings, and when he stands the fork up on the wood it makes a long note. We hum the note and sing about the British getting out of Ireland.

Ó ró sé do bheatha 'bhaile . . .

It's a funny song and very polite. It says to the British that we hope they'll keep healthy and have a good trip home. When you sing this song you feel strong. You sit in your desk with all the other boys singing around you at the same time and feel strong in your tummy, right up to your heart, because it's about losing and winning.

The master says Irish history is like a hurling match in Croke Park with his team, County Mayo, losing for a long time, right up until the end of the match when they start coming back and win the game at the last minute. He says that's the best way to win, to lose first. He tells us the story of a man named Cromwell who was winning and sent the Irish to Connaught or Hell. But they made one big mistake, leaving lots of dead people in Ireland to keep talking in the graveyard. The fools, the fools, he says, because then the Easter Rising happened and there was lots of fighting and dying and the British had to go home, even if they didn't want to. Then the game was over and the British flag had to be taken down in Dublin Castle. Michael Collins arrived late and kept the viceroy waiting, but he said the British had kept him waiting for eight hundred years so a few minutes wouldn't make much difference. The master taps the tuning fork and we sing again. Even when we're not singing the song in our class, you still hear it coming from another class somewhere else down the corridor.

My brother gets in trouble because he writes with his left hand and the master wants everyone in Ireland to write with the same hand. Franz can only eat with his left hand and write with his left hand. He's a *ciotóg*, the master says. My mother has to go into school and tell the master that

Onkel Ted was a a *ciotóg*, too, and now he's a Jesuit. But that makes no difference and the master ties Franz's hand behind his back to make sure he can only write with his right hand. All that comes out on the page is a scribble. I want to help him, because the master laughs and says it looks like a snail has crossed the page with ink.

I know what it's like to lose, because I'm Irish and I'm German. My mother says we shouldn't be afraid of losing. Winning makes people mean. It's good that the Irish are not losing any more. It's good to love your country and to be patriotic, but that doesn't mean you have to kill people who belong to other countries. Because that's what the Germans did under the Nazis. They tried to win everything and ended up losing everything. Like a hurling match? Yes, she says slowly, like a very brutal hurling match.

The master says I'm a dreamer and that's worse than being a *ciotóg*. He says I'm always disappearing off to some other place. He wishes he could tie my head down, but that isn't possible, because no matter what happens, you're still free to go anywhere you like inside your own head. You can travel faster than the speed of light to any place you want in the universe, but now it's time to be here in the glorious Republic of Ireland, he says. He bangs his stick on the desk and asks me what blasted country I'm in at all. Germany? So then he has to come down to my desk and drag me back home to Ireland by the ear. The only way that he can stop me from emigrating again is to tie my head down with a poem after school. I have to stay behind and learn a big poem about a priest who was hanged long ago in the town of Ballinrobe where the master comes from in Mayo. We sit in the classroom alone when everyone else has gone home and learn all the verses about the priest being hung, drawn and quartered because he spoke against the British.

I can see that the master has hair growing in his ears, like grass. I think of blood on the grass in Ballinrobe.

There are gangs in the school. At lunchtime, they fight each other in the yard and it's all about winning and losing. One of the gangs is called the cavalry and they are looking for Indians to kill. When you're in a gang, you feel strong in your tummy. You run and shout and everyone else is afraid. But they don't want me any more because I'm a dreamer, so it's best to stand with my back against the wall and make sure they don't get my brother. One day, I saw them running through the yard and they punched a boy right in the stomach. The boy was eating lunch and when they hit him, he dropped his sandwiches and opened his mouth. There was no sound, only a piece of sandwich that came out and dropped on the ground, too. He stayed like that for a long time, leaning forward with his mouth wide open and a dribble coming down. I could tell they were jam sandwiches because the white bread was coloured pink. I thought of his mother making them and now they were wasted. Somebody came and picked them up but he didn't want to eat any more, only cry. Then you could hear his voice coming out loud, like a high screech with lots of pain.

Back in class, the master said there would be no more gangs. The boy who was hit by the cavalry had gone home and the master made a big speech about the potato famine in Ireland. He said the people had green mouths because grass was all that was left to eat. He said it was a disgrace to hit anyone in the stomach while they were eating. I looked out and saw the sandwiches still lying on the ground. The yard was empty. I stared at the seagulls screeching and fighting over the jam sandwiches.

And then the master bangs the desk again, as if he wants

the stick to be a tuning fork and give a long humming note. He says he's fed up with me dreaming and not knowing what country I'm in, so now there's trouble and I feel like going to the toilet quickly. He's going to punish me, but not with the stick, and not with a poem about Ballinrobe or a song about the famine. Instead he's going to send me over to the girls' school and that's the worst punishment of all, to go over there with ribbons in your hair. He takes me by the ear and we travel at the speed of light over to the girl country. I sit at the back of the class and see the girls looking around and giggling, until it's time to go home.

At home, my mother says we have started doing strange things again. When it was nearly dinner time, she told us to put the bowl of mashed potato on the table. My father was talking to her in the kitchen and she was listening and cooking at the same time, so I carried the mashed potato up to the room where we play and took the lid off. With the spoon, I threw a bit of the mash at the wall. It stayed there and we looked at it for a while. I threw another spoonful at the ceiling and it stuck as well. It made a strange sound each time, like a click. It made a different shape each time, too, sometimes like a little cloud, sometimes with a spike pointing downwards.

Maria said she was going to run and tell on me. But I told her that we had to make a sacrifice. I closed the door and said it was our duty to do this for Ireland. We had to make as many shapes as we could. Franz took lumps out with his hand and together we tried to cover the whole ceiling. Sometimes a lump came unstuck and fell down again and Maria screamed. We laughed and threw more and more of it up, until it was all gone and the whole room was covered. My mother came in and saw the glass bowl, empty on the floor. She said we were going out of our minds. My father rushed into the room and looked at bits of mashed potato on the ceiling and said they would never come off. They would be there for ever. We were in real trouble. But my mother wouldn't let him hit us. Instead of getting angry, she said you couldn't punish a thing like that because it happened only once in a lifetime. My father was still frowning, but then she put her arm around him and said it didn't matter going without mashed potato for one day. She said they were lucky to have children with such imagination. She smiled and said you had to have an imagination to do something as mad as that.

Fifteen

I was sick again. The dogs were howling in my chest. At breakfast time I could not even eat the porridge. I looked at the ring of milk around the rim and smelled the warm steam coming up into my face, but my eyes were blurry and I couldn't breathe. My father said I was trying not to go to school. He was a schoolteacher once and he knew when people were making things up, he said, and if I was really sick I wouldn't have to prove it. But when it was time to go to school, my legs were soft and I couldn't walk. I heard Franz say that my face was white, so then my mother and father had to help me up the stairs, one either side. And halfway up my head dropped down on the step in front of me and I felt the cold wood on my forehead. I heard the sound of buzzing in my ears and the sound of my mother calling me from far away. Then I fell asleep.

When I woke up again my father was gone. Only my mother was there sitting on the stairs waiting for me to come back. She asked me if I was ready to go on and then she helped me the rest of the way up to bed. She stayed with me and sat on the bed repairing a jumper, pulling a blue woollen thread across the elbow. Some boys in school had leather elbows, but we had dark blue elbows. She told me stories to make the howling go away. So I lay there watching her, and sometimes I fell asleep and woke up again later, only to see that she was still mending the same spot and telling the same story, as if no time was going by.

She told me about the time there was a big fire in Kempen. She was afraid of fire, she said, because her sister Lisalotte's hair once caught fire on a candle. When you see something like that happening with your own two eyes, when you see it happen to somebody else it's much worse and you remember it more than when it happens to yourself. She can't forget the time people came to set fire to the synagogue and she hopes I never have to witness something like that with my own two eyes. That was the time Germany was sick and took a long time to get better.

My mother had to leave school early and go to work. Onkel Gerd had no more money once he lost his job as lord mayor. She got a job in the Kempen registry office and had to learn typing and filing names in alphabetical order. She remembers people coming in to find out if their grandfathers or grandmothers had ever been Jewish. She remembers how happy one old woman was, how she had tears in her eyes and put her hand on her heart when she found out that she was one of the lucky ones. Other people were not so lucky. Every day, they came to make sure they were not Jewish. Every day, Ta Maria wondered if the Catholics would be next. It wasn't long afterwards that the Nazis closed down the convent in Mühlhausen and wrote dirty words all over the classrooms.

My mother had long plaits at that time, down to her waist, like two dark ropes. But Ta Maria said it was time to cut them. It was time to grow up and look like an adult. So one day she stopped being a girl. She asked the hairdresser to give her the Olympia Roll, because that's what all the women were wearing in the films, but, by then, her hair had already been cut too short and she had to wait for it to grow again. She says it's funny how you can get so upset about something like that, how important those things can be and how you can sometimes cry more about little things than all the big things put together. She had to wear a hat and Ta Maria promised to go down to Krefeld with her and make up for it with new shoes.

My mother says she was at work when the trouble happened and saw nothing herself. She only heard about it later from her youngest sister Minne. But she smelled the smoke in the streets that afternoon. The synagogue was on fire and the fire brigade was standing by, doing nothing. Men in brown uniforms had gone around to the Jewish houses and Minne saw them going by with red batons. She said the curtains were flapping out through the broken windows and there were books lying on the pavement. Somebody's private letters were flying around in the street like litter and there were children walking around the town with black and white ivory keys that belonged to a piano.

Onkel Gerd said they could not be part of this. You couldn't watch something like that. People in Kempen blew their breath out slowly and thought how lucky they were not to be Jewish. That same evening, they all went to the big Catholic procession in the town where hundreds of people quietly passed through the Buttermarkt square with candles and torches, praying and singing hymns as if they needed to be especially close to God from then on.

The next day Ta Maria brought my mother to Krefeld, but you couldn't buy anything that day. When they entered the shopping street they saw shoes thrown out on to the ground. The Germans would regret this one day, Ta Maria said. It was not so long ago that they were wearing newspapers around their feet. And now there were shoes lying everywhere on the ground and people stepping over them. You could smell the leather. For a moment it even looked like a shoe paradise where you could just pick them up and try them on. This was the city where my mother's mother sang at the state opera house. Now people were stopping to look through the broken shop windows. A man with a clapper board was walking along the pavement advertising ladies' stockings as if nothing had happened. It made no sense. Expensive shoes. Brand new. Some of the best quality. Some still in their boxes, or only half out, on display. Some other boxes trampled flat, and the thin, blue-grey paper that goes to wrap new shoes blowing up and down the street as if nobody cared, as if nobody needed footwear any more, as if they hated shoes.

I couldn't breathe very well. My shoulders were going up and down trying to get air. My mother stroked my head and listened to the howling in my chest. She prayed that I would get better. She smiled at me and said everything would soon be fine again, because her oldest sister Marianne was coming with her daughter Christiane. And Tante Marianne was very good at helping people breathe. She helped people in Salzburg when it was hard to breathe.

For days and days my mother was cleaning the house. She polished the stairs and every piece of wood in the house was shining. She put fruit in a bowl on the table and baked a cake. Tante Marianne was going to get my room. It had no wallpaper any more, only pink plaster and some long cracks, but my mother said it looked clean and friendly, and that's all that mattered. And as soon as Marianne walked in the front door, she would see the old oak trunk that came from their house on the Buttermarkt and think she was at home.

My mother put on her blue suit with the big white collars. She put the big number 4711 on her wrists and wore the green Smaragd snake. We put on our best clothes, too, with no blue elbows, and kept looking out the window until Tante Marianne and Christiane arrived in a taxi with suitcases. Then my mother dropped her apron on the floor of the kitchen and ran all the way along the hallway smiling and crying at the same time. Tante Marianne was smiling and crying, too, as they embraced and stood back to look each other up and down.

'*Ja, ja, ja*,' they kept saying. And then, '*Nein, nein, nein*.'

They could not believe their own eyes. They shook their heads and wiped their tears and embraced each other again. *Ja, ja, ja*, and *nein, nein, nein*, and *ja, ja, ja*, until Tante Marianne turned around to look at us. She knew our names from letters and photographs, but she had to kneel down and look at us properly, one at a time. She knew everything. She knew about Maria's picture of my mother with the arms going all around the walls. She knew that I slapped the schoolteacher. And she knew about the mashed potato on the ceiling.

My father carried in the suitcases and smiled at everyone. Christiane talked to us and Tante Marianne talked to my mother as if they couldn't waste a minute. They went through each of the names one by one – Ta Maria, Elfriede, Adam, Lisalotte, Max, Minne and Wilhelm, and all the children, as if they had to travel around Germany in their heads until every question was asked and every story was told. My mother had to hear everything twice and clapped her hands around her face as if she could not believe what she heard.

Tante Marianne brought new perfume into the house. Everyone wanted to be close to her all the time and sit beside her at the table. Maria followed her everywhere. My mother and Tante Marianne could not be separated either, because they kept talking, even when they were not in the same room. Even when Tante Marianne was upstairs and my mother was in the kitchen, they kept remembering things out loud, calling up and down the stairs as if they were at home again in the house on the Buttermarkt square. Tante Marianne called her Irmgard. We still called her Mutti, and it was like having two mothers in the house, because they had the same teeth and the same eyes and the same hair. They had the same words and the same way of laughing out loud until the tears came into their eyes. They had the same way of peeling an orange in strips along the side and the same trick of cutting the peel into the shape of teeth. Two mothers playing the monster with big orange teeth while my father was out getting coal for the boiler.

'Vooo, vooo, vooo, vooo . . .,' they both said. Then they started laughing so much that they couldn't stop any more. Laughing and shaking, so that my father stopped pouring coal into the boiler to come and see what was happening.

Tante Marianne's suitcase was full of toys and books for everyone. There were lots of gummi bears and chocolates and biscuits that you would never get in the shops in Ireland. She brought a spirit level for my father, and a toy train for me and Franz. Some other presents were wrapped and put away immediately, for Christmas. There were biscuits to be eaten now and biscuits to be kept for later. One by one, Tante Marianne took things out with great care, explaining where they came from. We were allowed to read the *Mecki* books immediately, about a hedgehog who travelled all over the world in a hot air balloon with his crew – Charlie Penguin, and a cat called Kater Murr. Nobody in Ireland knows about Mecki, and they laugh at us because we don't know who Red Riding Hood is and we don't realise it's the same as Rotkäpchen.

Everything in our house was German again. Around the table every evening, all the stories were German. Tante Marianne's daughter Christiane had plaits tied up over her head and she wore a dirndl like in fairy tales. Maria got a dirndl as well. Tante Marianne said it was lovely to see Franz and me wearing lederhosen and Irish sweaters, German below and Irish on top. She said it was remarkable that we could speak three languages. My mother told her how we sometimes got things wrong and how Maria came home one day and said: *Ich kann es nicht believen*, which is a mixed up German and English way of saying: I can't believe it. Tante Marianne said our German was different, softer, more like the old days. And she wanted to hear some Irish spoken, so we said a prayer and she said it sounded different too, not a bit like English.

I wanted Tante Marianne to stay in our house for ever. I went with her down to the seafront. I showed her all the street signs that had been changed into Irish. I showed her where the doctor lives and where the shops are. I told her that when you pass by the shoemaker's shop you get an echo, because when you shout in, the shoemaker shouts back without looking up. She laughed and said it was just like something her father would do. People stopped to speak to her. The man in the fish shop recognised her immediately and said: 'You must be the sister.' He talked to her for a long time and Tante Marianne had to explain that she was from Germany, too, but that she was now living in Austria, in Salzburg.

'Salzburg,' he said. 'I know the place you're talking about.'

We went with her on the bus to Glendalough to see the round tower. We had tea and cakes in a hotel and helped her stick stamps on lots of postcards. She said Ireland was so beautiful. She envied my mother living in a country where the people were so friendly and spoke English all the time. But my father didn't like her saying that. He tried to stop himself being angry at the table that night. He didn't want to make any trouble while there was a visitor in the house, but there was something Tante Marianne didn't understand yet about Ireland, something that had to be explained.

'One day, the man in the fish shop will speak his own language,' he said.

Tante Marianne said there was nothing wrong with speaking English. But my father shook his head. He said we were the new Irish children and soon the whole country would be speaking Irish in the shops. He said children were the strongest weapons, stronger than armies. But then Tante Marianne had an argument with my father. She said all the things that my mother can't say. She said it was wrong to use children in war. She kept her arm around Maria all the time as if she was going to protect her for the rest of her life.

'In Germany,' she said, 'they used the children, too.'

That was the only argument in our house while she was there. On the last evening, before she was going away, she showed us a photograph of the house where she lived in Austria. It was a house with a small wooden fence outside, near the castle on the hill called the Mönchberg. One day we would go and visit her. And then they talked about all the other well-known visitors that came to stay there every summer. People like Oskar Kokoschka, the famous painter. People like Ernst Rathenau, whose cousin Walther was assassinated by the Nazis in Berlin. My mother looked at the photograph and said it was a good place to breathe in deeply. She said you could look out the window and see the castle above you every morning, as if it had just grown out of the rock overnight.

When Tante Marianne was gone home again, Christiane stayed with us so that she could go to school in Ireland and learn English. My mother told me the story of going to visit her sister Marianne in the snow. It was during the war, when nobody had much food. My mother took a train all the way to Salzburg and walked up the Mönchberg in winter with a bucket of sauerkraut, because Marianne had nothing. She says she remembers the thick snow all around and the silence. Tante Marianne was always very strong, even though sad things happened in her life and her husband Angelo never came back from the war. My mother and Marianne met Angelo on the same day, when they were out in the country one time, on holiday. And afterwards Angelo sent a parcel to each of them with the exact same gift inside, a book by Thomas Mann. But it was Marianne who married him while the war was still on. They married by proxy, my mother says. One day Marianne sat in the house in Salzburg with a picture of Angelo and a glass of wine in front of her, while Angelo sat around with his friends in Split and a picture of Marianne in front of him. They got married miles and miles apart. And that's why they're still so close, even though she heard nothing more and no more letters came home. She waited and waited, but he never came back from the war. And then one day, Marianne started up a guest house. And that's why all the famous guests like Ernst Rathenau and Oskar Kokoschka are coming to stay in her house on the Mönchberg, because

Marianne was kind to people with bad lungs who couldn't breathe very well in Germany and now they're being kind back to her.

I was better again. The howling stopped. But there was trouble for us on the street. Everybody knew that we were German again. In the fish shop, the man leaned over the counter to look at us and say the word *Achtung*, as if all the people in Ireland were going to speak German from now on. Everybody in the shop turned around. He tried some more German words and I know he's only joking, because he's a nice man with a red face and who laughs so loud that it echoes around the fish shop. Other people are the same, they keep asking us to say things in German. But we're afraid. I pretend I don't know any German. I pretend I'm Irish and speak only English. But the boys outside the shops can see us wearing lederhosen, so they call us Nazis.

'*Donner und Blitzen*,' I hear them shout. With one arm up in the air they keep saying: '*Sieg Heil.*'

I know they get all those words from reading comics in the barber shop. My mother says that's all they know about Germany. My father says there's always somebody laughing in Ireland. He doesn't let comics into the house because they are in English and have Germans dying on every page.

Then it's time to talk about Christmas. Because Christmas is something German, too. My mother tells us that pink skies are a sign of the angels baking. The angels leave sweets on the stairs. My mother sings '*Tannenbaum*' and then, as if she asked for it, the snow started falling. Thick flakes coming down silently and we hardly even noticed it. We ran into the street and looked up at the snow falling past the street light. One or two flakes fell on to my eyes and gave me white eyelashes. Franz opened his mouth and tried to eat some of the snow as it came down and he said it was like free ice pops. My mother came out and said we should all wash our faces. She scooped up the snow from the wall with her bare hands and rubbed it against her face. Wonderful, she said, and we all did the same after her, even my father, cleaning our faces with the new white snow.

Sixteen

It was a new snow country. It snowed right through the night and by Christmas morning, when I woke up and looked out the window, I could see Germany. Everything was covered over and swollen with snow. The roofs of the houses, the cars, the trees, the garden walls, even the rubbish bins were white and clean. On the way to Mass the street was like a silent room and Maria said the snow was talking under our feet. There was a lost glove which somebody had stuck on a spike in the railings so that the person who owned it could come back and find it again. But now it was covered in snow like a big white hand saying stop.

I knew that snow was not just for children, because my mother said it turned everybody into a child, even my father. He didn't want to let on that he was excited. He didn't want to make snowballs or anything like that, but I could see that he was happy because when they got married at Christmas in Germany, they travelled all the way down along the Rhine together in the snow. Snow was something German, he said. Normally the winter was too mild in Ireland and the only snow that you would see was in pictures on biscuit tins, or else as cotton wool on the crib or as icing sugar on cakes. It was the Gulf Stream, he explained. He laughed and said that Ireland would rather belong to a different climate because people had started growing palm trees in their gardens. Guest houses along the coast were called Santa Maria and Stella Maris, and there were lots of streets like Vico Road and Sorrento Terrace that made you feel like you were in a warmer country. But on Christmas morning all the streets should have had German names because everything was wrapped in white, even the palm trees.

The only thing different was the Christmas lights blinking on and off in the windows. I knew that my mother and father would never have fairy lights on the tree. Instead we had candles, because that's what they did in Germany and my mother even had special candleholders that clipped on to the branches. We had hanging chocolate angels and lots of other things that had come in a big parcel from Germany. I knew that other children had Santa Claus and they knew what he was going to bring them. Sometimes people in the street would ask us what Santa was going to bring and we didn't know. We never talked about that. One of the neighbours once brought us to see Santa in one of the shops, but I could see his brown fingers from smoking. He was coughing a lot and I saw him afterwards having a cup of tea with his beard off. I knew who he was, too, because I saw him coming out of the Eagle House another time and he wasn't able to walk very well and had to hold on to the wall.

We had Christkind instead and everything was a secret anyway until the very last minute. We were not even allowed into the front room for Advent, because some of the gifts were already laid out in the corner behind the sofa under a big brown sheet of paper. We were only allowed in to help with the Christmas tree, and once, when my mother had to leave the room to get something, I wanted to look under the brown sheet, but I was afraid the Christkind would take all the presents away again. My mother said it was not the gifts that would be taken away but the surprise, which was worse. I knew that other children were getting guns and cowboy suits, but we never got guns or swords or anything to do with fighting. Instead, we got a surprise, as well as something made by my father and something educational, like a microscope.

It was hard to wait. We stood in a line in the hallway, the youngest first and the oldest last. My father was in the front room lighting all the candles and we could smell the matches. When everything was ready, he opened the door wide and the candles were reflected in his glasses. My mother started singing '*Tannenbaum*' as we slowly walked into the room and found all the gifts and sweets laid out on the chairs. There was even a trail of sweets on the floor as if the Christkind had been in a hurry at the last minute. Then everything was a surprise. There were toys and games and books from Germany and I knew I was so lucky that we were German at Christmas. We kneeled down to say thank you, and then my father put on the record of the Cologne Children's Choir so that the whole house filled up with the bells of the Cologne Cathedral ringing out across the sea to Dublin. We might as well be in Kempen, my mother said, with the taste of *Pretzel* and *Lebkuchen* and marzipan potatoes rolled in cinnamon.

Later on, we went out to play in the snow. We built a snowman in the front garden, and it was only when we saw other children on the street that we realised where we were. There were marks where they had scraped snow off the pavement or off the walls and you could see Ireland underneath. A car had skidded, too, and left two black streaks on the road. We went from one garden to the next looking for new untouched sheets of snow, where the ground was still under a dream. And when all the other children had disappeared inside for Christmas dinner, we went as far as the football field to see how deep the snow was there.

But then we were ambushed by a gang of boys. We had never seen them before and it looked like they had been waiting for us. We were trapped in the lane and couldn't get home again. Maria and I ran away into the field through an opening in the barbed-wire fence, but they chased after us. The others had already caught Franz and pushed him up against the wall, holding a stick across his neck. They twisted his arm up behind his back and made him walk towards the field where Maria and I were caught, too, near a line of tall eucalyptus trees. One of them was forcing snow up under Maria's jacket and she was starting to cry.

'Leave us alone,' she said, but they just laughed.

Franz said nothing. He just stood there and waited in silence. He was doing what my mother always said we should do, to pretend they didn't exist. I did the same. I tried to pretend that standing in that spot in the football field was exactly what I wanted to do at that moment. I remembered what my mother said about fighting. Maria stopped resisting, too, and they gave up putting snow under her jumper because it was no fun any more. They were not afraid of anything. They pushed us back against the wire fence of the football field with sticks. The leader of the gang was not even afraid of the cold, because he picked up snow and caked it into a flat, icy disc while the other boys all blew into their cupped red hands for warmth.

'Nazi bastards,' he said.

They made a circle around us and whispered among themselves. One of the boys was pushing a dirty piece of brown snow towards Franz with his shoe, saying that he was going to make him eat it. But Franz ignored him. I knew Franz was saying the silent negative in his head. Then Maria started crying and I wanted to cry as well only Franz stopped me.

'Don't indulge them,' he said.

They repeated it a few times in a German accent. And for some of them it was a sign to start speaking in a kind of gibberish that made no sense. *'Gotten, Blitzen, fuckin' Himmel.'* One of the boys started dancing around, trampling a circle in the snow with *'Sieg Heils'* and I suddenly wanted to start laughing. I thought they were very funny and I wanted to be Irish like them, to laugh and make up some of these stupid words, too, all the stuff they had collected from the comics and from films where the Germans were always losers. One of them tried to speak German by himself with his face all contorted with pain.

'Rippen schtoppen . . . Krauts. Donner und Blitzen, Himmel, Gunther-Schwein . . . Messerschmidt . . .' he said in one long burst. Then he suddenly died in the snow, falling back and shaking as if he was riddled with bullets. *'Aaargh . . .'*

I couldn't help laughing. I could see myself as part of the gang, joining in and walking around the streets with them, laughing at everything. It made me feel soft in my tummy to think that I could be friends with them. But the leader didn't like it. He wanted me to be the enemy and to see how tough us Germans really were. So he flung the snowball and it hit me in the eye with a flash of white, like a hard lump of icy stone. I couldn't see anything and I rubbed my eye, but I didn't let myself cry because I didn't want to let my brother down. I showed them that nothing could hurt me and that Germans didn't feel pain.

They continued to talk among themselves, trying to

decide what to do with us. I heard one of them say that we should be put on trial.

'Yeah, put them on trial,' they all agreed.

'Guilty or not guilty?'

I knew that whatever they said about us we could never deny it. Whether it was true or not didn't matter any more. They said things about the sinking of the Bismarck or the gas ovens but we didn't know anything like that yet. I wanted to tell them what my mother said about the silent negative, but I knew they would only laugh at that. It was no use. We were at the mercy of their court in the snow. There was nobody else in the world to say who was right or wrong. Everybody was inside on Christmas day and we were alone on the white football field with a breeze pushing the tops of the trees behind us. Above the tall goal posts, the sky was grey and green again and it looked like there would be more snow. Low on the sky there were flashes of white or silver seagulls and I knew we just had to wait.

'We have to go home now,' Maria suddenly said, as if she could just bring this whole thing to an end by acting like an adult. She tried to move forward, but they only pushed her back again.

'Execute them,' one of them shouted.

They didn't even have time for a trial. Maybe they were numb with the cold like us and wanted to go home to eat sweets and play with toys, so they decided to get on with the sentence and started to make snowballs. One of them said to pack them hard and another one of them included the discoloured piece of snow in his armoury, and when they all had heaps of white cannon balls ready beside their feet, we waited for the order and watched the leader of the gang raise his hand. It seemed like an endless wait. I thought of all kinds of things that had nothing to do with being a Nazi. I remembered that the words in Irish for grey and green are the same. I thought of marzipan potatoes. And the peculiar skull-shaped design of plum pudding. I thought of the bell on the wall of my father and mother's bedroom that didn't work any more, and I thought of the three little dials on the gas meter under the stairs, until the hand eventually came down and a shout brought with it a hail of blinding white fire.

'It's only snow,' Franz said.

He had his hands up over his eyes. Even after they were gone and the football field was empty and silent and it was already starting to get dark, he still had his hands up.

We might as well have been in Kempen, sitting in the front room eating Christmas cake, while my father lit the candles on the Christmas tree one more time. We sat on the carpet and played a game of cards where one person was always left with a picture of the black crow and had to be marked on the nose with a piece of charcoal, until everybody was a loser once and had a black nose. My father stood up and opened the door of the big bookcase to take out the bottle of Asbach Uralt. He took out the cork with a tiny, high-pitched squeak that sounded like a hiccup and poured two glasses so that the room filled up with a smell of cognac, along with the smell of pine needles and matches and candle wax.

'A cognac-een,' my mother called it. She liked to make things sound smaller than they were, like they did in Irish, too, because everything was better when it was small and harmless and less greedy. She sipped slowly and closed her eyes so she could think about what she was drinking. She said it was like a little kiss from God above. She laughed and said it again, like a tiny, little kiss from God.

My father then put on a record. He took it out of the

sleeve and made sure not to touch the music with his fingers as he placed it on the turntable. He frowned as he did it, but I knew that nobody could be angry, because it was Christmas. When he dropped the needle down lightly with his index finger, you could hear a crackle before the woman began to sing in German, a high voice that was so beautiful, my mother said, it was like silver coins falling down the stairs. And at the end, there was a single note that rose up so high in the air that it stayed in the room long after the song was over.

Sometimes a candle crackled and spluttered. And outside it was dark. I knew the football field was empty now and there was nobody out in the world. More snow was covering the footprints and it was easy to forget what happened. We had been executed but we were warm and there was a nice smell of the Christmas tree in the room, so it was easy to forget how cold and numb your hands could be outside. We had orange juice to drink and chocolate angels to eat. My father was putting on another record and my mother sniffed the cognac-een. Everybody was safe now and we were lucky to be German, but I knew it wasn't over yet.

Seventeen

I keep thinking of things not happening.

If you lie in bed and think hard enough, you can pretend that lots of things don't happen. I can pretend that I'm floating above the bed and that my feet are miles away across the sea. I can pretend that I can't use my left arm, that I only have one arm, like Mr Smyth in the vegetable shop. I can pretend that my father has no limp. And I keep thinking there was no such thing as Hitler, or the Nazis, because then my mother would not fall on the ice and break her teeth. The day we go down to Mass early in the morning, when it's still dark and there's ice on all the roads and we have to hold her hand, I keep thinking that didn't happen.

My mother says I'm a dreamer and it's true what they say about me in school. I'm the boy who lives a million miles away in outer space. She smiles at me with all her new teeth and says goodnight. But she's the one who is dreaming and still hoping that some things didn't happen at all, because she stays in the room after she's switched off the light, just to stand at the window for a while before she goes downstairs again. The light from the street outside makes the branches of the trees blow across her face. It's very quiet and she doesn't say a word for a long time.

'Nobody can force you to smile,' she says.

'What?' I ask. But I know she's not even talking to me, only to herself, as if she's the last person left in the room.

'They can make you show your teeth, but what good is that? Nobody can make you smile against your will.'

It's hard to find out what she means sometimes, but I know that she's talking about the bad film in Germany when the houses and trains were on fire. She's standing there with the black and white branches moving across her face and across the wall behind her, as if she's stuck on the screen, standing under the light waiting for somebody.

I know that she had lots of men who wanted to go out with her in Germany, but they were all 'brown', which meant that they were Nazis and she had to wait for something better. Ta Maria kept saying that it wasn't a good time for men. I'm glad I'm not looking for a husband myself, she often said. I'd rather a soldier with a missing leg any day than one of those young house-devils in brown uniform. So my mother said no to them all. And then she always laughs and sings the song about the man kissing the dog.

Ich küsse Ihre Hand Madam, und denk es wär Ihr Mund.
Ich küsse Ihren Mund Madam, und denk es wär Ihr Hund.

I kiss your hand, Madame, and wish it was your mouth.
I kiss your mouth, Madame, and wish it was your hound.

So she waited and carried on working at the registry office in Kempen, until one day when she went on holiday with Marianne to the Eifel mountains and they both met Angelo.

He was a good man. He was serious and had great humour. It was hard to know which of them he was more interested in at first, because he paid them both the same amount of attention. He had read the same poems by Rilke that they had also read. He was polite and eager not to leave either one of them out of the conversation. If he spent a morning walking through the fields with Marianne, then he would make up for it in the afternoon coming back with her younger sister. At night in their campbeds, they whispered about him as if he was the last good man left in Germany.

I know they were the best two weeks that my mother ever spent in her life, because she still likes to talk about them. And sometime later, she received a parcel from him with a scarf inside and a book. She was so excited about the gift that she went around and told everyone, even all the old people working in the registry office, until Marianne wrote to say that she too had got a scarf, and the same book. So then it was time to give way, my mother says, because that was Angelo and he married Marianne later on and never came home from the war.

And then she's gone. The branches are still waving across the screen, but she's downstairs again, clacking on the typewriter, putting down all the things that she can't say to anyone, not even my father. Things you can't say in a song, or a story, only on the typewriter for people to read later on sometime, on their own, without looking into your eyes.

She got a new job in Düsseldorf, working in the central employment office. She was glad to be in a city at last where things were happening and you could go to the theatre and meet new people. The office was run by an energetic man named Stiegler who arrived every morning smelling of aftershave, dressed in a lovely suit with the newspaper already read and folded under his arm. He wore good shoes and always had his hair combed. He greeted everyone by name and shook everyone's hand, clasping it in both of his with great warmth. She was the youngest and the older women in the office said he was a good boss who liked a joke from time to time, unlike the crusty old boss that went before him. Herr Stiegler was human, they said, and not bad looking at all. He was modern, too, because even though he was married himself, that didn't stop him flirting harmlessly now and again, just for the fun of it. And whenever it was somebody's birthday, he made sure that it was remembered.

I know that she didn't like the work very much, but Herr Stiegler praised her and said she was intelligent. He was good with compliments. And if she made a mistake in her typing, he would not shout or humiliate her in front of the other women, but instead just point to the misspelling so that she could quietly go and do it again. It was a matter of being obedient and efficient, however boring and senseless the work was. Even when she once made a big mistake and he should have been really angry, he just smiled and said quite honestly that it was pigs' work. He expected more from her. And the way he said it was so inspiring that you could only vow to do better in future.

There was little contact with the other workers outside the office hours. They all went home to their families. So one evening, Herr Stiegler invited her out to the theatre to meet his wife. And Frau Stiegler was so kind and kept the conversation going afterwards over a glass of wine at a nearby café. They were cultured people, she discovered, and some days later, when Herr Stiegler noticed a book of

Rilke poems in her bag at the office, he was able to discuss them with her and even went on to suggest that she should read a poet named Stefan George, a real German master. He said the greatest poets were also the greatest patriots.

In Düsseldorf she didn't feel so much like an orphan any more. She was a grown-up now. At nineteen years of age, her other sisters envied her because she was able to do lots of new things, like going to concerts and watching the latest films that would take years to arrive in a small town like Kempen. She bought new clothes and changed her hair. The Olympia Roll didn't quite suit her any more and she decided to wear it more casually, in natural curls that other women in the office said they would give their right eye for. Everyone admired her, even Herr Stiegler, though he didn't comment openly. He waited until he found a big mistake in her typing and then he came right over to her desk and informed her that he was a little disappointed with her work.

'But the hairstyle,' he whispered, 'that's a big success.'

My mother says if we could all see into the future and tell what's coming then it would be a wonderful world altogether. Lots of things wouldn't happen at all. If you could tell the future then you could stop trains crashing into each other. She says the Germans are very good at finding out what's going to happen and being ready for it because of all the things that have gone wrong before. But lots of things in this world still happen for the first time and sometimes people just don't expect it.

Everybody must have known that there was another war coming. Herr Stiegler was away a good bit after that, setting up new recruitment programmes in various towns and cities in the region. It was all in the newspaper, too. The women in the office cut out a picture of Herr

Stiegler, smiling and saluting along with leading figures in the Nazi party.

And then one day, he picked her out to set up an office in the town of Venlo, on the Dutch border. The whole thing had to be restructured and he would need a dynamic assistant. Out of all the women in the department, he chose her for this important job. She was very happy and a little embarrassed to think that the others in the office were giving her jealous glances. She got ready and took the train to Venlo and started working immediately with energy. There would be no more typing errors, she vowed. She got a small room at the top of the administration building where she would stay and it was nice to have the whole house to herself at night.

On the second night, Herr Stiegler came back to the office because he had forgotten something important. She heard him downstairs. He was very polite and came up to her room, just to make sure that she didn't get a fright, hearing somebody in the office below. It was only him, he assured her. When he tried the handle of the door and found that she kept it locked at night, he laughed and said she had nothing to fear. But even then she didn't open the door, because it wasn't right to let a man into her room at night.

Herr Stiegler went downstairs to look for what he needed. And afterwards he came back up once more to speak to her again through the door. He said he had forgotten to mention it before but that he had brought something for her, just something small, a book of poetry. It was Stefan George. She said thank you very much, it was very kind of him, but that she had already gone to bed and she hoped she wasn't being rude by waiting for it until the morning in the office. So then Herr Stiegler said he just quickly wanted to point out a line or two in the book.

'My wife is downstairs,' he said. 'I better not keep her waiting.'

'She's here, in Venlo?'

'Of course,' Herr Stiegler said.

So then she had to get dressed quickly and open the door. And before she knew it he was in the room, reading out one of the poems and telling her what it meant. She was nervous and didn't like the way he talked about the poetry. He was breathless. She was afraid that Frau Stiegler would suddenly come upstairs and there would be trouble.

'I must ask you to leave now,' she insisted, but he just smiled at her and asked what she was so afraid of.

'Come on,' he said. He put the book down and stepped towards her. She could smell the cognac on his breath as he put his hands straight on her waist. She tried to push him away. She tried to remind him that his wife was downstairs waiting.

'Frau Stiegler . . .,' she kept saying, but that didn't stop him.

'Come on, Fraülein Kaiser, don't make such a big fuss,' he said. And then she was afraid because she knew what was coming but she couldn't stop it.

I can see the branches dancing across the street light outside. I can see them swinging from side to side along the wall in my room. I can hear my mother clacking downstairs on the typewriter, putting everything down on paper for later. She can't stop what's happening, but she can write it down instead, how she struggled to keep Herr Stiegler away from her. All she could think of doing was to call through the open door, down along the empty corridor.

'Frau Stiegler,' she shouted. 'Upstairs.'

But that made no difference, because she realised at last that his wife was not there at all. He had come alone. The whole building was empty and there was nobody she could call for help. Herr Stiegler had planned it. Maybe he had even planned the whole office expansion for this. She said she was an honest woman. She threatened that she would go to the police, the Gestapo, but he didn't seem to care. Nothing would stop him, not even when she started screaming and she could hear the echo of her own voice going through the whole building. There was nobody to hear it. Then he just slapped her across the face, twice, very hard, for making such a big pantomime out of it all. Her face was stinging and she got the salty taste of blood.

'You have to be able to make a sacrifice,' he said.

And that was the worst thing of all, that he accused her of not being able to make a sacrifice. So then she started crying helplessly, because she knew that he was much stronger and that she was trapped now and could not stop him doing what he wanted. There was nothing more that she could do to resist. She repeated the silent negative in her head again and again until it was over. Then Herr Stiegler said she should smile.

'Give me a little smile,' he kept saying afterwards, but she couldn't. And then he forced her to smile. He ordered her to smile. He put his fingers up to her mouth and pushed her lips apart so that she had to show her teeth.

There was lots of ice on the road and it was still dark as we went down to Mass. The street lights were still on and I could see a shine on the road where the ice was slippery. My mother told us to hold her hand, Franz on one side and me on the other. And when we were crossing the street, my mother suddenly pulled her hand away and fell forward. I heard her falling and I heard a click when her mouth hit the ground. Franz fell, too, at the same time and he was sitting down in the street. I tried to help my mother to get up, but she stayed there on her knees, looking around as if she didn't know where she was, as if she had just woken up in Ireland for the first time. She said nothing. She was looking for something, feeling the ground with her hand in the dark as if she was blind. She took out a small white handkerchief that she sometimes wipes my face with at the last minute before going into the church. She started picking things up and putting them into the handkerchief.

'Mutti, are you all right?' Franz asked, because he was the only person who could speak. My mother nodded and put her hand on his head. But when she stood up I could see that there was blood in her mouth. I could see that she had no front teeth and no smile. She put her hand over her mouth and we started walking again, very slowly this time. And when we got to the church we didn't go to Mass at all. We just blessed ourselves and said a quick prayer and then a man came to take us home in his car. All the way home the car was skidding over to the side and the man said it was lucky there were no other cars on the road.

My mother smiles at me with her new teeth and says it's all forgotten now. Everything can be repaired, she says, except your memory. A lot worse happened to other people, things we should not forget. The Germans broke their teeth, she said. But you can't be thinking about things not happening. You can be careful to make sure it never happens again, but you can't be still trying to stop things after they've happened. She laughs and smiles again, with her eyes, too, this time. And then she starts singing the song about the man kissing the dog.

Eighteen

My father took over the *Kinderzimmer*. That's the room we play in and keep our toys in, the room most people call the dining room. It's the room with the mashed potato still on the ceiling. Now my father says he's going to start a new factory and he needs a place where he can make things. First of all he built a workbench in one corner that's so heavy it can never be moved again. It has a vice at one end and lots of space underneath for spare pieces of wood that might be needed later. Then he made a press on the wall where he could hang up lots of tools like chisels and a saw and a wooden mallet. And before you start buying anything like wood or glue or screws, before you even start measuring and sawing, you have to have an idea. You have to draw a plan.

My father has great ideas for things that are badly needed in Ireland, like *Wägelchen*. They have lots of them in Germany, my mother says, but none in Ireland. So he drew a picture of one that looked just like a box with lots of measurements. He can see it in his head. He can see exactly what it will look like when it's finished, a German boxcar with stickers of forests and mountains and fairy tales stuck on to the sides. He calls it the prototype and we're allowed to watch while he works every evening after he comes home.

'Is it for us?' Maria asks.

'Yes and no.'

'Is it for Ireland?'

'Yes and no.'

He keeps frowning as he works. He has to concentrate hard and you can see the tip of his tongue coming out the side of his mouth. He says you have to measure everything twice because you can only cut once. Then you see the sawdust falling on the floor like snow. You see wooden curls falling like blond hair. There are some thin, cut-off pieces of wood, too, that look like swords for us to fight with. Sometimes you can hear him whistling a tune as he works every night until it's very late. Even long after we go to bed you can still hear the sound of the hand-drill squeaking and sometimes the mallet banging, until my mother goes into the *Kinderzimmer* to put her arm around him and tell him the world wasn't made in one day either and there's plenty of time tomorrow. But he still wants to finish one more little thing and after that it's quiet again with everyone asleep.

One night he was working so late it was after midnight. You could hear him sanding all the time and it sounded like he was telling everyone to be quiet.

'Shish . . . Shish . . . Shish . . .' he kept saying.

Then there was a smell of paint in the whole house that was nicer than any other smell in the world. And in the morning when we got up, the first *Wägelchen* was standing all ready in the hallway, painted red with black wheels and a rope for pulling tied at the front. My mother clapped her hands and said it was beautiful, just like one of the toy trolleys she had when she was small. There was a new baby in our house called Ita and everybody was always gathering around her and trying to make her smile. My mother took the baby and laid her in the new red *Wägelchen* so that we could make her smile and my father could take a photograph. And then it's time for him to go to work with the trolley under his arm and a list that my mother typed up of all the things that went into it, how much everything cost, from the wood to the wheels, down to the cheapest thing which is the glue.

In the shops in Dublin, they kept saying it was beautiful but too expensive. Even when my father told them it was made in Ireland, even when he showed them the list of materials and explained how long he spent working on it, they still shook their heads and said nobody in Ireland had the money to spend on a boxcar. A boxcar is not something people buy in shops, no matter how beautiful it is. When he walked around the city at lunchtime every day with the *Wägelchen* under his arm, people stopped to ask him where he got it. Which doesn't mean they want to buy it or that the shops want anything that's handmade. But that doesn't stop him either. Every night after he comes home on the train he goes into the *Kinderzimmer* to work on the next one. Because one day, he says, Irish people will stop buying only things that are made in Britain. One day Ireland will have its own great inventions.

Everybody in our house is busy working and inventing things. Franz is making a bridge with Meccano and Maria is learning how to knit. If my father is not busy making more trolleys, then he's in the greenhouse sowing trays of seeds so that he can plant as many different flowers as possible when the summer comes. There will be lots to eat as well like cabbage and peas and tomatoes from the greenhouse. My mother is busy all the time, too, trying to make the new baby talk and eat up, but Ita just keeps moving around and my mother has to chase her. She sits on the potty all day and my mother is still trying to make her eat the last spoon. Ita knows the fastest way of getting around the house, sitting on the potty and pulling herself along by the heels of her shoes without saying a word because she still hasn't swallowed the last spoon and her mouth is full. My mother is trying not to spend money, and one day she bought a big tongue from the butcher, a cow's tongue which she said was very cheap and tasty. We got up on the chairs to look at it curled up in a big jar on the kitchen windowsill, beside Our Lady. It was purple and grey, with lots of little spikes and cracks. Maria stuck her own tongue out to look at in the mirror and I thought of what it would be like to put your tongue in the vice, because that's what my mother said she would have to do with the cow's tongue. She said she would boil it and press it in the vice.

Some days when my father is at work, I go into the *Kinderzimmer* and make my own inventions. I put lots of things into the vice and squeeze them as hard as I can until they change shape. Franz, too, likes to crush down the hard-boiled sweets to dust. I have some English words in my head that I want to keep saying out loud because I like them. Don't forget the fruit gums, chum. I get bits of wood and spare buttons to see how long it takes before they bend or break. And all the time I say my secret words, don't forget the fruit gums, chum.

One day I got a splinter in my foot from running on the floorboards in my bare feet. But my father knew what to do right away. He got a needle and told me to put my foot up on the table. He took off his glasses and started to sting me with the needle, until I pulled my foot away. I thought it would hurt, but he said nothing hurts except what's in your head. Then he slowly lifted the skin with the needle and got it out without hurting, and afterwards he showed me the tiny splinter that caused so much trouble and everybody was smiling because there was no pain at all.

'There's no such thing as pain,' my mother said. 'The only pain is when you're ashamed. When you're ashamed, everything hurts.'

It's true because one day when I stole money out of her coat pocket, she brought me into the front room and tried to hit me on the legs with her hand. It didn't hurt because she's not very good at it. But I was ashamed and I had nothing to say. I just felt sorry and that was much worse. My father is better at punishment, and one day when he heard that I brought English words into the house, he was very angry. I couldn't stop saying 'don't forget the fruit gums, chum' and hitting other people like Franz and Maria because the words were stuck to my mouth and I had to keep hitting people even if I didn't want to. My father knew what to do. He picked out a stick in the greenhouse and said we had to make a sacrifice. He brought me up the stairs and my mother closed all the doors in the house so that nobody would hear anything. When we got up to the landing, my father said we would kneel down and pray that he was doing the right thing for Ireland. We kneeled down and asked God how many lashes he thought was fair and my father said fifteen. I was hoping that God said no lashes, because I didn't mean it and maybe it was better for Ireland to give me a last chance. But my father heard God saying fifteen and not one less. So then he brought me into a room and told me to lie down on the bed and take down my trousers. I heard the stick whistling through the air, but it didn't hurt at all because I knew I was making a sacrifice. My father told me to count up to fifteen to make sure that he didn't forget what number he was on or leave one out. I wish I never learned to count in Irish and when it was over we had to kneel down again and say thanks to God. I was ashamed because I thought everybody in the world was laughing at me now. That's worse than anything that can happen with a stick, when everybody is laughing. Even if you squeeze your finger in the vice, even if you squeeze your tongue in the vice, it's not as bad as when you're ashamed and can't speak.

I know that people laugh at our family. I know that we are funny people because we don't speak English while we're eating our dinner or playing with cars on the granite steps outside the house. We are funny because my father goes into a hardware shop to buy wood in Irish from a man who can also speak the language. We're funny because we're German and my mother just closes the doors and keeps saying the same things over and over again and telling everybody that it's not good to win and it's better to pretend that there's no such thing as pain and nobody can make you smile and you should keep saying the silent negative all the time. On the street I feel ashamed because they know I got the stick on the backside and I can't speak English. My father says we don't care about the people outside, because we'll show them how to be Irish. We have to be as Irish as possible and make a sacrifice.

Then my father sits down and tells me the story of his grandfather again, Tadhg Ó Donnabháin Dall, Ted O'Donovan Blind. He was called O'Donovan Blind, not because he was blind himself but because he was the son of somebody who was blind. He was an Irish speaker with a beard who wrote books, a land-surveyor by profession and he travelled a lot around west Cork all his life and loved poetry in the Irish language.

In Munster where my father comes from, there were lots

of poets who spoke and wrote their own language. But that was long ago when people still spoke Irish all over and poets were welcomed in every house and treated like kings. If a poet came to the door of a big house where the noble people lived, my father says, they were offered food and a bed for the night. If you were nice to them, if you had a party and made them feel welcome, then they would write long poems telling the whole world how generous and how cultured you were. But if you were mean and turned them away, they'd write bad poems about you that would put you to shame. They were called the bards, and what happened one day was that the people who looked after the poets, the earls and all the other noble people, lost the war with the British and had to leave their houses and flee to France. There was no place for the poets to go, so they disappeared as well and Ireland was left without any poetry for a while.

After that, the Irish people didn't know where they were going any more, because the names of the streets and villages were changed into English. People lost their way because they didn't recognise the landscape around them. Léim Uí Dhonnabháin became Leap. Gleann d'óir became Glandore and Cionn tSáile became Kinsale. People's names were changed, too. Ó Mathúna became O'Mahony and Ó hUrmoltaigh became Hamilton. My father says the Irish were all stumbling around, not knowing who they were or who they were talking to. They could not find their way home. They were homeless. And that was the worst pain of all, to be lost and ashamed and homesick.

And that's how my great-grandfather became blind, because he was descended from a poet who had lost his way and went blind. Ted O'Donovan Blind got a job as a surveyor and travelled around west Cork all his life, speaking Irish and reciting some of the old Gaelic poems to make people feel at home. But it was too late, because most people were already speaking English and following the English road signs. And nobody wanted their children to speak Irish any more for fear that they would not be able to find their way in places like America and Canada and Australia.

Gaelic in Ireland is called Irish, so that Irish people will remember what country they're living in. Some people say that the Irish language reminds them of the big famine when they had nothing to eat except the old poems in Irish. My father says people transferred everything they owned into English, their stories and their songs, even all their memories and their family photographs. They deny that Irish has anything to do with them any more, but some of their ways of saying things come down from the old bards, even if they don't know it. Time didn't just begin in Ireland with the English language, he says. And just because they all speak English so well doesn't mean the Irish are not blind any more or that they know where they're going. There are some things you can only remember in Irish.

'One day the Irish people will wake up and wonder if they're still Irish,' he says.

And that's why it's important not to bring bad words like fruit gum into the house. That's why it's important to work hard and invent lots of new things in Ireland and fight for small languages that are dying out. Because your language is your home and your language is your country. What if all the small languages disappear and the whole world is speaking only one language? We'll all be like the Munster poets, he says, lost and blind, with nothing to welcome them only doors banging in the wind. We're living on the eve of extinction, my father says. One day there will be only one language and everybody will be lost.

'The world will be full of homesick people,' he says.

In the evenings, my father stays outside in the garden as long he can because it's still bright. It's time to plant all the flowers and vegetables, and to get rid of flowers like dandelions that he doesn't want. There are pink and white flowers growing out of the granite walls, too, that look beautiful but everybody hates them, because they're wild and wreck the walls and make a good hiding place for snails. There are bushes that only grow by the sea with purple flowers, too, and leaves that keep growing from the inside so that when you peel off the outer leaves it's never-ending, until you get to a tiny green bud inside. My father says all plants were wild once and he's growing sweet peas. And then he always lights a fire that crackles and whistles. You can't see any flames, but you can see lots of smoke going all over the garden, as if he's sending a message all around the world.

Inside, my mother is boiling the cow's tongue and there is a strong smell all around the house. That evening we watch as she wraps the tongue up in a white cloth and puts it into the vice. She winds the lever around and presses the tongue as hard as she can. Then she leaves it there for a whole night.

The next day we sit down to dinner and my mother brings out the tongue on a plate, all pink and pressed into a square shape by the vice and some glue around it as well. My father takes the knife and begins to cut. Everybody gets a slice along with cabbage. Franz wants to know if you eat a cow's tongue, will you start saying moo. My mother laughs, but now it's time to stop the jokes and eat. I don't like the taste of tongue. It's like eating rubber. I look around at Franz and Maria and they have stopped chewing as well. Maria is allowed to spit hers out on the plate because she's going to get sick, but we have to keep eating until it's finished and learn not to be afraid of new tastes.

'It's just exactly like ham,' my mother says.

She eats it and my father eats it and they nod to each other.

'Excellent,' my father says.

But I don't think they like it either. I think they're just pretending because they don't want it to go to waste and people to know they're wrong. We have to keep chewing, even though I nearly want to get sick, too, and I can't stop thinking of biting my own tongue and all the glue coming out from inside it. Everything comes to a standstill. There's a big lump in my mouth and I'm like Ita on the potty, not swallowing the last spoon and not saying a word, until my mother says it's all right, we don't have to eat any more as long as we finish all the cabbage.

'I suppose you don't want to eat something that somebody else had in their mouth already,' she says.

And then I can see her shoulders shaking. She starts laughing so much that she can't even eat any more either. My father is laughing, too, and he has to take off his glasses. He has tears in his eyes this time and they keep laughing for a long time, until my mother tells us to clear the table and promises that we will never have to eat tongue again as long as we live.

Nineteen

The reason my father has a limp is that when he was a boy he got a very bad disease called polio. And that's the end of it, he says. Except that it's not true. It's not a lie but it's not the truth either, because he never told us about going to the doctor or staying in hospital and getting sweets. He never had polio, because Onkel Ted told me once that my father had a limp when he was born. So maybe his mother only made up that story about polio, because people were afraid of anyone who was deformed at birth and it was better to say you had a disease like everyone else. Or maybe my father made it up himself because they were always laughing and limping after him on his way to school and saying that he had a father in the British navy.

Sometimes on Sundays we go to visit our relations. Tante Roseleen smiles at me all the time with her eyes. Onkel PJ has a wristwatch with a silver cover on it to protect the glass from breaking if you go to war. Tante Lilly has two sons called Jimmy and Pat who toss coins up in the air and show us how to play cards. And sometimes they all come to our house and bring red lemonade, then Tante Kathleen comes up from Middleton and Tante Eileen comes up from Skibbereen with Geraldine and Carmel. Then the house is full of smoke and English. I'm still afraid to bring bad words into the house, but then my father starts telling stories in English, too, and everything is all right as long as the visitors are still there. They say that nobody in Ireland can bake a cake like my mother. They say nobody can build a wooden toy trolley like my father and there are no children as lucky as we are with three languages, because we'll never be homeless. They sit around the table and talk until it's very late, but nobody ever says anything about my father's limp. We don't know what questions to ask, until one day when I told Onkel Ted that the worst disease in the world was polio because it makes your legs shorter and you get a limp.

'Polio,' he said. 'Is that so?'

My mother says some things are hard to talk about, some things are private.

'You remember the stick in the water,' she says. 'You remember the day we were down at the sea where the dog was barking and there was a stick in the water that was crooked. You know it's not crooked or broken. It's an illusion, but that doesn't mean it's a lie.'

There is nothing in the whole world that my mother hates more than lies. She wants us to be honest and to tell the truth when you're asked, because lies are worse than murder and nobody will trust you. You won't even trust yourself any more. She wants no more lies, not even a small one, not even an Irish one. Irish lies or German lies, it makes no difference to her, it's always wrong. And anyway it's impossible to tell a lie in our house because my mother has a good nose and she can smell something burning. My father has a very good ear for music, too, and he can hear the creaks in the floorboards from miles away, even in the office in Dublin where he works with the ESB. One day I started looking in his wardrobe again. I was on my own this time and I found the picture of the sailor that he didn't want me to see. I found the photographs of HMS *Nemesis* and all the medals from the British navy. When my father came home from work that evening and we all sat down at the dinner table, he knew it and had a frown on his forehead.

'What did you do today?' he asked.

'Nothing,' I said.

'Nothing,' he said in a loud voice. 'That's the oldest answer in Ireland.'

He knew every answer in Ireland because he was a schoolteacher once. I could see myself twice in his glasses, but I couldn't see if his eyes were soft or hard. He was waiting for me to talk, so I told him that when I grow up I want to be a sailor. I told him I want to have a uniform and go all over the world on ships.

'Have you been looking in my wardrobe?' he asked.

'No,' I said.

I knew that nobody would ever trust me again because I said a lie. My father asked me the same question once more. He said I was the champion of wrong answers and he told me to think hard because he wanted the right one this time.

'Never be afraid of the truth,' my mother said.

I thought she was able to smell burning. And my father was watching the way I was buttering a slice of bread with hard butter, tearing big holes and making a mess of it.

'No, I didn't,' I said again.

'We have to believe him,' my mother then said, but after dinner when everything was cleared away from the table, I had to stay behind with my father looking at me. He can hear what's inside your head. He waited for a while and then asked me if there were any questions I wanted to ask him.

'No,' I said.

'Then why were you looking in my wardrobe?'

I wasn't sure which questions would make him angry and which questions would make him smile. He sat facing me for a long time until he had to get up and go outside into the garden because it was starting to get windy. He told me to sit there and think. I could hear him in the greenhouse rattling with sticks and I thought it was for me again and that we would be going up to pray for Ireland. I heard the back door banging in anger. But then I heard him outside in the garden with the sticks, tying down the new trees. I could hear the wind blowing. I could hear my mother talking to him and it was dark by the time he sat down at the table again. Then he looked at me and just smiled. He wasn't angry any more. He said it was wrong to tell lies and it was wrong to be more interested in the past than in the future. It was no use looking back all the time and he would show me something else instead.

'I'm going to show you the future,' he said.

I waited for him to say what it was but he just smiled.

'It won't be long, wait till you see. We'll be going there soon.'

That night there was a big storm. The window was rattling and the rain was tapping on the glass. Sometimes the wind pushed so hard that even all the rattling stopped and I thought the glass would break. I could see the shadow of the trees on the wall, shaking so much that they sometimes disappeared altogether. It was so wild and angry outside that I thought the roof would lift off the house. I thought the front door would blow in and everybody would be able to walk inside and see us. I heard my father coming up the stairs with one hard foot and one soft. My mother came to say goodnight and told me to pray for all the people out on the sea, and then I thought the house was moving like a ship.

I know that when my father was small he was called Jack after his own father John. He didn't know anything about his father until his mother told him he was a sailor with soft eyes. The sailor had a soft voice, too, she said, and he always called her 'baby' because she was the youngest in her family. He was away at sea all the time, even at Christmas, and the only thing that my father could remember seeing was the sailor's uniform, laid out all ready one night on the kitchen table. The next morning he was gone again and there was nothing left only the picture over the mantelpiece and all the letters he wrote home that were kept in a tin with roses on the lid.

Every time there was a storm she stayed up all night praying for all the people out at sea. And then she knew everything was all right when she got a postcard from Gibraltar with a short message.

Dear Mary Frances,
Rough crossing. More homesick than seasick,
all my love, John.

It was the last card he sent. He must have put it in the mailbox before he went out to work on deck. A wave must have come from the side and caused the ship to lurch, they said, because he fell over the railing down on to the lower deck. He would have fallen overboard and drowned if not for his friends pulling him to safety and bringing him inside to lie down on his bunk to sleep for a while. But when he woke up, he could not remember anything. He didn't look ill or have any broken bones and there was nothing wrong at all until he walked off the ship in

Gibraltar and got lost. He was like the Munster poets and kept going around and around the town in circles with no idea where to go, until the captain realised that he was missing and sent a search party out to arrest him for being a deserter.

The first thing that Mary Frances heard was some weeks later when she got a letter from Manchester saying that her husband was in hospital there. He had fallen and lost his memory on HMS *Vivid*, they said. She wasn't able to go and see him so she asked a cousin who was a nun in Liverpool to go to see him instead. And after a long time he was allowed to come home to Leap. He never wore the sailor's uniform again and he would never be seasick again because he was invalided out of the navy. There was no money coming from the British navy either to anyone who was invalided and he couldn't work at anything else in Leap. So Mary Frances looked after him and went up to Mass with him every morning to try to bring his memory back. He remembered her face and her name, but then after a while he started forgetting even that much, so that he could do nothing at times, only hold his head in his hands and say that he wanted to go home. He was a stranger in his own home. And then he lost his mind altogether one day, because he took a knife in his hand. My father was still a small child and he was crying so much that the noise went into the sailor's head like a nail into the wall, so he stood up and said he would kill him if he didn't stay quiet. Everybody in west Cork knew it wasn't like John Hamilton to do a thing like that, but his head wasn't right after falling on a British ship. He stood in front of his own picture in uniform, holding a kitchen knife in his hand and shouting, until Mary Frances had to stand in front of him, in front of the man she loved more than anyone else in the world and tell him to kill her first.

Sometimes it's a mistake to be born the son of people who love each other too much. Mary Frances went to see him at the hospital in Cork as often as she could. Once, after Ted was born, they all went up to visit him together, but he didn't recognise any of them any more and just turned away in the bed. Then a priest had to come and he died alone. Onkel Ted says it was a very cold day in winter when his body was brought on the train to Skibbereen and from there in a carriage to the graveyard on the hillside in Glandore. After that there was only the picture of the sailor over the mantelpiece and the box with the last card he sent home. After that Mary Frances had nothing in her mind only to pray and fight for a pension from the British navy, no matter how long it took, so that she could educate them and make sure they didn't have to go into the navy or emigrate to America. It was the biggest day of her life when her two sons came back to visit her in Leap, one an engineer, the other a Jesuit.

'It's no good looking back,' my father says. He is sitting across the table from me at breakfast time again and smiles. 'You should be looking forward. You're like a blank piece of paper and you should only look forward.'

Maybe that's why he had to put the picture of the sailor with the soft eyes in the wardrobe, along with all the medals and the box with the homesick postcard. Maybe that's why he doesn't want anyone to know that he has a limp, because we're living in a new country now and we can never go back again to the past. And maybe that's why he changed his name to Irish, so we'll never be homesick.

'Ten more days and then we'll be in the future,' Maria says.

The storm was gone. There was no wind at all any more and the sun was shining, but when my father went out to work he saw the broken slates on the ground and said there was a hole in the roof. There were fallen branches all over the road, too, and he told us never to touch any wires. Down at the seafront, the waves had thrown lots of sand and seaweed on to the road as if it were part of the sea, as if Dublin were going to be living underwater soon.

The man came to fix the roof. His name was Mr McNally and when I came home from school I saw the ladder in the house going up to the skylight. My mother said he had been up there on the roof for a long time and if he was any longer it would be infinity. I knew that infinity was even further away than the future, but I didn't know that infinity was in the past as well. She said she could not wait for him to come down, so she stood at the foot of the ladder and called up to him.

'Mr McNelly,' she called, because she says everything with a German accent. 'Mr McNelly, I have a cup of tea ready for you.'

In Ireland, you can't ask people anything, she says. It's not like Germany where a question is just a question. In Ireland people get offended by questions, because it's a way of saying what you're thinking. The only way to ask Mr McNally something politely was to offer him a cup of tea. My mother was not able to go up the ladder herself, so she kept calling up through the skylight. She said that the longer Mr McNally stayed up there, the bigger the hole in the roof would get and the more money we would have to pay.

Now and again, the phone would ring and it was my father calling from the office to ask where Mr McNally was now and how big the hole was. He could not come home early and go up the ladder himself, so my mother had to go back up the stairs and call up into infinity, saying the tea was already made and was now going cold. As well as that, there were homemade German biscuits, too, just out of the oven, covered with icing and hundreds and thousands. And when Mr McNally still didn't come down, she called him from the back garden, and after that from the gate in the front garden as well. Everybody on the whole street knew the tea was ready and my mother was getting worried because nobody had ever failed to come down for her biscuits before. When the phone rang again she told my father that maybe Mr McNally had a problem hearing things. And all the time the hole was getting bigger and bigger, the longer he was up there, so my mother said the next time there was a problem with the roof she would have to get two people to fix it, one man to do the work and the other to go up and call him down for tea and biscuits.

In the end she took off her apron and told us all to hold the ladder while she tried to climb up herself. The sun was shining down through the skylight and she didn't go very far because the ladder started shaking, so she came back down again. She said I had nothing to be afraid of, because she was holding the ladder herself and nothing would happen. So I climbed slowly up into infinity and put my head out over the roof, but it was so bright out there that I was blind, and I could see nothing. All I heard was the sound of snoring.

My mother could not understand why Mr McNally would not prefer to lie down and sleep on the sofa instead of sleeping on the roof. She likes things to be done properly, in the right place, and the roof is no place to fall asleep.

Mr McNally was very friendly. He smiled and said the hole in the roof was not half as big as he thought it was. It could have been much bigger. Some of the damage he had seen on other roofs was shocking, he said. He sat down at the table with the newspaper and looked at a list of horses' names. Then he rolled the paper up and put it away in his jacket pocket and drank the tea. He ate some biscuits and then lit a cigarette. He was talking to my mother all the time and he asked her if she knew what the feeling was like not to be able to remember something, like the name of a horse or a football player. My mother nodded her head as if there was something she could not remember either. Sometimes, Mr McNally said, he thought he was losing his memory. He said it was the worst thing of all, not knowing what you couldn't remember. Then it was time for him to go and he said he hadn't eaten biscuits as nice as hers before. He said he was hoping there would be another storm soon, so he would have to come back and fix the roof again. My mother smiled. He hit me on the head with the newspaper and said I was a lucky devil, and after he was gone we counted the biscuits that were left over.

My mother smelled the blue smoke and looked out the window for a long time to see if she could remember what it was she had forgotten. But it was only something that she could not put out of her head. Something from the time in Germany that she had almost put away by writing it down in a diary for her children. Still, it came back again and again. Sometimes it was there at the back of her mind and she didn't even know what was upsetting her, until she sat down and remembered. She smelled the smoke and thought about when she was trapped in the past, as if she were still unable to move on and she would never see the future. She would live her whole life in the same moment, when Stiegler was coming up the stairs, and it felt like helpless infinity. At first she tried to resist. She said she would go to the police, but Stiegler said that it wasn't a good idea for her to contact them because he had too many friends in the Gestapo. They would never believe her.

'I'll tell your wife,' she said, but he wasn't even scared of that.

'I wouldn't advise that,' he said.

He had power in his words and she had none. Every night he came up the stairs and she would hear the sound of his breathing outside. She would see the door handle turning. Then he stood inside her room and she could not stop it or help herself. Sometimes she tried to believe that it was right and that this was the sacrifice she had to make in her life. There was somebody she knew who had joined the Nazi party just so that the rest of the family didn't have to. So maybe she was going through this so that nobody else in her family had to endure it. It was all her own fault and she had brought it on herself. This is what she had wanted, she thought, what she had dreamed of so often. Maybe it wasn't quite what she had imagined, but if you're weak and stupid and have been misled, it's still your own fault and you can only blame yourself for what happens next. If you can't stop something at the beginning, then you may not be able to stop it later on either and you deserve everything that follows. So she was in a trap, with Stiegler coming to her room every night. He took off his clothes and placed them neatly on the chair. He even folded his tie. He even put each sock neatly into each shoe. He took off his watch and looked at it briefly before he hung it on the back of the chair. It was never too late to resist. She still felt that she could threaten to go to the police again. But he put that out of her head and closed off the last escape route that she had.

'A lot of people are being taken away these days,' he

said. 'You don't want to go with them, now do you? Nobody comes back, you know.'

Afterwards, when he put his clothes on again, he seemed to do everything in reverse order. The watch was first, the tie last. Then he lit a cigarette, every time, as if he wanted to keep her company for a while longer. He smoked his cigarette and sometimes he would tell her to smile. Where were all the smiles, he would ask, and then he looked at his watch and said he had to go. My mother sits in her chair and smells the smoke and stares out the window as if she will never escape.

Twenty

I keep asking my mother questions about the future. What language do they speak there? Do they have cars and buses and streets like here? Will you have to walk any more or will people have legs like wheels? Will people be able to live without breathing? Will there be shops with machines outside where you put in a penny and twist the handle for chewing gum? Will there be money or will people just be able to draw things and sprinkle salt on the picture to make it come true? She stretches her hands out in the kitchen and says she can't look into the future, only saints can do that. All she knows is that the future is far away and it will take a whole day to get there, first on a bus, then a train and then another bus. It might rain there a bit, she says, so she has to go out and buy a rain mac for each one of us.

Everybody is busy preparing for the journey. I watch my father making the last of the trolleys, concentrating hard with his tongue out the side of his mouth and saying nothing, only yes or no. Then I go upstairs and watch my mother laying everything out in rows on the beds first before she puts it all into the suitcases. We'll be sleeping in new beds, she says, so we'll need new pyjamas. Maria keeps counting and saying that there's only one more sleep and one more bowl of porridge before we go. Ita keeps mixing up words in every language in her mouth, like *bye bye Baümchen* and *go go maidirín*. She is very kind to everybody and always wants to give you things, even things that you didn't ask for. But you have to say thank you and then she goes off again to get something else. She goes around the house and comes back with a pencil and a cup and a broken umbrella. And those things have to go into the suitcase as well, my mother says, it's all coming with us.

Then everything was packed and ready in the hallway. My father lined up the trolleys one by one – blue for Franz, green for me, red for Maria, and the pram at the back for Ita. Each trolley had a rope at the front and pictures on the side. Each trolley was packed with a colouring book, a box of crayons, plasticine, sweets, biscuits and a grey, plastic rain mac. Behind the trolleys and the pram were the suitcases all in a single line, like a long train ready to move out of the station. And before we went up to bed for the last time, I felt strong in my tummy because we looked back from the stairs and saw how close we were to leaving.

The next morning we got up and had breakfast very early. When it was time to go we all kneeled down in the hallway first to pray for a good journey, then my father carried each trolley down the granite steps, followed by the pram and the suitcases. My mother stood with us on the pavement, while he went back in to lock the front door from the inside. We heard the big bolt sliding across and waited while my father closed all the windows and doors in the house and made his way out the back door, across the garden wall and all the way around the lane to meet us again on the street. There was nobody up and nobody there to see the Irish-German train heading off into the future, nobody to hear us squeaking and rattling down the street with my father out front carrying the suitcases, wearing his tweed cap and his own grey, plastic rain mac and with the umbrella hanging around his neck.

It took a long time to get down to the bus stop because one of the wheels came off Maria's trolley and had to be fixed. But there was no shortage of time, my father said. The bus conductor stacked the trolleys carefully one on top of the other under the stairs, and then we were moving at last with a long ticket flapping like a white flag out the window. On the train we had a table where we could take out the colouring books and draw. In Galway we sat by the river and looked at swans while we were eating our lunch. Then we got the bus to Connemara and my mother said it was more like being on a roller-coaster because the driver had a cigarette in his mouth and drove so fast it was impossible to see around the next turn or over the next hill. She said the bus drove itself. Chickens were scattering off the road. Sometimes a dog ran alongside, barking and trying to bite the back wheel, and my mother called them *Reifenbeisser*, tyre-biters. People waved at the bus and one time an old man sitting in the long grass held his cap in the air without even looking up to see, as if he knew it was the bus passing by and everybody on the bus knew it was him. Once or twice the bus had to stop because there was a cow in the middle of the road that wouldn't stop chewing. But then we were off again, going further and further into the empty brown land, full of rocks and stone walls that my mother said looked like a place on the moon.

It was the evening by the time we arrived and there was a man waiting for us. It was Seán De Paor, the postman, and we were going to stay in his house. He smoked a pipe and there was a smell of turf all around and sometimes you didn't know which was which. The place was called

An Cheathrú Rua, which was true because that's the Irish for 'The Red Quarter', the land that's brown red all around. There were no road signs because everybody knew the names of the streets in Irish. We followed him up the road past the handball alley, up Bóthar an Chillín to his house, and all the way the trolley train rattled so much that people came out of their houses to tell the dogs to stop barking.

My father was speaking Irish all the time and laughing and I knew he would never be angry again. There was Fear an tí, the man of the house, and Bean an tí, the woman of the house. There were two boys called Seán and Máirtín who had never seen plasticine before. Everybody said lederhosen were the best trousers they had ever seen and wanted to know where they could be got. All the men wore caps like my father and asked you what story you had. Some of them even wanted to learn German, so my mother had to give them German lessons on the road through Irish.

It was like being at home in the place where we all wanted to be for the rest of our lives. Every day we went for long walks down to the sea, down to the beach beside the graveyard with all the Irish names. We met the old people who could remember as far back as infinity and didn't even know any English, my father said. We didn't understand them either because they spoke very fast with no teeth, but my father took photographs of them outside their houses with thatched roofs, to make sure they wouldn't disappear. Sometimes we walked further up to Pointe, to the little harbour where the lobster pots were stacked up and where you thought you were standing on the furthest piece of land, looking right out across the bay to the Aran Islands, like black whales coming out of the sea.

This really was the future, my mother said, because

when we were playing on the rocks, there was lots of seaweed that looked like the tails of crocodiles and some like the tails of lions. We laughed and dragged the lion tails across the sand behind us. It was the future because sometimes the tide went out so far that you thought the sea had run away and disappeared altogether. The water drained away and left the land behind, silent and deserted, with black seaweed draped across the rocks like hair. As if everything had gone to sleep. As if we were the first people ever to discover this place. Sometimes there was nobody out under the sky and we didn't see anybody for hours. It was the future because when we climbed up the hill it was like walking on the moon, with nothing but grey rocks and rusty brown colours all around. And behind us the black line of the coast going in and out as far as your eyes could see.

It was a place where you could live on your imagination, my mother said, a place where everything was simple and you didn't need possessions, not like some of her sisters in Germany who had to own more and more things all the time, until they could only talk about what they didn't have and what they still wanted. It was a place full of things you could not pay for with money, a place where you could be rich with nothing but silence and landscape. All you needed was sandwiches and milk and the wind at your back, she said, and my father repeated the same thing in Irish, only the other way round, with your backside to the wind.

'*Tóin in aghaidh na gaoithe*,' he said.

So we laughed with our backsides to the wind and nobody ever thought of going home again. When it rained we got out our macs and sheltered behind the stone walls. The best shelter of all we learned from the sheep, when we were so far away from any house or any walls and the rain came so quickly that we just copied them and crouched down behind the rocks. Sometimes we found shelter in a doorway and stood watching the rain coming down at an angle. There was nothing to say and I saw my father going into a dream as he stared out into the rain without a word. My mother, too. All of us dreaming and sheltering from the words, speaking no language at all, just listening to the voice of the rain falling and the sound of water gurgling between the stones somewhere behind the barn. Then afterwards you could see the steam rising on the road when the sun came out again as bright as ever and the water continued to whisper along the roadside like the only language allowed.

One day my father met a man at the harbour whose name was De Bhaldraithe, and he had invented a dictionary of English words in Irish. It was a great book, my father said, as good as the book about people talking in the graveyard, because now at last everybody could learn Irish again. And that night they were invited over to a house where people gathered around to drink whiskey and sing songs. My father told lots of stories in Irish and my mother had to sing a song in German. The man who made the dictionary knew some German, too, so he was able to speak a few words to her, because nobody could speak any English.

And after all the singing and talking, there was a discussion about the state of the Irish language and everyone agreed it was still alive, more alive than ever before. They said people were putting the Irish language in a coffin and bringing it to the graveyard, but they didn't realise that people can still talk in the grave. One man said Irish speakers in Ireland were being treated like people from a foreign country, from another planet. But as long as there were people like De Bhaldraithe and my father who made their own children speak it, the language would never die out. They drank whiskey and smoked pipes and passed around plates of ham sandwiches. It was a great night because nobody was laughing at the Irish language, except one woman who disagreed and said nobody could live on their imagination for ever. It was no use being poor, the woman suddenly said, and everyone in the house went so quiet that you could hear the turf hissing in the fire and somebody's stomach murmuring. The woman said she was sick to death of seeing people coming down from Dublin for their holidays and all they wanted was the people in Connemara to stay living in thatched cottages with no toilets inside. What was the use in speaking Irish if you couldn't put food on the table? But then my father made a speech in Irish that made everybody hold their glasses up in the air to him. He said he could see the woman's point of view and it was no fun to be poor, but that's why people in Dublin were busy working hard and making a sacrifice, too, so that Ireland could live on its own inventions and its own imagination. And in the end, he turned the argument around to say that toilets inside the house and food on the table were no good if you lost the language. Your stomach could be full but your heart would be empty.

They came home along the road in the dark when all the lights in the houses were already gone out. My mother says you could not even see your own shoes it was so dark. And one time, they stopped and whispered to each other because there was somebody standing right in front of them on the road just breathing and staring at them and not letting them pass by, but it was only a donkey that suddenly got an even bigger fright himself and ran off.

It was the best night of all, my mother said, except that

in the middle of the night something funny happened. My father had to get up and go to the *leithreas* outside. The toilets in Connemara were all outside in a small wooden house with lots of flies and a bad smell of newspapers that always made me want to get sick. Inside there was a big box with a wooden lid and a hole in it. Underneath there was a bucket that Fear an tí sometimes brought to a field nearby where he could empty it out and bury it all underneath the soil. That night my father had to feel his way along the walls to go out the back door into the darkness. He found the *leithreas* and locked the door shut behind him. But then, as he turned around, there was no wooden board and he fell right down with his backside in the bucket.

At first everything was silent. It was dark all around and everybody in Connemara was asleep. My father couldn't lift himself out. He was stuck in the bucket with his legs hanging out over the wooden box and his pyjamas around his ankles. He had his shoes on, but no socks, and his laces were undone. He thought he would be stuck like that for ever, so he started calling for help in Irish. Nobody came and all he could do was to keep shouting and banging on the side of the shed, until there was so much noise, they said the dogs were barking as far away as Casla. Everybody in the house woke up and Fear an tí went down at last to rescue my father from the *leithreas*. He first had to break down the door to get in. Then he had to put his arms around my father to lift him out and get the bucket off his backside and tell everybody, even the neighbours across the road, to go back to bed, it was nothing at all. He offered him a cigarette and a pipe and some whiskey, but my father just said he was going back to bed and after a long time the dogs stopped barking and everything was quiet again.

In the morning we could see the door of the *leithreas*

lying on its side and the lock broken. Nobody said a word about what happened. Maybe Fear an tí was afraid that my father had hurt himself and wasn't saying anything. Maybe Bean an tí was even more embarrassed, because if they all spoke English and had a proper toilet inside the house, it would never have happened. Maria kept saying that she was never going to the toilet again as long as she lived. She was holding her knees together and we started pretending that we were falling into the *leithreas* all the time. Going down the stairs or walking around the house, Franz just suddenly said 'Oh' and fell down into an invisible toilet. We did it again and again and kept laughing.

Even at breakfast around the table, it was hard not to think about the *leithreas*. It was Sunday and my father came down all ready for Mass in his best suit. Nobody said a word. Franz was trying not to laugh and had a very cross face with his mouth closed tight. We knew my father couldn't be really angry because all the people in the house would be watching him. Every time I looked at Franz I couldn't stop myself from making a snort with my nose, until my father looked at me with hard eyes and my mother told us it was not nice to laugh at people's misfortune.

'It's not fair,' she said. 'Because your father made such a good speech last night . . . and then he fell into the toilet.'

That was the end of it and everyone was silent again, until my mother's face went completely red. I saw her shoulders starting to shake and then she made a big snort with her nose, too, and suddenly had to run upstairs. We were left at the table with my father looking at us. We were afraid to laugh any more and everything was so quiet in the house, until my father spoke up at last to make conversation. There was a sign near the door with a well-known phrase in Irish that said: *níl aon tinteán mar do thinteán féin*: there's no fireside like your own fireside. So my father turned it around and tried to make a joke of it. *Níl aon tóin tinn mar do thóin tinn féin*, he said, which meant that there's no sore backside like your own sore backside.

Then everybody in the house suddenly laughed out loud at that. Even though it was an old joke that everybody had heard a hundred times before, they still thought it was the funniest thing they ever heard in their whole lives. My mother came back down again and said the best thing is to laugh at yourself before anyone else does. My father says that if you laugh against yourself the whole world will laugh with you, and if you laugh at other people, you laugh alone. But my father is not good at laughing at himself. And he never laughs at other people either. He's much better at making a sacrifice. After Mass, we met the dictionary man and all his friends again outside the church. My father was afraid that he would be famous all over Connemara for falling into the *leithreas* rather than for his speech. But there was no mention of it and everything was forgotten, because there were too many other things to remember and Irish people don't say everything that's inside their heads.

We were going back home to Dublin the next day, so my mother asked us what we wanted to do most on the last day. We went back to the sea and played with the lion tails and then up the hill behind the house to be the last people to look out over the sea to the Aran Islands. We sat on the grass with the sheep all around us, waiting for the sun to go down. We looked out along the coast where the sea was just mixed in with the land, with inlets and islands and peninsulas as far as you could see. The sun went down and An Cheathrú Rua was even redder than it ever was before. My father said it was time to go, but my mother said we would wait until the very last minute, until it was completely dark, until all the colour had disappeared and there was nothing left except the lights in the houses and the smaller twinkling lights further away along the coast that told you where the land was.

Nobody was sad to go home the next day because my mother said we would remember this place for ever. Nobody was sad because my father said we would be coming back again soon. Nothing would change, he promised, not one rock, not even one stone wall. We would come back and see that everything was still there in the same place as it was before. Nothing was going to be in the past.

Twenty-one

That summer the garden was full of flowers. There was so much fruit, too, raspberries and blackcurrants and plums, that my mother started making jam again. And there were so many tomatoes in the greenhouse that we had to give lots of them away to the neighbours. There were flowers on the table every day and my father said we should keep bees. He started buying books on beekeeping and said it would make sense to put a few hives on the roof of the breakfast room where they could fly straight out to collect the honey and pollinate the fruit trees.

The same things were forbidden in our house as always. There was a song on the radio that said we had all the time in the world in the deepest voice in the world. My mother liked the song too, but only when my father was out at work. Ita started saying 'good morning' to all the people on the street, and when there was nobody else to say good morning to, she said it to the lamp-posts and the gates, all day until she was back in the kitchen saying 'good morning' to the cooker and the washing machine as well. My father said the rules had to be obeyed even though she was still a baby. So then there was trouble because Ita went on hunger strike and wouldn't eat or speak any more, and my father had to hold her head with one hand and try to force her mouth open to push the spoon in with the other. All the time she was shaking her head and I thought it was funny because Ita was winning. But my mother didn't want us to see what would happen next, so she closed the doors and brought us outside and told us to run down to the shop to buy ice cream until it was over and Ita stopped crying.

My father said he couldn't understand why the stick wasn't working any more. He said he was doing his best. Everything was for us. He made the trolleys, he made a wooden see-saw, he was even building a real puppet theatre, and if we kept on breaking the rules he would have to find new ways of punishing us that would hurt more. Sometimes I tried to punish Franz and Maria to see if they would feel pain, so my father said anything I would do to them he would give me back a hundred times, and I said anything he would do to me I would give back to Franz and Maria a hundred times, until nobody could feel any more pain. He brought me upstairs and we kneeled down again to pray in front of Our Lady that he was doing the right thing. But that didn't work so he had a better idea, something that would make me ashamed. He confiscated the braces on my lederhosen and I had to go down to the barber to get my hair cut, holding my trousers up with my hands in my pockets.

In the barber shop we sat on the wooden bench reading the comics. Most of them were torn and falling apart, but it was good to see them, even the ones I had read before. I didn't like the comic called *Hotspur* as much as the *Dandy*, and I didn't like it either when somebody was punished and put across the teacher's knee. There were lots of other boys waiting and reading comics, too, but none of them noticed that I had no braces and couldn't walk around without my hands in my pockets. The barber kept clicking the scissors all the time, even when he was not cutting hair, and there was a huge pile of hair swept into one corner on the floor. We waited and read as many comics as we could and pretended that we were Irish and spoke English like everyone else, even though everybody could see that we were from a different country.

When we came out I tried to speak English to Franz but he was afraid. The barber, Mr Connolly, always gave every boy back a penny, so you could buy a toffee bar. But that day we put our pennies together, along with other pennies that Franz still had from Tante Lilly, and we bought a brand new comic called the *Beano*. We took turns reading it and spoke Irish to each other in between. My mother said it was good to buy something that lasts longer, not like a liquorice pipe that's gone within minutes and can't be remembered, but there would be trouble if we brought the *Beano* into the house. So we pretended it wasn't our *Beano* and hid it in the hedges of Miss Hart's garden.

At night I thought of Mr Connolly still clicking his fingers, even when he was having his tea and there were no scissors in his hand. I thought of all the hair mixed together in a large wig, like the mane of a buffalo. I thought of Mr McNally reading his paper with crooked glasses held up only by one stick over his right ear, and I thought of Mr Smyth from the vegetable shop getting undressed and going to bed with only one arm. Downstairs my father was building the puppet theatre and my mother was making the costumes and the curtains. Outside it was raining and I thought of the *Beano* getting wet and all the colours washing out.

After that, my mother said we were all starting to go crazy because one day I told Maria to climb up on the wall in the front garden and show her backside to the wind. She did it because she trusted everything I said, even things she didn't want to do, even things she knew were not right. I promised that we would do the same after her, but she had to go first because she was younger and everything in our house was always done from the youngest to the oldest. So Maria stood on the wall and laughed with her backside to the wind for everyone to see. Then one of the neighbours came over and told my mother it was not very nice to do that in front of Irish people, Catholic or Protestant. So we all had to stay inside for a day and my mother said we were living on our own imagination too long and we needed friends to play with.

My father said we could only play with children who could speak Irish. He contacted lots of people and first of all we played with a boy nearby whose name was Seán Harris, the son of a painter and decorator, but their Irish wasn't good enough. Then one day my father brought us across the city on the bus to Finglas and we played with a boy called Naoise. Once or twice, children were brought over to our house by bus from other parts of the city, and there were some older boys who came to play in German but didn't say much. They stood around looking at our things and not even playing with them, just eating the biscuits that my mother made. There were some boys from our school who came over, too, but even they thought it was stupid to play in Irish and didn't want to come back again, even for the biscuits. You couldn't be cowboys in Irish. You couldn't sneak up behind somebody or tie somebody up to a chair in Irish. It was no fun dying in Irish. And it was just too stupid altogether to hide behind something and say 'Uuuggh' or 'hands up' in Irish, because there were some things you could only do in English, like fighting and killing Indians. My father was no good at making friends, so my mother took over and told us to join the altar boys. But they only wanted to kill Germans, so we served Mass and just went home again.

One day I was playing with the umbrella in the hallway, trying to kill all the coats with one arm behind my back, and Franz was outside on the street with his scooter. He was listening to the trains pulling into the station, waiting for my father to come home. But then he saw some other boys playing on the street with sticks and guns. They ignored him and didn't call him any names, so he stood there with one foot on and one foot off the scooter, looking at them from a distance, even though he couldn't join in. They were cowboys fighting and killing Indians. Franz was pretending that his scooter was a horse and that he had a real gun in the side pocket of his lederhosen, until my father came around the corner with his limp and his briefcase swinging. Then Franz turned around and tried to scoot back to the house as fast as he could, but it was already too late. I heard the key in the door and I saw Franz coming in with nothing to say. I saw my father turning around to look at the boys on the street before he closed the door and put his briefcase down. My mother came to kiss him, but that didn't stop him saying that Franz had to be punished for pretending to be with the other boys on the street.

'Now why is that?' my mother asked.

'He was listening to them in English,' my father said.

'My God,' she said. 'Are you not taking this too far?'

My father shook his head. She tried everything she could to stop it. She tried to distract him by saying it was the feast of St Brigid and that the curtains were finished for the puppet theatre and that she got a letter from her sister Marianne. She tried to say that we should phone Onkel Ted and see what he would say. And when my father still shook his head she tried to put her arm around Franz to stop him from feeling pain.

'Not with violence,' she begged him. 'Please, not with violence.'

So instead, my father confiscated the scooter and carried it upstairs. That meant there were now two scooters in my father and mother's bedroom. My scooter was there for days because I was listening to songs on the radio.

'Two horses up there eating grass,' she said to us afterwards.

I knew she was making a joke because there was no other way out of it. But I knew it wasn't over with the scooters either and after dinner, when we were gone to bed already, my mother tried to get my father to put on some music and pour a glass of cognac. They were talking for a long time and he said he was not going to be tricked into changing his mind, because that was like going backwards and letting the strongest languages win over the weakest. She said that punishing the innocent and confiscating things was going backwards. Then she laughed and asked how anyone was going to be able to sleep with two horses in the bedroom. But he just got angry again and she asked him to go up and give us a sign that everything was still positive in our family. She wanted him to go up and kiss us on the forehead.

'I love each one of you,' he said, and I could smell the cognac on his breath. 'You are like no other children in the world.'

And some time in the middle of the night, my mother got up and brought the scooters back down the stairs, one by one, because they were there in the hallway the next morning waiting for us. It didn't mean everything was all right again, but at least we had our horses back and soon we would be starting swimming lessons.

After that my mother kept asking people in the shops if there were any children that we could play with and one day she met Dr Sheehan and he had a boy called Noel who had red hair and glasses that were wrapped around his ears. So she brought us down to his house to play in a huge garden beside the church with bulldogs and apple trees. He was our friend and his house was the best place in the world to live. There were bicycles that we could ride around the path like a racetrack, and we could reach up from our saddles and pick apples from the trees above us any time. Sometimes the bell from the church rang and you could hear nothing at all except one of the dogs howling. One time Franz found a tap in the garden and drank some water, but then his mouth was full of earwigs and he thought he would die. And one time we found a wasps' nest and started throwing stones at it until they got very angry. We played in English all day until Noel's mother asked us to stay for tea. She had trouble with breathing and spoke very gently to say that she had phoned my mother. There was nothing my father could do to stop it. Even when we were walking up the road on our way home at the end of the day, Franz and me still kept talking English as far as we could, until the last lamp-post.

Then my father wanted to know if Noel could speak Irish. Before he could come and play in our house, he would have to sit an exam first in the front room. Next Saturday, my father asked him lots of questions in Irish, like what his name was and how old he was and what his father did for a living. We stood around watching and hoping that Noel could answer them, wishing that we could whisper and help him, but he knew no Irish at all. He just kept smiling and blinking behind his glasses and repeating the only thing he remembered from school.

'*Níl a fhios agam*,' he said. 'I don't know.'

That was the oldest answer in Ireland and my father started shaking his head. It was not good enough, he kept saying. But then my mother had a great idea.

'He wants to learn Irish,' she said. 'Dr Sheehan wants him to learn. It's his only chance.'

My father looked very cross, but my mother kept trying. She said Noel was not so good at Irish yet, but he would soon become a native speaker if he was allowed to come to our house. And then who knows, maybe his family would then become a full-Irish fireside and maybe even Dr Sheehan would begin to speak Irish to his patients and then everybody in Dublin would love their own language. It would be a pity to miss this opportunity.

So then we had a friend for life. We learned swimming and diving and went down to the public baths every day for the whole summer. We saved up and bought goggles so that we could dive down underwater and have contests picking up pennies from the bottom of the pool. We would throw the penny into the deep end and watch it turning as it sank out of view. Then we dived down to reach it underwater, where there was no language only the humming bubbles all around. We timed each other to see who could stay down for the longest and I was nearly always the winner because I could stay under until my lungs were bursting, until I nearly died and had to come up for words. I was the champion at not breathing. Sometimes the three of us went down together and shook hands, and it looked like you could live down there, just sitting on the bottom of the pool signalling to each other. When we got out of the water, our knees were purple. We had purple hands and purple lips and our teeth were chattering. Then it was time to go home and we bought chewing gum. Noel found there was still water in one ear and he had to lean over on one side to let it pour out like a jug. We were friends for life and walked home with our towels around our necks, slapping the swimming trunks against the walls and leaving wet marks behind, like signatures all the way home. Then we waited till we got to the last lamp-post before we stopped speaking English.

Twenty-two

You stand behind the puppet theatre with the puppet in your hand, completely hidden. Nobody knows you're there. Then you pull on the string to open the curtains and make the puppet walk out in front of the audience. You can say anything you want. You can change your voice and make up any story. You can hide behind the story, and it's a bit like being underwater because everything you say goes up like bubbles to the surface.

'Have you seen the dog?' Kasper the puppet asks.

'What dog?' the puppet man answers.

'The dog that has no name and belongs to nobody and barks all day until he's hoarse and has no voice any more?'

My mother helps us to make up a story. She goes upstairs to get the hairdryer. She takes out a thin blue scarf from her dressing table and when she comes back down she goes in behind the puppet theatre with me. She plugs in the hairdryer and the blue scarf starts crashing on to the beach and the dog starts barking and biting at the waves because he doesn't know any better.

Everybody has a story to hide behind, my mother says. In the vegetable shop one day, Mr Smyth started talking to her about a wall in Germany. He doesn't normally talk very much, but that day he was talking about a wall and that nobody had any courage left to stop it. Then he asked her when she was going back home to Germany, but she gave the oldest answer in Ireland and said she didn't know. Missersmiss, she calls him, because of her accent. He asked me if I had ever been to Germany. The little German boy who has never been to Germany, he said, and even though he only has one arm, he's able to keep talking and put the potatoes in a brown bag and take the money all with one hand. I wanted to know why he only has one arm and what story he was hiding behind, but we can't ask those questions. Sometimes he uses his chin to hold things like an extra hand. He picks up the bag of potatoes against his hip and slips it into my mother's net shopping bag. He said Germany was very far away. He spoke as if he had been there once himself, but couldn't say any more because of his missing arm. And my mother just kept looking at the Outspan letters hanging in the window, until Mr Smyth said 'please God', it would not be long before she could go back to Germany. He said he had brothers and sisters in America who would give anything to come back to Ireland even for a day.

Other people started talking about the wall and asking the same questions. After Mass one day, a woman whose name was Miss Ryan asked my mother about going home and she said she wasn't even dreaming about it. But that's not true because, later on, she said it felt as though people in Ireland knew what you were thinking, long before you even thought of it yourself. Before you opened the door to go outside, they knew what was on your mind, even something you had already put out of your head for good. She made up a story to hide behind and said she was nowhere more at home than in Ireland with her family.

Everybody knows how far away Germany is by looking

at our family. They know that my mother is homesick. They can see it in her eyes. They could see her dreaming again that morning. They could see us all from the back, standing at the seafront, looking out at the waves, until my mother heard the bells and remembered what time it was and what country she was in. On the way back, my mother was trying not to step on the cracks in the pavement. I was hiding in doorways and she was pretending that she didn't know where I was. Maria was talking to herself and stopping to point at a spot on the wall. Ita was smiling and saying 'thank you' to all the lamp-posts and gates. Franz went ahead and waited at the corner for us with his scooter, one foot on and one foot off, while Maria was still trailing far behind. Maybe we look like the children who are always thinking of home. The homesick children.

Outside the church the next day, Miss Ryan stopped to speak to my mother again and asked if she wanted to borrow the money to go back to Germany. There would be no rush in paying it back, she said, but my mother shook her head. They were whispering for a long time until all the people had left the church, until Miss Ryan told my mother to go home and have a think about it. But my father didn't want that. He says you can't borrow money from the neighbours and he doesn't want my mother to go home on her own because she might never want to return.

My mother said it was time to stop dreaming. Instead, she asked her sisters to send over lots of books and magazines about Germany so that she could tell us what was happening there. She showed us the pictures of people running through the streets with suitcases. She explained how the Russians had put up a wall right in the middle of Germany and there was nothing the British or the Americans could do except watch. There was lots of barbed wire and tanks in the middle of the streets. There were people climbing out the window and letting children down slowly on ropes. And when the wall was built, people still tried to escape to the other side but they were shot and there were pictures of them lying on the ground bleeding to death and nothing anyone could do to help.

Onkel Ted came to talk to my mother because she didn't know what to do. She told him that Miss Ryan offered her money to go back to Germany and that she would not have to pay it back or ever mention it again. There were two Miss Harts and two Miss Doyles and two Miss Ryans, and they always went to Mass in pairs on Sunday. The Miss Ryans said they had set aside the money as a gift, but my father didn't want money from the neighbours. After dinner and after the sweets in Onkel Ted's pocket, we went to bed and they sat in the front room until there was nothing more to say about it. I heard my father taking out the cognac and putting on some music. It was the record of the two women doing a duet in French. I could hear the sound of the two high voices, like two sisters singing together. I thought it was like the two Miss Ryans going up the stairs together, arm in arm, up one or two steps and then back down two steps, then up three or four more and back down two, until they finished on the landing at the top with their arms around each other, saying goodnight and lying down softly in their beds.

After that, Onkel Ted was only afraid that my mother was homesick so he started sending her more books and pieces about Germany cut out of newspapers. He wrote long letters, too, in German and she wrote letters back, but my father said that had to stop, because he didn't want Onkel Ted to be her friend for life, only himself. He didn't want anyone to know more about Germany or to read any more books than he did. He was able to read five books at the same time with a bus ticket sticking out of each one, but Onkel Ted was able to read so fast that he didn't need a bus ticket and a book still looked brand new when he passed it on to my mother. My father didn't like my mother reading books that he didn't read first himself. He didn't like her talking too much to the neighbours either or getting friendly with people in the shops or going to coffee mornings and getting ideas from other people, only Catholic ideas. He was afraid she would not listen to him any more. He started slamming all the doors in the house because he didn't like anyone else calling her Irmgard. And one time there was a French woman living on our street who kept dropping in and talking to my mother. Even though they were from different countries, they had the same questions and the same answers when they talked. She wanted to become my mother's friend for life, but my father stopped all that because she was talking about going back to France to get a divorce from her Irish husband who was friends for life with other women. That was the worst thing that could happen, if Irish people started getting French ideas. That would be the end of the family. That would be the end of Ireland, he said.

Then Onkel Ted sent Eileen Crowley out to talk to my mother instead. Her father PJ had a good business in Dublin, but his shop had to close down when he lent a friend some money and never got it back. They went into debt and had to sell everything and move house. My mother knew how bad that was, because her father had to close his shop, too, in Kempen. It was bad luck. My mother saw it as a failure, and Eileen would never call it that. They had different ways of seeing things. Even different words that led to misunderstandings. Maybe there was no failure in

Ireland, only bad luck, and maybe there was no bad luck in Germany, only failure. They were friends, and Eileen was good at helping people out of trouble. My mother didn't want our family to be a failure, because this was the last chance she had in her life. It would be her own fault if she was back on the streets of Germany with suitcases and children, like the people running away across the Berlin Wall. The family was a good story to hide behind and so she said it was time to stop dreaming. She went over to the Miss Ryans to put an end to it once and for all. She told them it was very kind of them to offer the money, but there were other people who might need it more, people who had nothing even to dream about, people who had nowhere even to be homesick for.

After that, everything was back to normal. The doors stopped slamming and my mother started writing in her diary every day because that's your only real friend for life. She collected lots more pictures of what happened in Germany. In some places, she said, the wall went right through the middle of a house, so that the back of the house was in one part of Germany and the front of the house was in the other. She showed us pictures of all the planes bringing food to Berlin and pictures of John F. Kennedy in the city. She said it was great to hear John F. Kennedy saying that he was a Berliner, because most American people were afraid to be German and changed their names from Busch to Bush and Schmidt to Smith and maybe you can't blame them.

Every day we played with the puppets and my mother said we would put on a play for our relatives and invite all the neighbours, too. We stayed inside to practise the play about the dog barking at the waves. There was even a book in our house about staying indoors. It was about what to do if an atom bomb fell anywhere near us like it did on Hiroshima. There would be nuclear radiation all around the streets. The radiation was always shown with red dots, like a disease in the air. It explained how to build a nuclear shelter, how to put sandbags in all the windows so you could stay inside living on tins of beans for a few years until the red dots were all gone again.

One day, Eileen brought Franz and me up to the top of Nelson's Pillar and my father said nothing, even though it was something the British left behind. When we came home, Onkel Ted was there with sweets in his pocket and we told him that we were going to put on a play for relatives and neighbours. He said it was a very fine idea and Eileen said we were full of talent. At the dinner table that night, my mother told a story about a family who had a puppet theatre under the Nazis. The father was afraid to say anything against Hitler. He was afraid that the children would go out and there would be trouble if they repeated what he said on the street. So every day they put on a puppet show in the evening after dinner, just for themselves. He would go in behind the puppet theatre with his children and make up story about a very bad man named Arnulf. And at the end of every play they always had to find a way to kill Arnulf, so that the other puppets were safe again.

'Remarkable,' Onkel Ted said.

He nodded his head slowly and said it was a great sign that people had courage. He had read lots of books about people like that, books that make you feel strong. There are no German songs that make you feel strong in your stomach but there are stories like that. Eileen was nodding because she was chewing a toffee in her mouth and my father had nothing to say either. They all just quietly swallowed the story and the room was silent.

My mother tells stories like that because there are other stories she can't tell. When it's silent, she thinks of all the things she has to keep secret. She wishes that she could have resisted more. For a minute, she sits there and everybody is waiting for her to tell another story. She is thinking about how she is trapped in Ireland now and how she was trapped in Germany once, and how nothing has changed. She wishes that she had thought of the puppet show killing Arnulf.

My mother was back in Düsseldorf, back in the same office, working as if nothing had happened. Nobody asked questions and she had no idea who to talk to now. One night, Stiegler even invited her out to the theatre again with his wife, as if it was all fine, as if the world could just go on as before. Frau Stiegler kissed her on the cheek as always, and it was like a cosy family, with everybody very happy not to say a word that might make things uncomfortable. My mother can't remember what the play was. She can only remember the lip biting and the helpless anger. She was thinking only about what happened in Venlo and how she wanted to go away and work somewhere else in a different place. She wanted never to see Stiegler again. She wanted a new life, maybe even in a new country. She even thought of running away and going into hiding because of the shame she might bring to her family if the story came out. She sat in the theatre with Stiegler in the middle and Frau Stiegler on the far side, dressed with a scarf made of fox, with fox eyes and fox paws hanging down. It was only at the interval, when Herr Stiegler left them alone for a moment, that my mother had the courage to say something.

'I think there is something you should know,' she said. 'About your husband.'

So then Frau Stiegler stared and listened to what happened in Venlo. It was hard to describe it in words, but my mother said Herr Stiegler must have planned it all and she could do nothing to stop it.

'What?' Frau Stiegler said, and it was like a little bark that the fox on her shoulders was making. She had angry eyes and my mother thought at last that there was somebody on her side again. Everything was going to be put right again. But, instead, Frau Stiegler looked at her with vicious eyes. The fox, too, as if they were not angry at Herr Stiegler at all, but at her. Maybe my mother was too polite. Maybe she didn't have words bad enough in her head to describe what happened to her. She didn't have a way of telling things that was ugly enough to describe Herr Stiegler and what he did, because Frau Stiegler just turned on her instead. It was as if she had started it all and Herr Stiegler was innocent. As if she had brought it all on herself and he could do no wrong.

'If I hear another word of this,' Frau Stiegler said, 'if you say a single word to me or to anyone about this, I will call the police instantly. I will not have my husband's reputation destroyed like this before my own eyes. Herr Stiegler is a good man, a respectable man, and how dare you even think up such a thing.'

They even sat through the end of the play and afterwards had the usual drink in a nearby café, but there was nothing more to say.

My mother is a dreamer and sometimes she just sits and stares, hoping that she will still find a way out, something she can say, some clever way that she can escape even now. She stays in the past for a few minutes and doesn't hear you sometimes when you speak. She's still thinking of running away.

Very late one evening, an envelope was dropped in the door. It was addressed to my mother and, when she opened it, she found it was full of money. There was no note going with it to say who it came from, but my mother knew immediately. She also knew that my father would not allow it and the trouble would start again and all the doors in the house would be banging. So she put the envelope away and said nothing. Next day she went straight over to the Miss Ryans to give the money back. She said it was so generous of them, but she could not accept it because that would be the end of the family and the end of Ireland. Then the Miss Ryans both stood at the door and shook their heads.

'What money?' they said.

They looked at each other and said there was some kind of mistake. Money in an envelope didn't automatically mean it came from the Miss Ryans. They don't go around dropping money into people's letter boxes before they go upstairs and lie down softly in their beds. My mother asked if it wasn't the Miss Ryans who dropped the money into her door, then who was it? So the Miss Ryans scratched their heads and thought about it for a moment and said the money probably came from God.

There was no way out but to bring the money back home again and there was nothing my father could do about it. My mother told him the money came from God and you couldn't give it back, unless he wanted her to put it into the poor box in the church, but he didn't want that either. There was no slamming doors this time, but he said she was still not allowed to go back home to Germany on her own. He said he had lots of cousins in America and South Africa who couldn't come home to Ireland any time they liked. So she put the money away and said she would wait until there was enough for all of us to go to Germany together.

Then everything was all right again and everybody in our house was dreaming and saving up money in jars.

My mother helped us to get everything ready for the puppet show. My father said we could use his desk-lamp as a spotlight. Onkel Ted came and Tante Roseleen and Tante Lilly, as well as Eileen Crowley and Kitty from Cork. Tante Eileen came up from Skibbereen with Onkel John this time, because he was attending the Fianna Fáil Árd Fheis and he knew all about politics. Anne was there and so was her brother Harry, and everybody was afraid of him going to the Congo, because the only thing the Irish army was good at was keeping the peace. Lots of the neighbours came, too, like the Miss Ryans and the Miss Doyles. There was a whole table full of sandwiches and cakes. People brought lemonade and there was even wine and whiskey and bottles of black beer.

All the chairs and seats in the house were brought into the *Kinderzimmer* and lined up in rows. My mother helped Maria to tie a box of sweets around her tummy as a belly tray, so she could go around offering them to the audience. Ita was sitting on Harry's knee trying to comb all his hair forward, and Tante Eileen from Skibbereen was showing everybody how to light a new cigarette from the old one. And when they were all sitting down, my mother closed the big wooden shutters on the window and switched on the spotlight. It was like a real theatre with people coughing in the audience and trying to stop making noise. My mother got in behind the puppet theatre with us and when everybody stopped talking and coughing, Franz pulled the string to open the curtains.

'Have you seen the dog?' Kasper said.

Then Ita suddenly started talking back to the puppets, because she believed everything they said and my mother had to put her head out and tell her to be quiet and not give away the ending. We continued and it was all in German, so nobody could understand what was going on except Onkel Ted and my father. Everybody else was in the wrong country and couldn't rescue us.

There was a man called Arnulf, like the story my mother heard about in Germany, and he would not let any of the other puppets speak. All the time, Kasper was walking along and meeting other puppets like Hansel and Gretel and the grandmother and the queen and the king and other puppets that we made up ourselves with papier mâché. But none of them could say a word to Kasper, because Arnulf said they were not allowed to speak to him. Kasper asked them where the dog was, but they were all afraid to say anything in case Arnulf would come and punish them. So then Kasper had to find a way of killing Arnulf so that all the other puppets could speak again. And when Arnulf was dead with his head over the side of the theatre, my mother switched on the hairdryer and the blue scarf started blowing across the stage. Then Kasper came to the seafront and found the dog barking at the waves. That was the end and when Franz pulled the curtain closed, the audience clapped for a long time.

Twenty-three

It's a long way to go to Germany. You have to go on two different ships and five different trains. My father shows us the tickets and my mother counts the luggage lined up in the hallway, six suitcases and four children. She laughs and claps her hands because we're going home and everybody is so excited that you feel nearly sick in your stomach. First you go on the ship to Holyhead. You go across the gangplank and my father laughs at the sign over the door that says 'Mind your Head' because it's like a warning to anyone who leaves Ireland to be careful, not to forget where you come from or do anything stupid. Outside on deck you can see the lighthouse going by and the land moving further and further away until it's out of sight. Maria wants to know if we're going to get seasick, because the ship is moving from side to side and you can't walk straight. The seagulls keep following us even though it's dark now and there's nothing more to see except some yellow light from the ship on the water. At night you take the train to London to see the black taxis. And the next morning you take another train and another ship to Holland and three more trains after that until you're in Kempen and we're back in my mother's film.

They were waiting for us at the window. Ta Maria came out and threw her arms around my mother for a long time without a word. Then it was Tante Lisalotte's turn and she wouldn't let go. They stood outside on the street, hugging and looking at each other up and down, again and again, and they just kept saying '*ja, ja, ja*' and '*nein, nein, nein*' as if they didn't believe their own eyes. The suitcases were forgotten on the ground. They shook hands with my father and called him Hans, as if he was going to be German, too, from now on. They knew all our names, but they kept saying '*Ach, Du lieber Himmel*', as if they thought my mother had only gone away to Ireland for a few days and come back with four children.

Then it was time for coffee and we were sent over to the Kranz Café to get cakes. The smell of baking was like a warm pillow in your face when you walked in the door. All the women in the Kranz Café asked us questions and said we had soft voices, like German children long ago before the war. They said we were the long ago children with good manners and straight backs and no chewing gum. The cake was wrapped in the shape of a church so that the paper didn't touch the icing on the top. They told us to hold the parcel flat so that it would arrive on the table the way it left the café, and Ta Maria even had the same silver trowel that my mother has, so you could lift a slice on to the plate and make sure it had never been touched by human fingers.

My mother walked around the town with us to look for all the things that had not changed. The church with the red steeple was there, just like it was in the photographs, as well as the cinema with the name Kempener Lichtspiele and the windmill on the Burgring. The shops had everything laid out in the windows just like the day that she left. The only thing that was missing was the house on the Buttermarkt square where she lived when she was small. The fountain was still there outside, but the house was gone. There were new doors on the houses and new windows. My mother said everyone had new kitchens and new cookers, and that's what happens when you lose the war and you never want to look back at old things. Everything has to be new. The streets and the people still had the same names in German, but she was sometimes lost and couldn't find things she remembered.

It was like being six years of age again and maybe she was homesick in her own home town. Or maybe we had been away too long, she said, and we were getting used to living by the sea, because she was expecting to see a bright blue glass of water at the end of every street. And late in the afternoon when we walked so far that we were nearly in the country, there was a high breeze in the trees that sounded like water. At the edge of the town we stood looking at the flat land going out for ever and watched a car travelling all the way across the horizon behind a line of tall trees.

There was lots of talk about making the evening meal and who would be eating what. Did Irish children like *Wurst*? Was there anything we didn't eat? They had black bread and black jam, and plates made of wood. They kept tidying up even while they were eating because nobody likes the table to be '*abgegrasst*', like a field where the cows have already eaten all the grass. Then there was lots more talk about who would be sleeping where. Everyone was counting heads and spaces in beds. In between, they would sometimes remember a story and laugh so much that they had to lean on something to stop themselves from falling down. '*Zu Bett, zu Bett wer ein Liebchen hat, wer keines hat geht auch zu Bett*' – 'To Bed, to Bed if you're in love, to bed if you're on your own.' The soap was different, and so were the basins and the toilets. The pillows were square and there was a big duvet instead of blankets. I was allowed to sleep on the sofa with the curtains moving slowly and the light coming in from the street outside like my mother's film on the wall, and when I woke up the next morning I found that I was still in Germany with my arm hanging over the side.

It was like being at home because they were always talking about things to be cleaned. There was a smell of washing and the white sheets were hanging out on the line outside so that you could run through them with your eyes closed, like running into the smell of baking in the Kranz Café. Tante Lisalotte kept checking through our things, examining the collars, picking up shirts and asking if they had been worn, as if she wasn't happy until she found something to wash. And then we had to help with the sheets and everyone picked a corner each and walked in towards the centre like Irish dancing, until they were folded and ironed and counted and put away again.

Tante Lisalotte was the aunt with a cravat-making factory in the house, so we got a coloured cravat each. She was married to Onkel Max and they had two boys called Stefan and Herbert who showed us how to throw water bombs out the window. They had a box of matches and a cigar in the basement, but Tante Lisalotte could smell trouble and came down before they had a chance to light it up. Four boys in lederhosen, she said, like *Max und Moritz* multiplied by two. Tante Minne was a doctor who wanted to collect lots of valuable antiques and Onkel Wilhelm was an optician who had hundreds of guns and antlers covering all the walls of the house. He was the uncle who kept a bottle of schnapps hidden in the aquarium of his surgery, behind artificial plants and the two lazy carp swimming back and forth. They had two children called Mathias and Ursula who also wore lederhosen and taught us new words in German. Ursula had blonde plaits, too, and knew how to whistle with two fingers in her mouth.

All our aunts in Germany had the same nose, so they could sniff what was going on anywhere, even things that had not happened yet. My mother said it was a gift that the Kaiser girls inherited down through the generations and that maybe all the Germans had. They could sniff every warning signal, every danger and every possible misfortune. My mother could sniff a lie from a million miles away and Tante Lisalotte could sniff trouble around the corner. Tante Minne could look at you for a long time and sniff what was inside your head. They knew if you had brushed your teeth or whether you had washed your hands. They knew if you had said your prayers or not. They could walk into a room and tell what you were talking about. They could sniff where you had been and they knew if you were wasting your money on chewing gum. The Irish aunts and uncles gave you money but the German aunts never gave you money, only clothes and toys. The German aunts and uncles told you not to spend any money, even the money that the Irish aunts and uncles gave you.

My father was different in Germany. He wore a cravat and a new suit, and he also got a new pair of glasses from Onkel Wilhelm that had a brown tint and made him look more German. He stopped wearing his tweed cap and his face was brown from the sun, right down to the collar of his shirt. He smiled a lot and one day Maria even made him eat chewing gum, just to try it. He liked talking to people about technical things, about all the new inventions in Germany. He had lots of new friends, like Onkel Willi, the priest who drove too fast with a cigar in his mouth and played chess with a box of cigars on the table beside him. I watched them one afternoon playing quietly until the room filled up with smoke and my father won and they shook hands like friends for life.

My father drank beer and sometimes he was nearly as German as any of the uncles, telling stories and laughing. With his brown face and his new cravat he looked so German that I thought he was going to buy a car and start smoking cigars as well. We didn't need to be Irish and there was no point in speaking Irish to people on buses in Germany. Tante Minne knew that Ireland was full of monastic ruins and valuable antiques, and Onkel Wilhelm knew it was full of rivers with salmon and trout. Onkel Max said it was a small country with lots of big writers. Onkel Willi knew it was full of priests and sheep and holy shrines along the road, and Tante Lisalotte knew it was full of rainbows and lots of trees bent over by the wind. They said Irish people were very friendly and very generous, but my father said that was because they didn't know how to own anything or keep money in their pockets. The poorer you were the more generous you were, he said. Irish people were so afraid of being poor that they spent all their money, while German people were so afraid of being poor that they saved up every penny.

My father said Irish people lived like there was no tomorrow and Onkel Wilhelm said the Germans lived like there was no yesterday. Onkel Max said that's why Germans were busy trying to invent lots of new things like cars and tinted glasses and the Irish were busy inventing stories and literature instead. My father said the Irish invented lots of other things, too, like the hunger strike and Irish coffee. Tante Minne said it was a pity nobody in Germany thought of going on hunger strike against the

Nazis. Onkel Wilhelm said it was a pity the Germans weren't more like the Irish and my father said it was a pity the Irish weren't more like the Germans. He said it was a pity that Ireland wasn't closer to Germany and Onkel Max said it was a pity that Germany wasn't surrounded by water. My mother said Ireland was a place where you still needed luck and prayers, and Ta Maria said Germany was a place where you made your own luck and deserved everything you got. They all agreed that the Irish never hurt anybody. They said the Germans tried to drive everybody who wasn't German into extinction, unlike the Irish who were nearly driven into extinction themselves. Would you rather kill or be killed, my father asked, and nobody knew how to answer that question. Would you rather trample or be trampled, he said, because one language always goes into extinction in the end and nobody knew how to answer that either. Instead they agreed that Ireland and Germany were both still divided countries. The only difference was that the Irish won the war and still hated the British, while the Germans lost the war and had nothing against the British. And then there was an argument because Tante Minne wanted Mathias and Ursula to practise speaking English to us, but my father said that wasn't allowed. So Tante Minne said my father was a welcome guest but he couldn't start making rules in her house.

'If you hate the British so much,' Tante Minne said, 'then why don't you teach your children the most perfect English.'

My mother didn't know how to fight back like that any more, even though she was in her own country. She had other ways of going around trouble. And anyway it was soon forgotten because it was time to start visiting more people and travelling around Germany. We took the train to Neuss to visit a bishop who had a large bowl of fruit on the table and a painting of a fruit bowl on the wall. He asked me if I preferred the real fruit or the painting of fruit, so I pointed at the bowl on the table and his housekeeper packed it all up in bags for us. He gave me his name too, Hugo. Then his driver drove us all the way to Cologne on the autobahn that went straight for ever. You could trust that there would be no cows chewing on the road and no '*Reifenbeisser*' dogs running out to try and bite the tyres. We saw the Cologne Cathedral and the railway station and the bridge that once fell into the river during the war and the big number 4711 lighting up at night.

Then we all had to split up. My mother took Maria and Ita on the train to see Tante Elfriede in Rüsselsheim and, after that, all the way up to Salzburg to see Tante Marianne and to meet all the writers and artists who came to visit there. My father took Franz and me to see the Drachenfelz and he was happier than he had ever been in his life before because it was like being on his honeymoon. We sat on a boat going down the Rhine and he talked a lot, much more than ever before, pointing at the mountains and telling us about how he met my mother. He wanted to explain everything and we had to listen. We drank lemonade called Miranda and had our dinner on the boat, watching other boats passing along beside us, some of them flat with lots of coal heaped up on them. The river was so wide it was like an autobahn with boats going up on one side and down the other.

It was evening by the time we got off the boat and started climbing up the Drachenfelz. We went up the steps and then walked along the path. My father was limping and it wasn't long before we slowed down, because it was very steep. We stopped to take a rest and turned around to look at the river below us with the ships still going up and down slowly without a sound, almost like toy boats. After a while, we continued back up the hill again but we were hardly moving at all. My father took off his cravat and put it in his pocket. He opened his shirt and you could see his white neck inside. He took off his jacket and carried it on his arm instead. But then he stopped to ask us if we still wanted to go all the way to the top. I knew how much he wanted to see the hotel again where he stayed with my mother. I knew it was a place you could not talk about, only see with your own eyes. He wanted to go back and see if it was still the same. And maybe then he was afraid to go back and find that it was not the same.

'Are you hungry?' he asked.

'No,' we said.

We carried on for a while, but then he stopped again and sat down on a bench as if his legs couldn't carry him any more. There wasn't far to go, but instead he started talking and telling us things that he had never told us before. He said it was not true that he had rescued my mother because it was the other way around. If it wasn't for her he would have joined the priesthood like his brother Ted. He said he once went to Rome to pray and ask God whether he should be a priest or get married. He went to see an Italian doctor who could hardly speak to him and used his arms a lot. The doctor said he should get married, because getting married and having children was the only way of getting rid of a limp. My father thought it was like God talking in broken English. He even cried and the doctor had to put his hand on his shoulder. Then my mother came to Ireland and rescued him from the priesthood. And that's why he could not go up to the top of the Drachenfelz without her. After that he was quiet and said nothing all the way back on the train to Kempen.

That night, back in Ta Maria's house, I was trying to get to sleep and I thought of what it would be like if we all came to live in Germany instead and all had the same language. Nobody would ever call us Nazis. My father would have lots of friends and my mother would have all her sisters to talk to. My father would be more German and my mother would learn how to argue and make the rules, like her youngest sister Tante Minne. I lay there and saw different shadows on the wall. I was back in the black and white film that made my mother so afraid.

'Please God, help me to get out of this,' she wrote in her diary.

She didn't know what to do any more. At night she prayed on her knees and walked up and down in her room. She was afraid of what was going to happen to her now. She was back in Düsseldorf, but she had nobody to speak to. She wanted to go home to Kempen, but she was afraid to make trouble for Ta Maria and Onkel Gerd. They had no money and they couldn't support her. She was afraid of being a beggar with no work. She saw Stiegler in the office every day in his suit and she could smell his aftershave. She had not learned the words to describe what happened to her in Venlo. She could not trust any of the women in the office and she didn't know how to go to the police either, because Herr Stiegler had lots of friends in the Gestapo and the Waffen SS. He could accuse her of not helping Germany and then she would be taken away instead. In the end, the only person she could go to was Stiegler himself, because she was only nineteen years old and sometimes you think the person you're most afraid of is the only person who can help.

One day, she had the courage to go straight up to his desk after work. The typewriters were all silent. Herr Stiegler sat looking out the window while she spoke.

'I'm glad you told me this,' he said.

Then he asked her to go home, back to her apartment room. He told her to wait there for him and not to say a word to anyone. He would come and discuss it with her there. He said there was nothing to worry about because he would personally see to it that everything was all right. She was afraid it would start all over again. She could not let him come near her. But he was so calm and so confident that she began to think everything was fine. She knew everything was going wrong but she wanted to believe it was right. As if it was easier to believe a lie. She went back to her apartment and paced up and down the room that night, wondering if she should just run away, just go and start again in a new city where nobody knew who she was.

It was about midnight when Stiegler came to her apartment. She heard his footsteps on the stairs. He was very quiet because there were neighbours living in the other apartments. He entered her room carrying a pouch under his arm that was black and shiny, with a rubber band around it. He told her to lie down on the bed and sat beside her. He held her arm and asked her where all the smiles were gone. He held her chin with his thumb and forefinger and told her to relax, it would only take a minute and then everything would be all right again. This was the solution. He would give her a small injection that wouldn't hurt at all. It might make her feel a little nauseous afterwards, but that would all pass over and she would be full of smiles and dimples and going out to the theatre again. She wanted to know what was in the injection and he said it was a simple preparation, made of purely natural ingredients like vinegar and alcohol. He was already rolling up her sleeve and rubbing a little swab of alcohol on her arm. He said he had received it from a very good doctor that he was friendly with. It would make her strong. It would wipe away all the sickness and disgust. It was an injection against disgust.

'There we are,' he said, like a real doctor.

He was very kind and very polite. He sat with her for a while stroking her forehead and there is no defence against kindness, my mother says. He kept saying he admired her strength and her courage. He said she was very brave and very beautiful, a real German woman. She could smell the cognac on his breath. Then she fell asleep and when she woke up, he was gone. She felt dizzy and sick. She tried to stand up, then she kneeled down, and then she lay on the floor as if nothing mattered any more. Even though she vomited everything up and her stomach was empty, the pain kept getting worse. She left the room and staggered to the bathroom in the hallway, holding on to the wall as if she were on a ship. She tried not to draw any attention to herself, and then she started bleeding and crying silently at the sight of her own blood all around her. She was afraid that one of the people in the other apartments would come out and find her there.

Stiegler came back some hours later. He found her lying on the floor of the bathroom. Her face was white and he could hardly wake her up any more. He was worried that something might go wrong, that she might die maybe and then he would have to explain himself. He had to do things quickly now. There was no time to clean up the blood in the bathroom. He dragged her back to her room very quietly so as not to wake anyone up. He left her on the floor and packed her belongings quickly into a suitcase. He lost no time on this and went straight out to arrange for a car to come and take her away. He had already discarded the needle and the doctor's pouch in various bins around Düsseldorf. When the car arrived, he got the driver to come up and help carry her down the stairs.

She woke up once or twice and saw that she was dribbling on to Herr Stiegler's jacket and there was a white mark on his collar like a new badge. Then they put her into the back of the car with her suitcase beside her and Stiegler handed the driver some money. She heard the engine starting with a growl. And as the car drove away she looked up and saw Herr Stiegler taking out his handkerchief to wipe his suit.

Twenty-four

Then it was the time of the bees.

My father had been preparing for a long time, talking to other beekeepers on the phone and planning everything like a new business. He worked out how much he would have to spend on one side of the page and how much the bees would pay him back with honey on the other. He bought a jungle hat with a wire cage around his face and leather gloves that reached all the way up his arms, past his elbows. He bought the hives and the frames and a smoke gun where you could put in a piece of rolled-up sackcloth on fire and shoot smoke out through the spout to calm the bees down. Everything else was free. The bees would fly out from the roof of the breakfast room from morning till night and nobody could stop them collecting pollen.

On the evening they arrived, my mother got out her special tablecloth, as if the bees were coming to tea like relations from Germany or west Cork. It was like having a party because she put flowers on the table for them and bought lemonade, too. From now on we knew we would never be the same as any other family, because we had friends who were bees and everybody on our street thought the bees were sitting at the table with us eating bread and jam. We even said a special prayer for them, and when the bell rang we all jumped up from the table together and ran to the front door. There was a tall man standing there with a straw skep in his hand. He smiled and spoke to my father in Irish. Then they both went up the stairs and through my bedroom, and we watched from the room above as my father stepped out the window on to the roof of the breakfast room with the cage around his head.

My mother had a picture in the diary of a man named John Glenn who was dressed like a beekeeper. He was the first man to go into orbit, but then he lost his balance in the bath one day and broke his middle ear and stayed in orbit for the rest of his life after that. My father looked like he was in space for ever when he came out in his overalls and his long gloves and with his heavy boots on. The tall man said there was no need to shoot smoke because the bees were very happy to come to our house. He banged the skep and threw them all out on a board where they marched into the new hive with their white tails up in the air.

My mother and father are not afraid to be different. Other families are getting a car and a TV and we want those things as well, but we're German and Irish and have bees as friends. They say we're lucky to be so different because bees were better for the world and better for us. Most other children don't even know the difference between a bee and a wasp. The TV kills your imagination and makes you stupid. But I know the other boys are not stupid, they just don't care if there's a difference between a wasp and a bee. They don't care about the famine either. They don't care about coffin ships and they don't care about concentration camps.

All they care is whether we can fight. They call us Hitler and Eichmann and they want to see if we can fight like Germans. They want to hear us saying aaargh and uuumph like they do in comics and films. We try and run away. One day when they came after us, I ran one way and Franz ran a different way. I got home first through the football field, back along the lanes and in the back door. I didn't know where Franz was. He came home later and stood at the front door with blood on his face and blood on his shirt.

'*Mein Schatz*, what happened?' my mother asked.

There was nothing we could do about it. She could not tell us to stop being German, so she brought Franz into the kitchen and began to clean up the blood on his face. She got some chocolate out of the press to make things better. She said it was good that we didn't fight back because we are not the fist people. We are the word people and one day we will win them over. One day the silent negative will win them all over.

When my father came home he was very angry, because nobody is allowed to hit Franz except him. He examined the shirt with the blood on it and said he could not let it go. I thought it was great because he was going to pay them back for what they did to Franz. Maybe he would get the boys who did it and make them kneel down to ask God how many lashes. He put his cap back on again and went straight down the road to one of the small houses and my mother tried to hold him back by the elbow at the last minute to make sure that he would stay friendly.

'I'm not going down with fists,' my father said.

Instead, he took the bloody shirt and brought Franz with him. When they got to the house and rang the bell, a woman answered the door and pretended that they had come to the wrong house. It was a funny thing to say, because the boy who hit Franz was hiding behind the banisters right beside her. My father smiled and said he didn't come with fists, but he wasn't leaving until somebody listened to him making a speech. So the man of the house had to come out in his slippers and his sleeves rolled up and a tattoo of an anchor on his arm. He was very tall, almost twice the size of my father. He had twice as many children as my father and their house was not even half the size of ours. He was tired and he had a stubble on his face, and it looked like he had no time to listen to speeches from people in bigger houses. The television was on in the front room and he was missing half the football match. My father didn't care how big the man was or how small his house was or if he watched TV all day. He wasn't looking for revenge. He just held up the shirt with the blood on it and let the tall man look down at it for a long time.

'This is your own blood,' my father said.

Then he recited pieces that he remembered off by heart from books he had read. He said it was time to fight for the rights of small people and small nations. He said the reason we were all on our knees was that others thought they were so great. He said it was no use fighting each other all the time because then Ireland would never have its own inventions and its own language.

The man with the tattoo started scratching his belly. He thought he was back at school. He had no idea why my father was coming down to his house to start reciting things from books and saying a few words, too, in Irish with a bloody shirt in his hand. Maybe he thought it was like a new religion or a new political party looking for money. Maybe he thought my father was a Communist. And that was even worse than being a Nazi, that was like the nuclear thing, when the air is full of red dots and everybody stays inside for the rest of their lives watching television. The man with the tattoo started looking down at the sour sallies that were growing beside his slippers at the door. Then my father said goodbye and insisted on shaking hands. He didn't even mention the boy who hit Franz. He just left it at that. He even closed the gate after him, the gate that was never closed in its life before because the man with the tattoo and his whole family just left it open all the time and didn't care how many dogs came into their garden to lift their leg and scratch the grass. As they walked away, my father told Franz not to look around.

'Did you win them over?' my mother asked.

'They laughed,' Franz said.

My mother said it didn't matter because they were the fist people and you were right not to fight back, otherwise you would become just like them. My father didn't even mind that they laughed and ignored his speech.

'What matters,' he said, 'is that a small man was able to walk up to a big man and not be afraid.'

I knew it wasn't over yet. I knew they would come looking for us again because I was Eichmann and I could do nothing about it. I wanted to be one of the fist people so that I could defend myself and not be afraid on the streets. From then on I wanted to be a real Nazi. I wanted to be so cruel and mean that they would be scared of me instead. In bed at night I thought of all the things I would do. I thought of bashing their heads against the wall. I thought of smashing a rock into some boy's teeth. I would be famous all over the place. People would be afraid even to go swimming when I was out. I thought of them running away and hiding in doorways when they heard me coming, shivering at the sound of my name. Eichmann.

I started practising on my own. I learned how to do the evil smile. I learned to laugh like the Nazis do in films, slowly, while I was getting ready to torture somebody. I spoke English to myself in a German accent. I kept saying things like 'my friend' and being so polite that people would be even more frightened when they realised that I was going to kill them. I stuck knives into puppets and grinned into the mirror. I threw rocks at cats. I practised torturing Franz and Maria. And one day, I even threw a chair at my mother and there was nothing she could do about it. So she left the chair there where it fell and said nobody else would ever pick it up again and it could stay there for a hundred years.

'Why do you want to be one of the fist people?' she asked.

'It's boring to be good,' I said.

I wanted to be as bad as possible. When you're bad you get a good feeling because people look shocked and worried and that makes you want to be even worse. If you're good nobody looks at you.

'I'm Eichmann,' I said. 'I'm going to kill people and laugh about it.'

She brought me into the front room and showed me a book where there was a picture of a boy in the street with his hands up in the air saying don't shoot. She told me about a place called Auschwitz and how Eichmann was the man in charge of the trains for getting people there. She could remember Jewish people in Kempen. They were called '*die Jüdchen*: the little Jews' because they lived in the small houses. She never saw any of them being taken away, but she said there was only one Jewish man who came back to Kempen after the war and he didn't stay. He just came to look around once and then he left again and now there are no Jews in Kempen. She said they were our people. Our people died in concentration camps.

I wonder what it's like for my cousins in Germany and if they still have to think about it every day like me. Is anyone calling them Nazis on the street? Here I have to be careful where I walk, because if they catch me then I'll go on trial and they'll execute me.

'I don't want to be German,' I said.

She had tears in her eyes and said the Germans would never be able to go home again. Germans are not allowed to be children. They're not allowed to sing children's songs or tell fairy tales. They cannot be themselves. That's why Germans want to be Irish or Scottish or American. That's why they love Irish music and American music, because that gives them a place to go home to and be homesick for.

'It's like a birthmark,' she said.

It was time for us to go down to the sea and look at the waves, because she had to carry on with her work. She stood at the door to watch us going across the street until we disappeared around the corner. I knew I was in the luckiest place in the world with the sea close by. The sun was shining and you could smell the dust in the air. There were tar bubbles on the road and further along you could see a shimmer, as if the ground was rising up in the heat. Some of the shops had canopies that were flapping in the breeze. The boats were out on the bay and there was a haze over the harbour. We went swimming, Noel, Franz and I. We dived under the water for as long as possible. I knew I could stop breathing longer than anyone else. I could stay down there until my lungs nearly burst. I was the champion at not breathing and not speaking. I could hear the voices around the pool, but they were muffled and far away. Down there it was blue and calm, like being inside a cool drink.

Sometimes the bees come into my room at night. They go after the light because they think it's daytime and they want to get as close to the sun as possible. They go mad and whirl around the light until they crash into the bulb in the middle of the room and fall down. Then they pick themselves up and start again, whirling around and getting more and more excited and impatient, until you switch off the light and they move to the window instead. Then they buzz up and down the window for ages trying to get out to the light in the street, until they get so tired they drop down on the floor and crawl around in circles. They always go in circles when they're dying, as if they're trying to make themselves dizzy. You can't let them out, and I have to sleep with my head covered up in case they come over and sting me in the middle of the night.

I know it's the smallest things that hurt most because I got stung in the garden one day when I put my hand down on a bee in the grass. He had been hit by a drop of rain and was going mad in circles. When I put my hand down he stung me and after that nobody wanted to play on the grass any more. My father says that stings are good for you and we'll never get rheumatism. If you want to reduce the pain, he says, you should take the sting out quickly to stop the poison going in. He explained that a bee sting is very different from a wasp sting, because a bee has a hook at the end of it and he showed it to us once under the microscope. He says we'll soon get used to bee stings and won't even feel them. And my mother says we shouldn't howl so much every time a bee stings us because the neighbours will think we're being tortured to death.

Sometimes when I'm inside the house I hear somebody screaming outside and I know it's a bee sting. Maria or Ita or Franz, everybody has a different scream. And sometimes they scream before they're even stung. If a bee goes near them they start shouting and running inside, as if they're going to die. It's not even the bee's fault. They fly out over the garden and come back with pouches so full of pollen, like heavy suitcases. And when the wind suddenly blows around the corner at the back of the house, they get pushed back down into the garden and find it difficult to pick themselves up again. Sometimes the wind blows them into somebody's hair and it's not their fault because they just want to get back up and carry the pollen home to the hive. Then they get tangled up in hair. You hear Maria or Ita screaming and running into the house even though the bee hasn't stung yet and is only trapped and buzzing like mad, trying to get back out.

One day it happened to my mother and we invented a way of stopping the bee from stinging. My mother came running inside and shouting that there was a bee in her hair. She held her hair tight to try and stop it from getting closer to her head. The bee was probably lashing out and stinging everything it could touch because it was trapped in a prison of hair, like a spider's web with no chance of getting out alive. But as long as it didn't get close to the skin, then there was still a chance of stopping it from stinging. She told me to get a tea towel and put it on the place where the bee was. I could feel the buzzing under my fingers and I pressed hard until the buzzing went up to a high pitch, like a motorbike far away. Then I pressed even harder until I felt a crack under the towel and the bee was dead. Nobody said anything about it afterwards, in case my father would get angry that we were killing all his bees. After that I was the expert at stopping stings. I was the sting stopper.

Twenty-five

After that we tried to be as Irish as possible.

There was a new baby in the house named Bríd. Onkel Ted came out specially to our church to say Mass in Irish and we were the altar boys, Franz and me. Some people coughed and walked out because they thought they were in the wrong country and couldn't pray to God in Irish. But Onkel Ted carried on without even looking around once. He baptised Bríd and poured holy water over her head, and afterwards there was a big cake in our house with a Celtic spiral made of Smarties. It didn't matter who walked out of the church with a bad cough because my father said Bríd was born and baptised now and those people would soon be outnumbered. My mother wanted to know why they were more afraid of the Irish language than they were of the bees, and Onkel Ted said maybe the sting is worse. Franz said Irish speakers don't sting and then everybody laughed and ate the spiral cake.

Then we went back to Connemara for three months to be as Irish as possible. We got new caps and new rain macs and went on a train with a group of boys who were all going to live in a full-Irish fireside. We were going to school in the Gaeltacht and we would come back like native speakers. At the station, a photographer came to take a picture for the newspapers and my mother kept it in the diary. Franz and me and the other boys waving goodbye on the platform, because we would not see or speak to anyone in our family until we came home fully Irish.

Franz went to An Cheathrú Rua and I went to a new place called Béal an Daingin, but I was sick again and the howling started up in my chest every night. The people in the house were very nice to me, but sometimes I wanted to go home because I couldn't breathe. I had lots of trouble with the dogs howling in my chest. The local doctor came and he said I would soon get over it. But I was coughing all the time and had to stay in bed. Then Bean an tí gave me cigarettes that were good for asthma. She bought a packet of Sweet Afton and put them beside my bed with a box of matches. She told me that if I felt short of breath I should light up a cigarette and smoke away like a good man, because that would help me to cough up all the bad stuff and not be afraid of the dark. Then I got better again and forgot that I was German and started learning how to live in Irish.

There was a boy named Peadar in the house who showed me how to get water and how to milk the cows. Bean an tí taught me how to find all the places where the hens laid eggs. I helped Fear an tí to stack turf against the side of the house and I learned how to say '*go dtachtfaidh sé thú*' which is the Irish for I hope it chokes you. I learned how to turn English words into Irish and to say '*mo bhicycle*' and '*mo chuid biscuits*'. I learned how to walk to school backwards to stop the hailstones stinging my legs. I watched men gathering seaweed and putting it on big lorries to be taken away to Galway and turned into cough medicine. I saw people laying out salted fish on the stone walls to dry them in the sun. I saw the tide going out every day as if it was never coming back, and I saw donkeys with their feet tied together to stop them running away and laughing at everybody.

There was a curly piece of brown sticky paper hanging in the middle of every room with dead flies stuck to it. There was a dog beside the fire who had his chin on the floor and his eyes closed and only lifted one ear to hear if anyone was coming. Every day a man named Cóilín came to visit and sit by the window. He was a cousin belonging to the woman of the house and he would look out at the road and tell them who was passing by. There was a radio in the house but there was no TV and no need for one, because the man at the window was the man who said the news. The woman of the house could carry on making the dinner and the man of the house could sit with his pipe by the fireside without looking up. That's Joe Phait going west now with his new coat on, Cóilín would say. Here's Nancy Seóige making her way back from the east now with biscuits for her sister. There were four different directions you could go – west, from the west, east and from the east. Sometimes they came in to visit and then the whole house was like a television programme, with the man at the window keeping everybody talking. Nancy Seóige came in to smoke a fag out of the wind and explain that the biscuits were for her sister, because she was ill in bed for a long time and the Sweet Afton were doing her no good any more. She came in from the east and when she finished her story she went back out to the west.

There's Tom Pháidin Tom going east now with his bicycle and his dog behind him, the man at the window said. Sometimes the woman of the house would ask questions, too, like what Tom Pháidin Tom was thinking about, and she was told that he was thinking he had spent long enough in his own company on the bog for one day, and he was going east up to Teach Uí Fhlatharta to buy pipe cleaners and tobacco for himself. The man at the window knew who was going by and who was not going by. He knew what everybody was saying in Connemara, and all the conversations that were going on in England and America even, as far away as Boston. I see the *sagart*, Father Ó Móráin has not gone up to see the Johnson family yet about their son in Birmingham. Páraic Jamesey must have gone up to Galway on the bus for the day, because they say he's great with a nurse from Inishmore working in the Galway regional hospital. They say that Patricia Mhuirnín Leitir Mochú is getting married in the spring in America, to a stranger.

The man at the window could tell who was up at Teach Uí Fhlatharta and what stories they all had. He knew that Tom Pháidin Tom was buying more than pipe cleaners because his dog was coming back from the east already and that meant Máirtín Handsome was surely up there as well and Tom Pháidin Tom would not be going home until it was late, unless Peigín Dorcha went up after him with her dark hair. He knew what all the living people were saying and also what all the dead people were saying in the graveyard. He knew that Tom Pháidin Tom's brother Páidin Óg was calling out from the grave, saying that his throat was like a dry stick and that if he was still alive and hadn't drowned out of Ros a Mhíl one day, then he'd be up there in Teach Uí Fhlatharta and nobody, not even the priest or the Pope in the Vatican or Éamon de Valera himself would get him out until he had sung '*Barr na Sráide*' and the 'Rocks a Bawn'.

One night I had to go up to Teach Uí Fhlatharta with a blue and white milk jug. The man of the house was not allowed to go up himself because the priest had told him never to go east or he would never come back west again if he did. So then I had to go east for him and he told me to be careful on the way back not to spill a single drop. It was dark and as I walked along the road towards the lights of Teach Uí Fhlatharta, I knew that the man at the window was telling the man of the house about me. There's Dublin Jack going in the door now carrying the jug with the blue and white stripes and there's Dublin Jack taking out the money and buying sweets instead, but that was only a joke.

Teach Uí Fhlatharta was a big shop with everything you could buy, like jam and sweets and things like cement and wood, too. There was lots of smoke and lots of tall men in wellington boots standing at the counter, all talking at the same time. They were telling all the stories in Connemara as far away as Boston. I saw Tom Pháidin Tom laughing and smoking a pipe that had a lid on it for the rain. I stood behind them waiting for a while and looking at the new brushes and buckets hanging from the ceiling, until one of the men turned around to take the jug from me. He told the man behind the counter to fill it up to the top because Dublin Jack was very thirsty. I put the money up on the counter and, when the jug was full, they passed it down to me and told me to hold it with both hands. There was cream on top to stop you from seeing what was inside the jug, but you could smell it. Then one of them came over to open the door, and I walked back slowly in the dark without turning the jug upside down or meeting any ghosts or falling down in the ditch or getting swallowed up by the ground and never seen again. I didn't spill a single drop. But when I got back, the man of the house looked into the jug for a long time. He asked me did I drink half of it myself, but the woman of the house told him I didn't. The man at the window wanted to know if I saw anyone with a tweed cap turned backwards and that was Máirtín Handsome. Then the man of the house drank from the side of the jug and started telling a ghost story that happened to himself one time when he was coming home from Teach Uí Fhlatharta in the dark.

When I was going back to Dublin again, the woman of the house went out and caught a chicken for me to take back with me on the train. She put it into a bag and tied it with a ribbon so that the chicken was looking out at one end and some feathers were coming out the other. I knew that the man at the window was still talking about me long after I was gone. There's Dublin Jack on the train now with the chicken beside him looking out the window at the stone walls going by. There's Dublin Jack going home more Irish than anyone in Connemara, talking to the chicken in Irish and giving it a bit of his sandwich.

After that we started going to a new all-Irish school in Dublin with the Christian Brothers. Every day we had to get a train into the city and walk past Nelson's Pillar and Cafollas and the Gresham Hotel. Everything at the new school was done through Irish – Latin, algebra, hurling and even English. The Christian Brothers wore black with a white collar and white chalk marks around their shoulders. One of them had brown fingers and smoked a piece of chalk all day in class, until his lips were white from talking. He asked me to read out a piece in a book and the whole class had to listen. He said it was a miracle how a Dublin boy could become so Irish. He escaped out of the classroom and took me by the hand, flying down the stairs three at a time and leaving all the other boys behind fencing with rulers. He said I had to go around and read in front of the whole school. I had to go to every classroom and show them what a native speaker was like, and the principal said I should be on television as an example of how history could be turned back.

Everybody was proud of me and I liked being Irish. But I knew all the boys in the school were laughing at me. Nobody really wanted to be that Irish. If you wanted to have friends you had to start speaking to yourself in English, so that nobody would call you a mahogany gaspipe or a sad fucking sap or think that you were from Connemara long ago. You'd never get into the Waverley Billiard Hall speaking Irish. You had to pretend that you had no friends who lived long ago like Peig Sayers. You had to laugh at Peig Sayers so that nobody would suspect you were really Irish underneath. You had to pretend that Irish music and Irish dancing were stupid, and Irish words smelled like onion sandwiches. You had to pretend that you were not afraid of the famine coming back, that you didn't eat sandwiches made by your own mother and that you had an English song in your head at all times. You had to walk down O'Connell Street and pretend that you were not even in Ireland.

There were celebrations everywhere in Dublin for the Easter Rising. It happened fifty years ago and my father said it should happen again because Ireland would never be free until we had more of our own inventions. He said the Irish people were forced to repeat their history because of all the things the British left behind. And one day we saw the Easter Rising happening again in front of our own eyes. They were making a film of it and I saw Patrick Pearse coming out and surrendering with a white flag before he was executed by the British. There were pictures of Patrick Pearse in the windows of shoe shops and sweet shops. The shops had Irish flags, too, and copies of the proclamation which we all learned off by heart. We sold Easter lilies and there was hardly a single person in the city who wasn't wearing one. In school a man came from the Abbey Theatre to put on a pageant and we got parts as croppy boys or redcoats and died every night. On the buses there were little torches and swords and all the lamp-posts in the city had flags so that everybody would remember how great it was that the Irish were free to walk down any street in the world, including their own. Nobody was telling the Irish when to get off the bus. Some people still thought it was the British empire coming back every time a bus conductor asked them for their fare. And some people thought it was the Nazis coming back every time an inspector came on to ask for their ticket. But the flags and the special stamps and the pictures in all the shops were there to remind everybody that the Irish were not the saddest people in the world any more, they were laughing now and nobody could stop them.

One day the whole school was brought out to see a film called *Mise Éire* which is the Irish for 'I am Ireland'. Some of the boys in the class were asking was Sean Connery in it and was there a woman smoking and blinking and wearing nothing under her dressing gown. But it wasn't that kind of film. There were no horses either rising up and whinnying. It was mostly about the Easter Rising, with black and white pictures of windows smashed and bullet holes in the walls. There was lots of big music that sounded like big country music from the end of a Western film and made everybody feel strong in their stomach. There were two boys standing guard and protecting the grave of O'Donovan Rossa with hurling sticks. There were people marching through the streets with hurling sticks on their shoulders and a deep voice saying 'Ireland unfree shall never be at peace.' It didn't matter that James Bond wasn't in it because Patrick Pearse was in it instead, and even though he got killed in the end, he put up a good fight.

I had new friends in school and one of them had a brother who worked in a gardening shop. One day he brought a bag of green dye into school that was used to mix with fertiliser, so that everybody would know it was not to be eaten. At lunchtime, we were not let into the Waverley Billiard Hall yet, so we brought the bag of fertiliser over to the new garden of remembrance across the road from the school. Then I had the idea to throw the dye into the fountain for Ireland. It turned green before we even got a chance to get back out of the garden again and the guards were sent for. The problem was that anyone who touched the dye had green hands and green faces, so it was easy to tell who did it. I tried to wash my face in the public toilets near the GPO but every time I put water on my face it turned even more green. There was a lot of trouble at school because I walked into the class late with my face all green, and I thought I would be expelled, but nothing happened because they said it was the right colour at least.

On the train home everybody thought it was part of the Easter commemorations and that every boy in Ireland was turning green. I wanted to be as Irish as possible so that I would never have to be German again. I wanted to belong to the saddest people and not the people who killed the saddest people. At home I tried to speak Irish to my mother again but she didn't understand a word, so then I sat at the window while she was working, and I pretended that I was the newsreader, like the man at the window in Béal an Daingin. I waited for my father to come home from the station and told her all the people going by.

There's Miss Ryan going east now to get minced meat

for herself and her sister. There's Miss Hosford going east, too, on her bicycle and nobody knows where she's off to at this time of the day with a rucksack on her back. They say that Mrs MacSweeney's niece is getting married soon in Dublin. They say that one of the Miss Doyles nearly got married to a stranger once, but she's happier now living with her sister till death do us part, and reading to each other every evening after dinner from an indecent book by James Joyce. Here are the Miss Lanes coming out and looking up at the Irish flag hanging from the front window of our house, and they think they're in the wrong country altogether. They look around the garden to make sure that nobody has kicked a football into their country and say that it's a shame more Irish people didn't die fighting the Nazis. They say the Irish were cowards because they didn't fight against the Nazis, but they forget that the Irish fought against the British. There's Miss Tarleton coming out now picking up bits of paper in her front garden and wondering why my mother didn't die fighting against the Nazis. But she doesn't know that my mother lived against the Nazis instead. They say that Miss Tarleton hates the bees more than the Irish language, except that they're good for the loganberry harvest. They say that Miss Tarleton went into the butcher's shop one day and asked Mr Furlong what the picture of Patrick Pearse was doing in the window beside all the meat. He said it was time to die for Ireland and she said that meant it was time to kill for Ireland, but my father says they're both wrong because it's time to live for Ireland and be Irish. They say that Mrs Creagh once went over to England for horse racing at Cheltenham and somebody asked her if the Irish still kept pigs under the bed, and she said it wasn't half as bad as having the pigs in the bed like they do in England. Here's Mr Clancy going down to the Eagle House and he once had a big argument with my father in the street. My father told him we were trying to be as Irish as possible. Mr Clancy said he was just as Irish as us and didn't speak a word of Irish. He said Irish was the 'aboriginal' language and no bloody use to anyone any more. So then my father told Mr Clancy he would soon be outnumbered and Mr Clancy said my father better have a lot more children. Here's my father coming around the corner saying that nobody is going to stop us speaking Irish or make us take down the Irish flag from the window until we feel like it. My father and Mr Clancy are going towards each other on the pavement and you think there's going to be a big fight and blood on the ground, but my father is not one of the fist people and neither is Mr Clancy, and they both nod to each other politely as they pass by.

One morning my father woke me up early and showed me the newspaper. He still had shaving cream on his face and he was breathing fast from running up the stairs. He opened the paper wide and pointed at a picture of Dublin after a bomb. It was a bomb for Ireland, he said. I rubbed my eyes and looked at the picture, but I didn't know what was happening until he read it out to me. It said that Nelson's Pillar had been blown up during the night. I remembered going up to the top of Nelson's Pillar once with Eileen and now it was gone and nobody would ever go up again. My father slapped the paper with the back of his hand and said the empire was crumbling. At last all the things the British left behind are disappearing, he said. At last we're living in our own country and telling our own stories and speaking our own language. When I went to school I saw hundreds of people standing around looking at the remains of Nelson's Pillar. There were no buses going up and down the street any more because there was rubble all over the place. The windows were broken and there was glass everywhere. People couldn't go shopping that day or pass by to get into the GPO either. I saw a shoe shop with glass all over the new shoes. I looked up and saw the stump of Nelson's Pillar like somebody's arm cut off. Nelson's head was on the ground and the dust of the empire was all around.

Twenty-six

I keep thinking this didn't happen.

One day I had to collect Bríd from school because she was homesick. The wind was howling in her chest so I had to go into the girls' school and bring her home. I had to go up the stairs past the glass cage with the stuffed birds and knock on the girls' classroom. They opened the door and I saw Bríd sitting down with three girls and the teacher around her. Her face was white and she was breathing with her mouth open. Her hair was wet from sweating and they were wiping her face with a towel, but she was happy and she smiled because I was there to take her home. I picked up her schoolbag and took her by the hand and we walked down the stairs very slowly. She was holding on to the banisters and sitting down sometimes to take a rest with her head down and her hair in her face as if nothing mattered any more.

When we got outside I had to carry her because she couldn't walk. She was leaning forward and stopping all the time to hold on to the railings, so then I hung the schoolbag around my neck and gave her a piggyback up to the bus stop. On the bus I got her to lie down on the seat like a bed with the schoolbag as a pillow, but she got up again, because she was coughing and crying for air with her arm around me. I knew she wouldn't be able to walk home from the bus, so I asked the conductor if he could get the bus to bring her home. He was clicking the money in his hand and said he wasn't allowed to do that, but then I told him that my sister was going to get sick and he talked to the driver. So the bus turned up at the Eagle House and all the people were lost because they had never been up that street before on a bus. The conductor explained that the bus was an ambulance now. He was still clicking the money in his hand to see if anyone hadn't paid their fare, but then he sat down like a passenger himself, until the bus got to our street with the red houses and the driver stopped because it was impossible to go any further. I told him it was all right because we lived in number two and that wasn't too far. Then the bus conductor carried Bríd as far as the front door and afterwards everybody was talking about the lost bus, because it took so long before it turned around and drove back down to catch up with the main road again.

The doctor had to come and we went down for the red medicine and twisted glucose sticks. Bríd took only one spoon because she wasn't able to swallow and the second spoon dribbled down her chin, down the outside of her neck instead of inside. My mother tried to make her go to sleep with a song about a donkey who said he was better at making noise than the cuckoo, but she kept sitting up in bed and trying to run away. So then we carried the bed down to the kitchen to make sure that she wouldn't be lonely upstairs. She fell asleep for a while and we walked around the house very quietly as if there was a cake in the oven. When my father came home he knew what to do. He sat on the bed and stroked her head. He got her to swallow another spoon of medicine inside her neck, and even when we were going to bed, he was still sitting there with her, trying to make her smile and asking her puzzles like the one about the man who came to a fork in the road and had only one question to ask. He gave her lots of clues, but she still didn't know the answer and he had to tell her in the end. We could hear her breathing up and down all through the house, and sometimes she was crying and putting her arm around my father to beg him to help her breathe.

'It's all right, *Tutti*,' I can hear them saying all the time. 'It's all right, *mein Schätzchen*, it's all right.'

The man named Gearóid still comes to our house sometimes on Saturdays and he says the only thing that would help Bríd is goat's milk. He comes in his Volkswagen and says we're a true Irish fireside and we should be drinking goat's milk anyway. He wants my father to start making speeches again and to write for the newspaper *Aiséirí*, like he did long ago. Everybody knows that the *Aiséirí* office is on Harcourt Street because you can see the blue Volkswagen outside every day with all the newspapers on the back seat, and sometimes you can see a goat tied to the railings as well to show the people of Dublin that the Irish are not afraid to be different. Gearóid keeps a goat in the city and we keep bees in the city, to remind people not to be so afraid of the country. My mother thought the goat was coming out to our house in the back of the Volkswagen but Gearóid said it would only eat up all the copies of *Aiséirí*, so the next time he came out he brought a canteen full of goat's milk instead and my father gave him a jar of honey in exchange.

The goat's milk didn't help Bríd. She spat it out all over the bed clothes because it looked grey and tasted like pee-pee. Some people said Bríd should not be drinking milk at all. Some said she should be living in the mountains in Switzerland, not by the sea in Ireland, because it's damp and sometimes you can't even look out the window. Miss Tarleton said Bríd would grow out of it because she had a really bad chest herself when she was a little girl, and look at her now, she's 78 years old and she can't remember the last time she had a cold or even a cough. But Bríd doesn't want to be like Miss Tarleton when she grows up with two different shoes on. The Miss Ryans said Bríd should go on a pilgrimage to Lourdes or Fatima but you have to be in a wheelchair for that. A German woman, who was not allowed to come to our house because she was divorced, gave my mother eucalyptus oil. And Mr Furlong told my mother it was good to have asthma, because then you would never get malaria. But Bríd is still sick all the time and getting thin because she doesn't want to eat anything any more, not even glucose sticks or cakes that my mother makes.

In the middle of the night the doctor had to come back again because she was trying to open the window and get air from outside. I woke up and heard her crying, begging my father for air, and my mother still saying 'it's all right, *mein Schätzchen*, it's all right. Come back to bed now.' Everybody was afraid because nobody in our house ever cried that much before. I got up and saw Bríd reaching forward with her mouth open. My mother and father were holding her arms on each side. I asked if I could help but my father told me to get back to bed. Franz and Maria were standing on the landing as well, and they ran back into bed as soon as they heard his voice. My mother came and told us to pray hard, so I listened to Bríd in the dark and prayed that the bad chest would come back to me instead. Then I heard Dr Sheehan's voice downstairs in the hall. He said Bríd was an angel and a saint and he gave her an injection to make her go to sleep. The next morning she was still going up and down all the time, but she was smiling again and my mother got her to eat some toast with jam.

Gearóid came again the next Saturday with the new *Aiséirí*. He's always dressed in a brown tweed suit. His knees are bent even when he's standing up, and, one time, me and Franz laughed because his trousers looked like they wanted to stay sitting down. He has bits of hair growing on his cheeks, too, where he stopped shaving, and a big smile when we answer him in Irish. He says Bríd is a *páistín fionn*, a blonde child, and really Irish underneath. She's a fighter, he says. Then they go into the front room to talk for a long time about all the things that are not finished yet in Ireland, like still only one pop song in Irish about a goat that went mad and had to be stopped by the priest, and lots of other things like street names still in English and no parking fines in Irish. What if somebody wanted to break the law in Irish? Gearóid said they were going to put him in jail for not paying motor tax on the Volkswagen in English. They were going to put my father in jail, too, because he was waiting to pay a fine in Irish. My mother brings in the tea and we can hear Gearóid's voice coming out under the door. He says he can't keep writing all the articles in *Aiséirí* on his own, and he wants my father to write something big instead of just writing letters to the papers.

One day my father wrote a strong letter to the papers to prove that what they were saying about Cardinal Stepinac was wrong, that he wasn't a Nazi at all and that he didn't even hate any Jewish people, even though he was a Catholic. It was a big mistake to believe Radio Éireann, he wrote, because they only repeated the rubbish that the Communists in Yugoslavia were saying. They locked Cardinal Stepinac up in his house and put him on trial because they felt guilty themselves. People who feel guilty point the finger, my father says, and they're just putting the blame on Cardinal Stepinac for everything that happened in the concentration camps. There were lots more letters in the paper after that and a Protestant man named Hubert Butler from Kilkenny once insulted the Papal Nuncio, saying that Cardinal Stepinac was guilty because the Catholic priests in Yugoslavia baptised children before they were killed in concentration camps. Nobody in Ireland could ever believe that priests helped the Nazis to kill children and save their souls. Nobody could ever believe Catholic priests helped a big SS man named Artukovic to escape to Ireland after the war and live in Dublin for two years before he emigrated to Paraguay. My father says Cardinal Stepinac should be made into a saint, and Gearóid said it was a pity my father didn't take up writing again because he was so good at making speeches and lighting matches and going around the country on his motorbike.

'His speeches had passion,' Gearóid said to my mother. 'He had them throwing their hats up.'

It's good to hear people saying that. It's good to think about my father standing up on a platform with crowds of people around him in the street throwing their hats up and not caring if they ever came back down again. It's good to like your own father otherwise you won't like yourself very much either. You want to believe that everything your own father says is always right.

'*Aiséirí*,' Gearóid said. 'Resurrection. What about the daily uprising?'

My father smiled and said he was still waking up for Ireland every morning, but he was very busy with other things, too, at the moment, like beekeeping and making German oak furniture and reading about how to cure asthma without listening to doctors., He was starting to translate a German book as well that Onkel Ted gave my mother about training children without sticks. He was also trying to write more letters about Cardinal Stepinac not helping the Nazis to kill children, as well as trying to write an article about Guernica to say that the painting of screaming cows and legs in the air by Picasso might be a masterpiece, but maybe it wasn't the Germans who did it. Gearóid says the Irish spent a long time building stone walls and saying the opposite and pretending the British were not there, and my father is a real Irishman with a gift for being against. He holds his fist up in the air and says my father could make anyone believe that day is night. He turns to my mother and winks at her because she is the audience and she says it's good that people in Ireland can't be kept quiet.

'Remember the article they tried to ban,' Gearóid said.

'What article?' my mother asked.

Gearóid punched his fist down on the side of the armchair and told her that my father once wrote a great article about the Jewish people in Ireland. He said they tried to stop them from printing it. They threatened to close down the office in Harcourt Street. The police came and took away lots of documents, but they were not afraid of going to prison and they went to confession and printed the article on the front page, because *Aiséirí* is the Irish for not sitting down.

'Did you never read it?' he said. 'It was very well written. Very balanced and fair-minded. Maybe it didn't even go far enough.'

After that my mother was very upset and she didn't even do the washing-up. She was using the silent negative all the time. She told Bríd she was going back to Germany. She said she was going to pack her bags and take Bríd with her to a place where she would be able to breathe.

There were lots of doors slamming in our house after that. Bríd jumps in bed when the door of the front room bangs shut. Sometimes we get a fright as well when there's a draught and the back door bangs shut in anger of its own accord. I know where my father is by the sound of the last door banging. One day I started slamming doors as well, but he said that wasn't allowed and it's not too late for him to get the stick and take me upstairs and close all the doors so that nobody will hear. My mother reminds him that he's translating a book about punishing children without sticks, so then he puts on his coat and slams the front door, and everybody thinks he's gone away and never coming back. Everything in the house rattles and then stays quiet for a long time. Then one day I told everybody I was leaving and slammed the front door from inside. It was a joke just to annoy them. I hid behind the oak trunk in the hall so that everybody thought I was gone for ever, but then Bríd started crying and my mother said she would start banging the doors, too, one day, then we would see how funny it was. And one night she did it. It was very late but she did it really and truly. My father came back and slammed the door of the front room without eating his dinner. He sat there staring at all the patterns in the carpet. My mother didn't want him to feel sorry for himself, so she went in to sit beside him and put her arm around him like a friend for life. She wanted him to say that he made a mistake, but he just pushed her away. Then she stood in the hall and put her coat on slowly. She went out and closed the front door very, very quietly, as if she was leaving us and going back to Germany for ever.

'Jaysus, what the Jaysus,' I said. Nobody ever heard a

door closing so much before in their whole lives. It was so quiet that you could hardly even hear the click of the lock, and this time we were really afraid that she would never come back. This time the silence was bigger than after the loudest bang. I ran to the window upstairs and looked out, but she had already gone around the corner out of sight. I thought I should run after her. But then I waited. The whole house waited for her to come back. And when she came at last, everybody was happy, even my father. He said he would never slam doors again as long as he lived.

My mother says it's the hardest thing in the world to say that you're wrong. She wants us not to be afraid to make mistakes, and, when we do our homework, never to use a rubber or tear a page out of the copy book. She wants everybody to honest and Onkel Ted comes out to the house specially because he's a priest and he's heard all the mistakes that have ever been made in Ireland. He always brings a book in German for my mother and you wouldn't think he's read it because it looks new. This time he brought a book about Eichmann and a book about a priest named Bonhöffer. They sat around the table in the breakfast room and didn't come out because they had so much to talk about. We went into the front room instead to listen to the radio and there was a song we liked called 'I Heard it Through the Grapevine'. We listened to the radio with one ear and listened out for my father with the other, to hear if he was coming with one soft foot and one hard.

The next day, when my father was at work and we were at school, my mother went upstairs very quietly to her bedroom with lots of clean laundry. Bríd was still breathing up and down, so my mother sat her up in the big bed where she could look out and tell her everything that was happening outside on the street like a newsreader, who was going east and who was going west. She put the light on because it looked like it was getting dark outside and the red houses on the far side of the street said it was going to rain. Bríd said there was a man from the corporation slicing the weeds off the path with a shovel. Miss Tarleton came out and threw some more weeds out on to the path while the man wasn't looking. And a dog came walking into our garden because the gate was open, but he just scratched the grass and went out again.

My mother opened up my father's wardrobe and put away lots of clean shirts and rolled-up socks. She left the doors open and started looking at all the things that belonged to him before they got married. She found the picture of the sailor with his soft eyes looking away that my father never wanted anyone in our house to see again. She found other pictures of my grandfather when he worked on ships that belonged to the British navy. She found the last postcard he sent home to his wife saying: 'More homesick than seasick.' There were rosary beads belonging to my grandmother Mary Frances and a box full of letters and lots of medals she got from the navy after he died on his own in a Cork hospital. There were more boxes of letters from people in America and South Africa who couldn't come home again. There were letters that Mary Frances wrote to my father when he was going to university in Dublin so that he would never have to leave Ireland and get seasick or have to work in America. Letters that my father wrote home to Leap to say that he got the money and a list of all the things he had to spend the money on, like the rent and razor blades and a penny for Mass on Sunday. Letters from his mother asking him to send home his clothes to Leap to be washed. Letters to ask him if he had heard anything from his brother Ted.

Bríd said it was raining and the man from the corporation left the shovel leaning against our wall. She said he was standing under the tree across the road taking shelter and smoking a cigarette. She said Mrs Robinson opened the door to hold her hand out and see if it was really raining, because there's a clock in her hallway that tells the weather, but it's not always right and you have to tap it with your finger. Bríd said it was raining hard now and there were big drops on the pavement and nobody on the street at all any more going east or west.

My mother sat on the floor and looked at photographs of my father before he was married. She found pictures of the time when Onkel Ted was becoming a priest and my father was becoming an engineer. She found German language lessons from Dr Becker and homework my father did. There were lots of things from the time during the war, when my father met Gearóid at university in Dublin and started the party called *Aiséirí*. There was a picture of my father walking down O'Connell Street at the head of a big march, holding a poster with the words: 'For whom the bell tolls, *Éire Aiséirí*.' There was another picture of my father and Gearóid in his tweed suit walking down Harcourt Street, smiling as if they were not afraid of the police.

There were boxes full of green leaflets to say what *Aiséirí* was going to do with Ireland if they were in control. They were going to stop people being greedy and getting rich on their own without sharing. People would not have to pay rent if they had to live with rats and not enough clothes or food for their children. Irish people would no longer have to go away and get seasick. They would get rid of all the things the British invented like county councils and slums and postboxes with the crown. They would take back all the things that belonged to the Irish, like the rivers and the big houses and the six counties in the north. It was time that the Irish took back the factories and the shops and put up the Irish word *Amach* on the doors in the cinemas instead of Exit. They were fed up with Irish people changing their minds all the time and not knowing how to start up a new country from the beginning. They said it was time for Irish people to stop sitting down and staring out the window as if they got an awful fright. What they needed was a big strong leader, not like Hitler or Stalin, but more like Salazar, because he was a good Catholic and Portugal was a small country like Ireland with stone walls and poor people living on their imagination.

My mother doesn't understand very much about politics so she can't tell the difference between the things that people say before elections. She knows they have nice hands and nice shoes and make lots of promises. She doesn't understand what difference *Aiséirí* would have made if more people had thrown their hats up in the air for my father and not kept some of the things that the British left behind, like the trains and the courts and elections. She found notes for all the speeches on O'Connell Street, written in tiny handwriting on cards. But they made no sense. There were notes about laziness and blindness and immoral practices. Notes about greediness and money lending. Notes about bringing horses to the water and making them drink. About biting the hand that feeds you and rubbing salt into the wounds. There were notes about how silly it was to live in Ireland and not be Irish, notes about people still calling themselves British. People calling themselves Jewish, too. Notes about Jewish people giving Irish people carpets and making them pay for the rest of their lives. Leaflets about an international conspiracy of Jewish bankers. One of the cards quoted a man named Belloc, asking if anybody had ever heard of such a thing as an Irish Jew. And then my mother found the newspaper that Gearóid was talking about. It was so old it was gone yellow and almost brown. The headline on the front page said: 'Ireland's Jewish problem'. The date on the top was 1946. There was a note in handwriting, too, from Gearóid saying: 'doesn't go far enough'.

When you're small you know nothing and when you grow up there are things you don't want to know. I don't want anyone to know that my father wanted Jewish people in Ireland to speak Irish and do Irish dancing like everyone else. I don't want people to know that he was foaming at the mouth. That the Irish language might be a killer language, too, like English and German. That my father believes you can only kill or be killed. It's the hardest thing to say that you're wrong.

One day when I was coming home from school I saw my father in the street. He was on his way home, too, buying a newspaper on O'Connell Street. He looked like a different man when he was outside, more like an ordinary Irishman going home from work, with his cap on and his briefcase in his right hand. I was standing beside a newspaper stand looking at all the books and the magazines. There was a book with a gun and a dead bird on the cover and I wanted to know what the story was inside. All the time the man was shouting 'Herald-ah-Press', with the newspapers under his arm. There was an echo coming from across the street where another man was doing the same thing, shouting 'Herald-ah-Press' back. When somebody asked for a paper, the man quickly took one out from the bundle under his arm and held his hand out flat so that people could give him the money. They could take the paper out of his fingers and walk away home quickly without wasting any time. The man's hand was black from the papers and there were black marks on his face.

Then I heard my father speaking right beside me. I got a fright because I thought he was coming to get me, but he was just asking for the *Evening Press*. He didn't know I was there at all. I looked up and saw him standing beside me, putting the money into the man's hand. I knew it was my father's soft Cork accent. It was my father's briefcase and I even knew what was inside – his flask and his rain mac and his book on Stalingrad, with the train ticket halfway through to show how much he had left to read.

'Vati,' I said. 'It's me.'

I waited for him to look down, but he didn't see me. He was thinking of all the things he had not finished yet and all the things he was still going to do when he got the time. He put the paper under his arm and walked away. I wanted to run after him as if he was my father. I wanted to tug him by the sleeve of his coat. I wanted him to talk to me about things like films or football. But he didn't know anything about that. And, anyway, I would have to pretend he was my friend and go all the way home on the train with him. We would have to talk Irish together, as if there was no other language in the world. Everybody would look at us. They would know that we were homeless and had nowhere to go, because we lost the language war. They would know that we were still locked in the wardrobe and didn't know any better.

I didn't move. I didn't run after him. I knew I was doing the same thing as he had done to his own father, the sailor. I stood still and heard the brakes of the buses screeching. I saw the people in a long queue waiting. I saw the windows of the buses steamed up and the places where people rubbed a circle clear to look out. I heard the man shouting 'Herald-ah-Press' and the echo still coming back across the street over the traffic. I watched my father walking away towards the train station like one of the ordinary people of Dublin. I watched his limp and his briefcase swinging, as if I had never seen him before in my life.

Twenty-seven

One day a man put a bomb in a briefcase and went out to work, like my father. He looked at his watch because he had an important meeting to go to and he wanted to be there on time. It was a hot day and he brought a clean shirt with him as well. Before the meeting, he asked everybody to wait a few minutes so he could change his shirt first. They told him to hurry up and waited outside while he went into a room and clicked open the briefcase with the bomb inside instead of his lunch and his flask. He took out the shirt and started getting the bomb ready straightaway. It was two bombs really, but he could only fix the fuse on one of them, because he had been injured in the war and only had one arm, like Mr Smyth in the vegetable shop. He could only see with one eye, too, because there was a patch over the other one, but he was not afraid to die and he took out a small set of pliers and did his best. Everybody knows how long it takes to change your shirt, even if you only have one arm. He was taking so long that somebody came to the door to ask what was keeping him and then his hand started shaking, so he decided, in the end, that one of the bombs would be more than enough. He changed his shirt quickly and came out again with the briefcase in his hand. The empty sleeve of the missing arm was tucked into the pocket of his jacket, like Mr Smyth. He didn't have to shake hands with anyone and nobody knew what he was thinking either, because he was like Onkel Ted and not afraid of silence. They didn't know that there was a bomb inside the briefcase for Germany, and when he got to the meeting where they were all standing around a table and looking at the map of the world, he gave the briefcase to another man and told him to put it as close to Hitler as possible. Then he walked away and heard the explosion right behind him. He thought Hitler was dead and everybody was free again, but that was a big mistake because, after all that trouble, Hitler wasn't even hurt and came out with only a bit of dust on his uniform.

'Make sure of it,' my mother says. 'For God's sake, don't just walk away and leave it to somebody else.'

The man who planted the bomb was arrested in Berlin very shortly afterwards. His name was Claus Schenk Graf von Stauffenberg and he was immediately taken out into a square to be executed by firing squad, along with some of the people who were on his side. Later on, his brother and all his friends were arrested, too, and put on trial for planning a puppet show against Hitler. They were put to death in a very cruel way and their children were taken away and given new names so they would forget who they were. One of the boys wrote his real name on the inside of his lederhosen, but they were all sent to a special school so that they would grow up as Nazis, and none of the puppets would ever try and speak against Hitler again.

Afterwards, Hitler went on the radio to tell everyone in the world that he was alive and still had two eyes and two ears and two of everything. In case there was a mistake and some people might not have heard the radio, they collected everyone together in halls and theatres and schools to tell them that Hitler never felt better. My mother says that she was on a platform waiting for a train when she heard the news that he was not dead yet and the war was still on. Her sister Marianne was working in Salzburg and had to go to a big meeting in the opera house to be told what happened, as if they were about to hear some music. When everybody was sitting down in their seats and all the coughing and whispering stopped, an SS man came out on stage to make a speech. He said there was some bad news. Somebody had betrayed Germany and tried to kill Hitler with a bomb. But there was nothing to worry about, he said, because Hitler was still alive and could never be killed, not even by a bomb in the same room. Then Marianne stood up.

'*Leider*,' she said out loud for everyone to hear. 'What a pity.'

The audience turned around to look at her standing up with her arms folded against the Nazis. Everybody in the whole opera house was waiting for her to be taken away and maybe even executed immediately. But then at the last minute, an older woman she had never seen before stood up beside her and spoke very calmly.

'*Ja, leider*,' the woman said. 'Yes, what a pity such a thing can happen.'

Then everybody thought it was just a mistake. Maybe Marianne wasn't a woman against Hitler with her arms folded, but a woman so much for Hitler that she was not afraid to stand up and say it out loud. Before Marianne could say anything more, before she could say that she really wished Hitler had been killed by the bomb and that his two of everything had been blown to bits, the woman pulled her back down quickly into the seat and told her to stop trying to get herself killed.

My mother says it's hard to tell that story, even it it's

true. Nobody will believe it any more, because lots of people made up things like that after the war. Everybody wanted to prove they were against the Nazis and never said a word against Jewish people in their lives and even saved lots of them from being killed. If all the stories were true, then how come Hitler was alive for so long and there weren't more Jewish people found all over Germany when the war was over. People who are guilty usually point the finger. It's the people who really were against the Nazis who don't want to boast about it. Most of the people who were against the Nazis disappeared and can't speak for themselves.

In the book she got from Onkel Ted about Eichmann, there is a story about a German man who helped the Jews in Poland. He gave them guns against his own country, against Germany. When the Nazis found out what he was doing, they killed him straightaway. And afterwards he was forgotten by everybody because what he did was not enough to stop what happened in the end. He might as well not have bothered. Nobody wanted to know. All the books and films are about the bad people, my mother says, not the good people. It was the same with the man who changed his shirt and brought the bomb in a briefcase to meet Hitler. He was forgotten and he might as well not have bothered either, because so many people were murdered by the Nazis that it's hard to think of anything else. He was not very good at making a bomb, because he was not very good at hating people. And it's hard to start boasting about somebody who was not very good at killing Hitler or giving away guns against the Nazis or standing up with your arms crossed and saying it was a pity Hitler wasn't dead.

There was fog everywhere outside that day. I looked

out the window of my mother and father's bedroom and I thought it was like net curtains hanging down. The fog was waving a little. I could hardly see the houses across the street. I was listening to my mother and I didn't know what country I was in any more. She was feeding the new baby on the bed, my small brother, Ciarán. When there was nothing more to say and she was finished telling about the bomb for Germany, we just listened to the foghorn for a long time and said nothing. Ciarán was smiling and shaking his head from side to side, trying to make himself dizzy and drunk. Ita and Bríd were playing with him and sometimes copying the voice of the foghorn until Ciarán laughed. Mrs Robinson pulled back her net curtains and looked out across the street at me and I waved, but she couldn't see through the fog. She lets us watch the television in her house sometimes and I know what her house smells like. Everybody's house has a different smell and some smells make you feel lonely and other smells make you feel like you're at home. Miss Tarleton's house smells like a greenhouse and boiling cabbage, and Miss Hosford's house smells like a chemist. Mrs McSweeney's house smells like toffee and shoe polish. The Miss Doyles' flat upstairs always smells of beans on toast. The Miss Ryans' house smells like washing and ironing and a bit of liquorice mixed in, and Miss Brown's house smells like the mixture of soap and cigarette smoke and the smell you get at the back of the radio when it's been on for a while. I don't know what makes the smell of each house so different, but our house smells of being happy and afraid. Our friend Noel's house smells like nobody ever gets angry because his father is a doctor and his mother never raises her voice and they have a dog. Tante Roseleen's house smells of red lemonade and the place where Onkel Ted lives smells like a different country, like the house with the yellow door and the custard, the place where you always feel homesick.

My mother said we would go down to find the foghorn when she was ready. We waited outside and you could not see the end of the street, only up to number six. She cleaned all the crumbs and bits of mushy biscuits out from the bottom of the pram and when she came out Ciarán was sitting up with a serious face and a hat on over his ears that has a big furry bobble on top. We walked down to the sea with Ita and Bríd holding on to the pram as if they were driving it. The cars and the buses had their lights on, even though it was daytime, and sometimes you could only see the yellow lights like a ghost coming through the fog. Everybody was travelling so slowly that you thought they were afraid of where they were going and what they might find in the fog.

It was like a new fog country where everybody was quiet and saying nothing. There were no more far away countries like Germany or England or America, because you could not even look out across the sea. There were no waves at all and the ceiling was very low. It was like a small room with net curtains. Like a bathroom with the bath filling up and seagulls floating on top and the mirror steamed up and funny voices echoing around you. When we looked back we could not even see the road or the cars or any houses either. Nothing was moving. Not even a piece of paper. The trees were pretending to be dead and the foghorn kept saying the same word all the time.

'Roooooom . . .' You could hear the word very clearly now. The same word all the time, as if it had only one word to say.

'Roooooom,' we shouted back. 'Room the roooooom.'

I ran across the green park in front of the sea until my

mother and all my brothers and sisters disappeared behind me. I heard them calling and I walked back slowly, like a ghost walking out of the fog. My mother looked different. I thought it was somebody else and I had come back to a different place. She had her back turned, looking out towards the sea, like somebody from a different country that I didn't know the name of and couldn't talk to. There was a ship coming in very slowly with the lights on. There was no wind and no language, and the only word left was the word 'room'. She stood at the blue railings with the brown rust, like an ordinary German woman.

We walked on towards the harbour and the foghorn kept getting louder and louder. We saw the lighthouse coming closer, too, and the light coming around every few seconds to point the finger at us through the fog. My mother said it was like a man carrying a yellow lantern. Bríd was afraid to go any further, so my mother changed her mind and said it was just the lighthouse winking at us. We counted the time in between each word from the foghorn and in between each wink from the lighthouse. We came to the place where you can shout into a hole in the wall and hear the echo. 'Jaysus, what the Jaysus,' Franz shouted and everybody else had to do it after him in a line, except my mother. 'Room the room and Jaysus what the Jaysus and down you bully belly,' we shouted. We walked all the way out along the pier and my mother said we had to be careful not to walk straight off the end into the sea.

We came to the place where there was a granite monument for the lifeboat men who were drowned while trying to rescue people from a ship, not very far away from the land. My mother said it was very sad to think of them getting up on a stormy night and leaving the house and saying they would be back soon. We stood looking at the names of the men written up and thought of them going down into the dark water so close to home without saying goodbye to anyone. When we came to the place with the wind gauge on top, the cups were stuck and not even moving at all, just waiting for the wind to come back so it could start spinning again. Any of the boats we could see in the harbour were not moving very much either and the foghorn was talking so loud that we could not say a word any more. Bríd and Ita had their hands over their ears and we could not go any closer because Ciarán started crying. We sat down on a blue bench and my mother took out a bar of chocolate. There was nobody else on the pier. We were like the last family in Ireland, listening to the silver paper and waiting for the chocolate to be shared out.

If Hitler had been killed, then everybody would have said it was a good bomb, a bomb for Germany. Instead, they said the people who planned the puppet show against the Nazis were liars and betrayers. They were bad Germans who were not very good at hating people. It was a bad bomb, they said, a bomb against Germany and they might as well not have bothered, because nobody would even remember it. Sometimes a good bomb can be a bad bomb and sometimes a bad bomb can be a good bomb. But this was a useless bomb and everybody had to wait until all the good bombs started falling on Germany. Then the trains were on fire and the streets were full of people running. That was near the end of the black and white film that my mother was in. She had to work for the German army like her sister Marianne. Her other sisters didn't have to, my mother says, because they already had children and Hitler didn't want mothers fighting in the war. That was the time when all the good bombs were falling on the cities and people were burned alive in their sleep, to make sure they learned how to hate the Nazis.

After the bomb that didn't even hurt Hitler, Marianne thought somebody was following her all the time. She was afraid that what she said in the opera house put her in trouble and that everybody knew she was against the Nazis. When she walked through the streets of Salzburg she sometimes had to look around and check to make sure that nobody was behind her. Sometimes they're after you because they think you're a Nazi and you feel guilty and you can't trust yourself any more. And then one day on her way home from work, she found out who was after her. It was the woman who stood up in the opera house and stopped her from killing herself.

'*Leider*,' the woman said and smiled.

My mother says everybody was afraid to smile and afraid to speak about things that didn't have to do with getting enough food and making sure that everybody in your family was safe from the bombs. The woman started talking about where to get butter and where to get eggs and how difficult it was to make a good cake these days. Marianne said it was impossible to get any meat at all. The woman was very friendly and asked her where she lived. Marianne told her that she lived on the Mönchberg, up high, the last house before the castle. So then the woman said how nice it must be to live up there on the mountain, away from everything, with clean air and no noise and plenty of tranquillity. They kept talking for a while, because nobody was afraid of talking about good air and bad lungs and living away from other people coughing.

'It would be a great place for a guest house up there,' the woman said.

Marianne said she had never dreamed of it. She was

expecting a baby and working every day with the German army and looking after her mother-in-law, too, who was very old. She was not afraid of work, but her husband was away in the war and she didn't know where she would get the food for the guests. And not only that, she didn't think anyone could afford to go on holidays any more.

'I know people with bad lungs,' the woman said. 'They would love it up there.'

'It's a long way up,' Marianne said, 'without a car.'

But that would even be doing them a favour, the woman said. It would be good for them to get the air even as they were walking up. And that's how Tante Marianne got the idea to open a guest house, my mother says. That's how people started coming to visit her from all over the place for clean air and tranquillity, that's how she has a name for keeping one of the most beautiful guest houses in all of Austria today, a place that has a long waiting list and you would never hear about from the tourist board, only by word of mouth.

It was thanks to the man with one arm and one eye who put the bomb in a briefcase. The bad bomb was good for one thing at least. It started a guest house on the Mönchberg where there never had been one before. It was strange that nobody had thought of it already, my mother says. It didn't start as a big business, not like a big hotel. Just one guest at a time, or two at the most. They could stay up there and breathe in deeply and pretend that there was no war on at all.

Tante Marianne didn't have to think about it for long, my mother says. She went home and got the place ready. And some days later, the first of the guests arrived, a Jewish woman who had no name and no face and no address. She didn't stay for long, only two or three days at a time, and then she moved on again to another house somewhere else.

My mother says you can't boast about things like that. You can say it to yourself. You can be proud that somebody had courage. But you can't go around telling the whole world your aunt helped to harbour Jewish people and made a safe haven out of her house on the Mönchberg. You have to remember all the people who were not saved, too. You have to remember all the voices speaking from the graves. I want to tell everybody that I had an aunt who was not afraid to lose and stood up against the killing. I want to run out and tell the whole world that she helped people to breathe in Germany.

'Maybe they won't believe me,' I say.

My mother says you know when something is true sometimes by the way nobody is boasting about it. Nobody is trying to turn it into a big story on the radio and asking people to clap. You know it's true that Tante Marianne kept the silent negative in her head until she could do something about it, because nobody is talking about it much. Because it's not written about in any newspaper.

The first Jewish woman to visit the guest house was not killed by the Nazis and went to America after the war. She never came back. But she told people what a wonderful guest house she stayed in on the Mönchberg. And later on, when other Jewish people like Ernst Rathenau started coming back from America after the war, they went straight to the Mönchberg on their holidays, as if there was no other place in the whole of Austria that had clean air. They came back to the guest house again and again, year after year, and they brought other famous people with them who were also against the Nazis, like the painter Oskar Kokoschka and the sculptor Giacomo Manzú and the singer Elisabeth

Schwarzkopf. You know it's true because why else would a Jewish man named Ernst Rathenau bring friends like that all the way up to the Mönchberg just for the air. And why would Ernst Rathenau, the cousin of Walther Rathenau who was assassinated by the Nazis before the war even started, come back from America and go straight up to visit a German woman who had lost her husband in the war? Marianne never heard from her husband Angelo again, but she had one daughter named Christiane. Ernst Rathenau even paid for Christiane to go all the way through university and become a doctor. Because Tante Marianne once did a favour to Jewish people and now they were paying her back.

My mother says you can only really be brave if you know you will lose. And the silent negative is not like any other silence either, because one day you will say what you're thinking out loud with your arms folded, like Marianne. You can't be afraid of saying the opposite, even if you look like a fool and everybody thinks you're in the wrong country, speaking the wrong language. Everybody thought the man with the bomb in the briefcase was an idiot and they only wanted to laugh at him. And Tante Marianne must have looked like a fool standing up in the opera house in Salzburg, trying to get herself killed and saying what a pity Hitler wasn't dead yet.

My mother remembers the steam from the trains like fog on the platform. She remembers the sound of the whistle echoing through the station. She remembers seeing people crying all over Germany. She shows me the photographs of cities in Germany that were bombed. She heard once of a woman carrying her dead child with her in a suitcase. Sometimes you can't think of anything else but the people you know. Sometimes people are afraid to look any further than their own family. That's when you have to be brave.

When the winter came, my mother was told to go to

Hamburg, to join a big camp full of women. From there they were sent mostly to the east to fight with the German troops. People were saying that it made no sense to go to the east because the war was lost already. Some people got a chance to go home one more time to say goodbye to their family as if they were never going to come back. My mother got letters from Tante Marianne asking for food and she wrote back to say that she would do her best. But it was nearly impossible to find anything, unless you were with the army going out to the war. My mother managed to get a bucket full of sauerkraut and instead of going back home to Kempen, she decided to try to get to Salzburg instead. She asked for a ticket to a different town called Kempten which sounds the same, and isn't in the Rhineland at all, but somewhere in Bavaria. She carried the last bucket of sauerkraut with her all the way and it was snowing heavily when she arrived to deliver it.

Nobody wanted to go back to the war. My mother says she wanted to stay on the Mönchberg and hide until it was all over. She thought of staying and helping Marianne, because she was expecting her baby and had a husband in the war and a mother-in-law who was ill. But then she would only have to eat some of the sauerkraut that she had brought and that would make no sense any more. Marianne would be worse off. So at least, my mother says, she helped her with the washing before she left. She got all the clothes and the sheets together and boiled up lots of hot water. There was enough soap and starch to do it properly, and because it was so cold outside they dried everything inside. My mother hoped it would all take longer. She hoped it would take so long that somebody would say on the radio that the war was over. When the sheets were dry, my mother helped to iron them until they were like new.

She laughed and helped Marianne to fold them together, taking one corner in each hand and dancing towards the middle like Irish dancing. The smell of the laundry made my mother think that she was a little girl again. She didn't want the dancing with the sheets to stop. It was only when it was over and all the washing was finished that my mother realised how many sheets there were. She counted them in her head and thought there were too many just for three women.

'Are you thinking of starting a guest house?' she asked, but that was a joke and Marianne didn't know how to answer. They didn't know how to talk about it. Everybody was afraid to say anything that didn't have to do with things like washing and ironing. And then it was time for my mother to leave. They looked at each other for a long time and said *ja, ja, ja* and *nein, nein, nein*, until my mother put on her coat and stepped out into the snow.

The walk down the Mönchberg was harder than the walk up, she says. It was icy and you had to hold on to the fence sometimes to make sure you didn't slip and break your teeth. At the station, the guards checked her papers and she was in trouble because she was very late and should have been in Hamburg ages ago. She was told to take the next train to Nuremberg, but there she was arrested and taken into a police station. They accused her of not following orders like everyone else in Germany. They asked lots of questions and she said she was just trying to bring some food to her sister who had a husband in the war and mother-in-law who was sick. They didn't believe her. They didn't think she looked eager enough to go back to the war. They said she was a deserter. *Fahnenflucht*, they called it, running away from the flag. They put her on a train to the east and locked the carriage door. They didn't tell her where she was going, but she knew it was to the east, that's all. She was locked in the carriage with a young soldier who was not much older than fourteen, my mother says, and he was chained to the seat by his ankles.

The fog is starting to disappear, but the foghorn keeps going just in case. It has begun to rain a bit, just a few drops on the window. It's dark now, but it's clear enough to see across the gardens to the next street. From my bedroom I can see the light and the branches in front of it. There is a bit of a breeze and the branches are dancing across the wall behind me and across my face, too. If anyone saw me, they would think there was something wrong with me. They would see spots all over my face from the raindrops on the glass. They would see a speckled face and say that I was diseased. Nobody would want to touch me. The foghorn is still going, but it sounds more tired, as if it's been saying the same word all day and now it's getting fed up with it. In my room I have some books that my mother gave me and that Onkel Ted gave her. I have some books about Irish history and some magazines that my father gave me, too, about geography, with stories about people in other countries like South Africa and Tibet that are still not free. Sometimes I read them and sometimes I just look at the pictures because I don't like any more words. I just want the one word from the foghorn to go to sleep with. 'Roooooom . . .'

I looked at the books and noticed that the picture of the man who put the bomb in a briefcase for Germany looked a bit like the picture of the man who started the Easter Rising for Ireland. I had to bend the books a little bit, but when I put the pictures together they looked alike. And they were facing each other, as if they were talking. Patrick Pearse was looking to the right and Claus Schenk Graf von

Stauffenberg was looking to the left. They seemed not to be even surprised to be in the same room together. Patrick was saying to Claus that he thought he was in Germany. Claus looked back over and said he was only here in Ireland for a short visit. There was a lot of trouble in Germany and he wanted to know if anyone in Ireland could help. He heard that the Irish were good at saying the opposite. And Patrick Pearse said he was having a lot of trouble with the British at the moment, and the only thing to do was to make a sacrifice. You can't be afraid of looking stupid.

They looked like brothers. Claus and Patrick. I sat up in bed and held the two photographs together. Claus was planning a puppet show against the Nazis and Patrick was planning a puppet show against the British. Claus knew that people might laugh at him in Germany and Patrick knew that people would surely laugh at him in Ireland. They both knew that people would say they might as well not have bothered. Patrick said that Ireland unfree shall never be at peace and Claus said long live the real Germany. Before they had to leave, they wondered if there was time to go for a walk down to the sea. Or maybe even a drink in the Eagle House. But they were in a hurry and there was no time to waste. They were not sure their plans would work either, because they were not very good at hating anyone yet. But they were not afraid to lose. They were not afraid of being put up against the wall and executed. And that's what happened to both of them in the end in different countries for the same reason. They met for one last time in my room with the foghorn still going outside. They shook hands and said 'Down you bully belly.' They laughed because they were not afraid to be Irish and not afraid to be German. I told them that Tante Marianne was going to save Jewish people who could not breathe very well and that my father was going to help people who wanted to breathe in Irish. When they were gone and the light was out, I lay back and listened to the foghorn going on and on, saying the same word over and over again until it was hoarse and had no voice any more.

Twenty-eight

Everything keeps happening again. Now I'm going down to the seafront and holding my little brother Ciarán's hand. We're going to look at the sea and throw stones at the big bully waves. I help him to walk on the wall and hold his hand to make sure he doesn't fall. He sings the same song that Franz sang when we were small and we didn't know any better. He says good morning to everyone that we pass by in English and sings 'walk on the wall, walk on the wall . . .' I'm Ciarán's big brother now, so I have to make sure he doesn't fall off and break his nose.

The dog is still there every day but he doesn't bark as much any more. Sometimes he just sits on the steps and says nothing, as if he's fed up fighting and he knows there's no point in trying to stop the waves. He still keeps an eye on them and maybe he's waiting for a big one, or waiting for somebody else to come and throw stones and then he'll start again, barking as much as ever before. He still has no name and belongs to nobody and follows anyone who pretends to be his friend for life. So we decided that he would belong to us from now on. We clicked and he came after us. We had a dog now that would protect us and we gave him a name, Cú na mara, which is the Irish for seadog. But that was too long so we tried Wasserbeisser instead, water-biter. But that was even harder, so in the end we just called him nothing and said: 'Here boy.' Every time we looked back he was still there. Even when we went into a shop to buy chewing gum and an ice pop for Ciarán, he stayed outside and waited. But then we met a gang coming towards us.

'Hey Eichmann,' one of them shouted.

They were not scared of the dog at all. They came across the street and asked if I had any cigarettes. I told them I didn't smoke yet. They called me a Kraut and wanted the chewing gum instead. They started kicking me and Ciarán was crying. The dog said nothing, but there was a man working in a garden nearby who stood up and told them to stop.

'Leave them alone,' the man said. 'Off you go about your business.'

They didn't have any business because they were the fist people. Instead, they tried to pretend that we were the best of friends. One of them put his arm around me and whispered into my ear.

'Listen, Eichmann. We're not finished with you.'

Then they walked away, laughing and eating the chewing gum that I bought. One of them whistled and the dog followed them instead of us. The man in the garden saved us and we were lucky. We were free to go home now, but I knew that wasn't the end. I know they're still after me.

Everything is happening again. My mother cuts out a picture from the newspapers of a man who set himself on fire because he couldn't live in the wrong country. She puts it into her diary, as well as pictures of Russian tanks on the streets of Prague. She remembers Prague with German troops. A new war started in Vietnam and my mother was cutting out pictures of a new kind of bomb there. She also has a picture of a black man named Martin Luther King who was assassinated in America. Now they want civil rights in Northern Ireland, too, and she cuts out pictures of people with placards and blood running down their faces. Some people even had to leave their houses because they were in the wrong country and had no names and no faces any more. So now the diary is full of pictures of Russian troops in Czechoslovakia and British troops in Northern Ireland and American troops in Vietnam. My mother says it's hard to believe how anyone thinks they can keep people quiet that way. Homesick people carry anger with them in their suitcases. And that's the most dangerous thing in the world, suitcases full of helpless, homesick anger.

In school, some of the boys made an effigy of Nelson's Pillar out of cardboard and blew it up on O'Connell Street with sodium chlorate and sugar. They made a little speech called 'Up the Republic'. The fuse was coming out the door where you used to go up the winding stairs to look out over the city. They lit it and there was an explosion that knocked the toy soldier with the sword off the top and set the whole thing on fire. Everybody going home from work in Dublin thought things were happening again. On the radio you can hear a song about people with the foggy dew in their eyes and another song called 'Up went Nelson'. On TV you can see a man in Northern Ireland foaming at the mouth about a spider inviting the fly into the parlour. You can see people marching with big drums that make so much noise none of the other puppets can speak. A boy at school told me that his mother came from Derry and she had her Holy Communion dress torn when she was a girl and never forgot it.

Up in the north the Catholics are called Fenians and the Protestants are called Prods. The Fenians are afraid to be British and the Prods are afraid to be Irish because they can't breathe very well in Ireland. People call each other names because they want to kill each other. People learn how to hate each other because they're afraid of dying out. In school they call you a Jew if you don't have any chewing gum to share. The British are called Brits and the Irish are called Paddies and the Germans are called Krauts and that's worse than being either British or Irish, or both together. They still call us bloody Krauts even though we're bloody Paddies. Sometimes they tell us to fuck off back to where we came from, but that doesn't make any sense because we come from Ireland. One day they called Franz a fuckin' Jew Nazi and held him against the railings of the Garden of Remembrance. He had no chewing gum, so they banged his head until it started bleeding. Brother Kinsella punished them all for it, including Franz who did nothing, and everybody was laughing about that for a long time, punishing the guilty and the innocent together. Brother Kinsella said it was the only way to stop things happening again, to hit the victims and the perpetrators equally.

My friend at school has stopped being my friend. I like him. I like the way he looks and the way he talks. And sometimes I want to be him instead of myself. He never called me names, but one day he stopped talking to me. He just walks past me in school without a word. Maybe he's punishing the innocent and the guilty, too, because he tells everybody that the Nazis turned people into soap and you can't deny that. He won't be my friend for life any more because he thinks I'm going to make chairs out of people's bones and I can't deny that either, even though I haven't done it yet. I know I can't have friends for life. It's better to be on my own from now on, because they'll find out sooner or later what I've done.

At home my mother wants to stop things happening

again. She says we're not the fist people, so one day she took all the sticks from the greenhouse and broke them over her knee in the kitchen until they were all in bits and my father had nothing to hit us with any more. He was still able to smack the rubber gloves into your face and give you the foggy dew. And he was able to throw pots, too, because he always did the washing up. But he was not able to take me up the stairs and pray that he was doing the right thing for Ireland, so then I started arguing with him at the table until he was blinking and I could see myself twice in his glasses. I like giving the wrong answers. One day, my father said there was nothing outside infinity. He said the universe was like a cardboard box with God sitting outside surrounded by light, but I wanted to know if maybe God was sitting inside another cardboard box with the light on, and how could anyone be sure how many cardboard boxes there are? My mother says I was driving him mad with wrong answers. He knew there were no sticks left, but there was a bowl of *Apfelkompot* on the table instead. He looked at it for a minute. Then he picked it up and threw it over my head. It was still warm. I felt it running down my face into the collar of my shirt. But I was smiling, because I knew that my father was losing the language war. My mother cleared everything up and tried not to laugh. She said you had to have an imagination to throw *Apfelkompot* over somebody's head and maybe she should make it more often if we liked it so much. But later on she told me never push people into a corner. She says there's too much fighting in our house and how can Ireland ever be at peace if we go on like this.

One day I ran away from home with another boy from school called Evil. We stayed out all night until it started raining and the only place we could find to shelter in the whole city was in the cab of a truck. It was so cold in the truck that we were shivering. In the morning we went into a church to get warm, and I knew that I never wanted to be homeless again. Homeless people are always hunched up with the cold and warm people stand up straight. I knew there was a boy living rough under the Top Hat. There's a dance hall called the Top Hat Ballroom that we pass on our way to school. It had a huge black top hat on the roof until it was blown off in a storm one night and the hat fell down into the laneway beside the dance hall. Now there's a homeless boy living under it and I don't want to be like him, hunched up with no language to go home to.

Instead, I went home and told my father that I would kill him. I said I would not speak any dying language any more, only killer languages, and then I asked him how would he like to be killed by his own son. He took off his glasses and told me to go ahead. But then I did nothing. I just said what they say in school when they're afraid. I said it wasn't worth wasting my energy. In any case, my mother said I would have nowhere to go home to if I did something like that. Once you kill somebody, you can never go back. So now she tries to keep us away from each other in different parts of the house with at least one or two doors slammed between us. She helps me to run away. Sometimes she lets me stay out of school and go to the cinema where it's dark and nobody knows who I am. Then I talk to myself in English. I pretend that I'm not German or Irish at all. But one night my father found out and he came up to my room when I was already asleep. He started punching me in my sleep and I woke up with him foaming at the mouth and my mother pulling him back by the elbow and Franz standing at the door calling peace. My father had lost the language war and everybody knew it. My mother says the people who lose become ugly and helpless with anger. Nobody wants to be a loser. Nobody wants to be left in the train station with a suitcase full of helpless anger.

Sometimes I argue with my mother as well. I start twisting around all the things she said and making no sense out of them. I ask her why she was trying to bring me up to live under the Nazis. We have to behave as if the British are still in Ireland and the Nazis are still in Germany. I tell her the silent negative is useless. She can't argue with me any more. She has other children to look after as well, she says, and so I tell her that she had too many children. Then she looked at me for a long time and waited for a moment to search for what she wanted to say next.

'Maybe I should have skipped you,' she said.

Then I threw an egg at her. I picked it up and threatened her with it, but she pretended that she didn't care. Go ahead, she said. I didn't want to hurt her. I didn't know how to hate very well yet, so I threw it softly so that she could catch it without breaking it. And then she threw it back to me and I caught it as well. So from that day on we started throwing eggs to each other every day and catching them, until we laughed and nobody ever had so much fun with eggs before without eating them.

I stand alone at the seafront a lot. Sometimes I throw stones at the waves. Sometimes I just sit on one of the rocks and think I'm in the luckiest place in the world, with the blue sea out in front of me and the sun stinging me in the back. Sometimes I think of escaping away to another country where nobody knows where I came from. And sometimes I am trapped, full of helpless anger. Sometimes I still hate everything, even the dog that had no name and no owner. He just followed the fist people when he felt like it. He was a betrayer. One day I found him near the harbour so I pushed him in and told him to drown.

There was nobody around and nobody to see what I was doing. I threw stones at him because I was Eichmann. I was the most cruel person in the world. I smiled as I watched him trying to rescue himself. I laughed like the Nazis in the films and would not let him up the steps again. I knew I was punishing the innocent instead of the guilty. He swam away to try and rescue himself somewhere else. I watched him scraping against the side of the boats, but it was no good. He swam helplessly around in circles looking for anywhere to survive and not die out. He was getting tired and then I started feeling really sorry for him, because he was an old seadog now. I wasn't angry any more, just ashamed. I said this was the worst thing I ever did in my life and I tried to save him. I ran over to the next steps and called him, but he wouldn't trust me any more and I could never trust myself again either. I was one of the fist people now. I didn't know any better. The dog had his mouth open, trying to get air and not drink any more of the seawater. He was starting to go down under and I couldn't look any more. I had to run away. I was sick of what I had done and I knew that I would never have any friends. My knees were shaking and I wanted to disappear and drown myself as well. I was so sick of what I had done that I ran home and scraped my hand on the wall so the skin came off and there were little black stones mixed in with the blood.

My father knows he's lost the language war because he's behaving more like other fathers now. He bought a television set and started watching programmes in English like the detective who pretends he knows nothing. He got a car, too, and buys petrol in English and even eats biscuits that are not made by my mother. Sometimes he looks like he's tired of fighting and tired of making sacrifices all his life, and he's sad because he might as well not have bothered. There's no point in keeping the waves back any more. He says he made mistakes. It's not easy to say that you lost, but he came to me one day and shook hands and said he wished he could start all over again because he would make different mistakes this time. Sometimes if you lose, everything is wrong. If you win, everything is right.

Then one day British soldiers shot people dead on the street in Derry. They had lost the language war, too, and shot straight into a crowd of people marching for civil rights. On television we saw a priest crouched down waving a white handkerchief and maybe the British people are afraid of dying out. My father watched it all on television and couldn't speak. He sat for a long time staring at all the things that happened in Ireland for hundreds of years and were happening all over again. Later he came upstairs and said he didn't want me to make the same mistakes again. He said he had never held a gun in his hand and there was no point in me doing it either. He said it was better to use the typewriter, because if you make mistakes, you can still correct them without killing anyone. I knew he wanted to make up for all the mistakes he made.

Onkel Ted came out and gave me a book called *Black Like Me*, about a man who changed his skin from white to black, just to see what it was like for other people. He said you have to be on the side of the losers, the people with bad lungs. You have to be with those who are homesick and can't breathe very well in Ireland. He said it makes no sense to hold a stone in your hand. A lot more people would be homeless if you speak the killer language. He said Ireland has more than one story. We are the German-Irish story. We are the English-Irish story, too. My father has one soft foot and one hard foot, one good ear and one bad ear, and we have one Irish foot and one German foot and a right arm in English. We are the brack children. Brack, homemade Irish bread with German raisins. We are the brack people and we don't just have one briefcase. We don't just have one language and one history. We sleep in German and we dream in Irish. We laugh in Irish and we cry in German. We are silent in German and we speak in English. We are the speckled people.

Twenty-nine

After that my father was killed by his own bees.

Every year in May the bees swarmed because they wanted a new place to live in, not just the same gardens and the same flowers and apple trees every time. Whenever there was a swarm, you could see it like a cloud in the air all around the house, with bees zigzagging like needles against the sky when you looked up. It was always a fine day, too, with the sun out and no rain. And they would never sting when they were swarming. My father said they were happiest when they were going off to find a new home because for them it was like going on their holidays to Connemara or Germany. You could stand underneath without any protection and not be afraid. You could watch the cloud until it started moving away from the house like a whirlwind. They would not go far at first, only up to a nearby tree where they would settle down and wait while the scouts went out to find a new address for them to live in. Then you still had a chance to catch them and bring them back before they emigrated and disappeared for ever. My father taught me how to do it. You could see the swarm like a black beard hanging in the tree and you could climb up with a straw skep and not be afraid to put it on top. You didn't need to have gloves on or anything. The bees would think it was a new home and move in. Either that or you could hold the skep underneath and shake the branch until the beard fell straight in. Then you put it on the ground and all the bees would settle down again. You had to be quick and calm at the same time. You had to do all this before the scouts came back with the new address and sometimes, when you thought you had caught them, the cloud would start swirling up in the air again and fly away over the roofs of the houses.

I was very good at catching the swarms when my father was out at work and he was good at making them move back into their old hives again as if it was a brand new home. But after a while the bees started getting very angry and they always wanted to go back to the country. My father said that maybe they were getting aggressive because of inbreeding. And one day, when he was out on the roof of the breakfast room checking the hives, they attacked him. I wasn't there to stop it. I wasn't there to do the sting-stopping trick with the tea towel and cracking the bees before they could do any harm. I was away, walking on my own all day, hanging around by the sea and thinking of going for a swim.

Nobody could stop what happened. My father was dressed for going on the moon with the cage around his head and the big gloves going up past his elbows. He was taking out the frames and trying to make sure they weren't thinking of running away again, so then the bees all went mad. They zigzagged all around him like an unhappy cloud. My mother knew there was something wrong so she closed all the windows and told everyone to stay inside. Maybe my father was not meant to be a beekeeper. Maybe he wasn't calm enough to be a father. Maybe the bees knew he was still fighting and thinking about the time when he was a boy and nobody liked him except for his mother. Maybe they could feel anger in the air from the time when Ireland was still under the British, or when Ireland was free and could remember nothing but being under the British. Maybe they could smell things like helpless anger, because they kept trying to kill him. And then one of them finally got in under the cage around his head and stung his ear.

My father thought he would never hear music again as long as he lived, so he began to panic and dropped the frame in his hands. The bees jumped up in the air like a black cat. They were humming like a furious engine now. He tried to get the bee out of his ear but they were already stinging the leather gloves. Every time he tried to stop them from getting under his cage, he was only letting more of them in. He nearly fell off the roof trying to beat them off. He shouted for help and climbed back in through the window to get away from them. My mother heard him calling and ran up the stairs with a towel, but there were bees all over the house by now. Everyone ran away to hide. Ita got into bed and covered herself up with the blankets and didn't come out again. Bríd took Ciarán into the bathroom to play with water and locked the door for ever. The whole house was full of bees. They were in every room, buzzing at the window, trying to sting anything they could find, soft things like curtains and pillows and coats that smelled like us.

My father was running through the hall with bees on his back and his arms. My mother was behind him trying to beat them off with the towel and getting stung herself as well. He was shouting and trying to get the cage off his head. They were both shouting, which is the worst thing of all because the bees know when you're not calm. That makes them even more aggressive. They stung him around his neck and close to his eyes and on his lip. They stung him inside his shirt, even under his arm, even in the other ear so that he couldn't hear anything any more. Then my mother just flung open the front door and ran out of the house, out on to the street, with the bees still following. They escaped from the house and left the front door wide open. She pulled my father across the road and waved at the cars passing by. Neighbours ran back into their houses because they were scared of bees and scared of the Irish language. In the end, a woman stopped her car to take them down to the hospital. But even then the bees got in with them and kept stinging my father. Even when he got into the hospital they came after him and kept stinging until he stopped fighting and couldn't say anything more. They were buzzing at the frosted glass of the hospital windows and around the neon lights. They were still trying to sting anything they could find, things like rubber tubes and plastic gloves. When the doctors and nurses started taking his clothes off they found bees underneath who were trying to sting him even though he was not moving any more. They found a bee right inside his ear. They counted 38 stings in all and that was more than anyone could live through with a bad heart.

When I came back I saw the front door open for anyone in the world to walk into our house. I knew there was something wrong because there was a hum in the hallway. Bees were at all the windows. They were dying on the floor and walking around in circles, making themselves dizzy. I knew there was something wrong because Ita was still under the bedclothes afraid to come out. Everybody was crying and you don't want your father to die. You still want to be friends with him, otherwise you won't like yourself very much either. I didn't want to have a father who was killed by his own bees before I could talk to him.

My father worked all his life with the ESB. He helped to bring electricity to lots of places in Ireland like Connemara and Mayo and the Aran Islands. It was called rural electrification. My father was responsible for all the wires hanging between the lamp-posts all around the country. He was respected with his long Irish name, the name that nobody could pronounce but that everybody remembered. And then he had one last job to do before he died, he had to buy some high tension cables in Germany. He was the only one who could speak German in the ESB, so he was sent over to get the best value. He visited factories and admired all the German inventions. He travelled all around the country and said the Germans were great people. And that's where he died. The bees followed him all the way and on the last day at Frankfurt Airport, when he was on his way back home again, they killed him. He was sitting down, ready to say goodbye to one of the men he was buying the cables from. Then he just fell over into the man's lap, stung to death.

The phone call came in the afternoon. My mother came out of the front room with shadows around her eyes. She walked around the house as if she was lost and didn't know where to go. His coffin came back to Ireland some days later. His suitcase, too, full of things that he had bought for us, presents from Germany to make up for all the mistakes.

I had seen other funerals before but I never thought it would be our funeral. At the church my mother looked so different. She's my mother, but when I saw her crying, she was a child again. She was thinking of all the things that happened in her life after she was nine years old and her own father died. Now she's an orphan again and everyone has to look after her. She was weak coming out of the church, so

Eileen and Tante Roseleen had to help her and hold her arms. There were lots of people outside the church that we didn't know. People shook hands with me that I never saw in my life before and I never knew my father had so many friends. Everybody was looking at us and whispering with the foggy dew in their eyes. People said there was nobody like my father left in Ireland now. They said he was the last person to be killed by his own bees and Irish people were only interested in things like cars and televisions from now on. Onkel Ted was there to help my mother into the black car for all the family because she had nowhere to go home to any more. It looked as if she had just arrived in Ireland and didn't know where she was.

After that it's sometimes hard to talk to my mother. She says she should have fought back earlier. She says she was trapped by my father and could not escape. If she had the choice she would still be born in Germany and she would still come to Ireland, but she would have changed things and made different mistakes this time. People sometimes come to visit her and ask her if there's anything they can do. Gearóid comes in his Volkswagen and his tweed suit, but she doesn't want to see him. Some of the neighbours invite her over but they don't always understand what she says in her German accent. Sometimes people come from Germany to visit and then the house fills up with the smell of cake again. But most of the time my mother prefers to sit in the front room and read books and write her diary, because that's your only friend for life. To my children, she starts off again. When you grow up I don't want you to say that you knew nothing.

My father is gone and our house is very quiet. The tall man came to take the bees away one day and there's nothing on the roof of the breakfast room now. My father's bee hat and his bee gloves are in the greenhouse. All the things in the house that belong to him are still there. Nothing has changed. His books are on the desk with a train ticket halfway through to let you know how much he has left to read. His tools are there in the *Kinderzimmer* and there is a dining-room cabinet waiting to be finished. Everybody is afraid to touch anything. Upstairs, his shirts and his Sunday suit are hanging in the wardrobe. I can walk out of the house now any time I like and go down to the seafront. There's nobody telling me what to do any more and what language to speak in. But sometimes I still think he's going to burst in the door any minute. I think he's back in the house and I can hear his voice full of anger.

You can inherit things like that. It's like a stone in your hand. I'm afraid that I'll have a limp like him. I'm afraid I might start sticking the tip of my tongue out the side of my mouth when I'm fixing something. I know I have to be different. I have to listen to different music and read different books. I have to pretend that I had no father. I have to go swimming a lot and dive underwater and stay down there as long as I can. I have to learn to hold my breath as long as I can and live underwater where there's no language.

I know they're still after me. One day when I was swimming on my own, they found me pretending that I was not a Nazi or an Irish speaker who was dying. They knew it was Eichmann gone swimming and diving underwater. There was a big gang this time and I couldn't run away. There was nobody else around either to save me. No gardener. No old man swimming with pink skin as if the water was not cold. It was Sunday morning with the bells ringing and rain coming. They started throwing stones at me, every time I came up for air. So then I had to come out of the water and they put me on trial.

I stood in the shed where you change. But I couldn't get dressed because they started kicking my clothes around. They laughed and asked me questions I couldn't answer. One of them had a knife and said he had ways of making me talk. They stood around, punching and kicking me to see if I was guilty or not.

I knew that was the reason why my mother came to Ireland in the first place. One day in the front room she told me that after the war she got a job in Wiesbaden with the American army. She worked in the de-nazification courts, she said, where they examined people to see if they were really Nazis or not. Before they could start working again and behaving like normal decent people, some of the Germans had to be put on trial and asked lots of questions to see what they had been up to in the war and if they had helped the Nazis. She had to make all the notes of what people said and then type them up afterwards. It was a good job and everybody said she was so lucky. Maybe she would even meet an American and get married. But one day, there was an old man before the court, a gynaecologist. He said he had no time for Hitler because he was only helping women with babies getting born. He said he didn't care if babies were German or not, they were all good babies to him. But they didn't believe him. In the end, a Jewish woman came home to Germany from England to speak up for him. She said he was always very friendly to her and that he helped her when it was difficult to have a baby. That should have settled everything, but afterwards when my mother was typing everything up, they came and asked her to change the words around. They wanted the Jewish woman to say he was always very angry and that he only wanted Nazi babies. But my mother couldn't. So then she wrote a letter to say that she would not work there any more. Everybody said she was mad giving up a great job like that with a flat in Wiesbaden and American food when everybody in Germany was hungry. But she could only think of the old gynaecologist sitting in court very quietly and not even trying to defend himself. He said he liked German music and German books, but that didn't make him hate other people. He was one of the last good men in Germany and they were trying to turn him into a Nazi.

She left her job and went away, on a pilgrimage to Ireland.

My mother says there are enough guilty people and we don't need to invent them. There are enough murderers left in the world today and we don't need to make up Nazis that didn't exist. And there's no point in turning the Nazis into big film stars either, because then everybody will be blind to all the other things that are going on now.

There's no point in telling any of that to the gang at the seafront. There's no point in saying that they're kicking the wrong person and that I'm not really Eichmann, that I was brought up to live against the Nazis and I don't want to kill anyone. There's no point in telling them that they're making a mistake and they don't know any better.

I had no cigarettes and no chewing gum to give them either, so then I thought the best thing was to try to be funny and Irish like everyone else. I tried to put on the slow grin that Nazis have in films. I stood up and shouted: '*Sieg Heil, Donner Messer Splitten, Himmel Blitzen.*' Some of them laughed a bit, but they didn't want me to start being their friend. They stood around, trying to decide how they would execute me. All I could do was stand under the shed and wait. There was a pool of water around my feet and I felt the cold stone under my heels. I tried to stop myself from shivering. There was rust on the blue railings and green seaweed on the rocks. There was a mist on the sea and the water was licking the steps, going up two steps and back down one, down two steps and back up three like a song. The seagulls were standing around on the rocks, just watching and listening, only one of them occasionally lifting his wings and screeching as if he was the judge.

I tried to talk to them. I tried to tell them my story but there was no point. I asked them did they not trust me? But they just laughed. And there was no point in trying to be innocent. My mother says you can only be innocent if you admit the guilt. You can only grow up if you accept the shame.

Then they started the execution. One of them kicked me so hard that I had to bend over. There was a black pain spreading up into my stomach and I thought I was going to get sick. I couldn't stop the foggy dew in my eyes, but I tried to look up as if Germans didn't feel any pain. One of them punched me in the face and I saw blood on my towel. I knew that they were learning to hate and that you're allowed to hate Germans. They wanted me to surrender.

I looked up to show that I was not afraid to be silent. And then I saw the dog. I nearly forgot about the execution when I saw the dog behind them, the dog that barks all day until he's hoarse. I couldn't believe it at first and I had to wipe my eyes to make sure. The dog with no name was coming down to bark at the sea as if nothing was wrong and he never drowned.

'Jaysus, what the Jaysus,' I said. 'It's the dog.'

They looked around as if I was trying to play a trick on

them and get away. They said all the Germans were gone mad because I was calling the dog over to save my life.

'It's the dog with no name,' I said again.

He didn't drown after all. He must have rescued himself. He must have got up the steps and shook the water off his back and forgotten it even happened, because he came right over to where we all were standing in the courtroom by the sea. The courtroom in the forty-foot gentlemen's bathing place. He started sniffing around my clothes and socks scattered on the ground. He came right over and sniffed at me, too. He didn't blame me for anything and I was able to pet him as if we were friends for life. I heard them laughing and saying that the Kraut has lost it completely now. I heard them saying they were going to execute me even more after that for being so stupid, but I didn't care and they could say it until they were hoarse and had no voice any more, because the dog was alive and I didn't kill him.

'Jaysus, what the Jaysus,' I kept saying. 'Jaysus what the Jaysus of a bully belly Jaysus.'

There was nothing they could do to hurt me now. So I picked up one of my shoes and threw it into the sea. It was the only thing I could think of doing, because I grew up being good at saying the opposite and giving the wrong answers. I was not afraid any more. Laugh at yourself and the world laughs with you. Execute yourself and nobody can touch you. I heard them say that I was out of my mind and the Nazis were mental. So I picked up the other shoe and threw it out as well, and then the dog with no name ran after it and started barking. My shoes were floating on top of the water and there was nothing they could do. They didn't know how to execute me any more. They couldn't touch me because the dog was alive and barking. He was trying to go down the steps and get my shoes back, barking and barking as if he never drowned.

On the way home I walked along the wall with the dog behind me. My shoes were squeaking all the way. There were white salt marks where they were already beginning to dry. The sun was starting to come through the mist and it was not going to rain after all. I looked back and saw the sun coming out. The water was so white and so full of bouncing light that I could see nothing at all. It made me want to close my eyes and sneeze. When I looked into the shadows under the trees it was so dark that I could see nothing there either. When you're small you know nothing. I know the sea is like a piece of silver paper in the sun. I can see people walking along the seafront with ice-cream cones. I can hear the bells and I'm not afraid any more of being German or Irish, or anywhere in between. Maybe your country is only a place you make up in your own mind. Something you dream about and sing about. Maybe it's not a place on the map at all, but just a story full of people you meet and places you visit, full of books and films you've been to. I'm not afraid of being homesick and having no language to live in. I don't have to be like anyone else. I'm walking on the wall and nobody can stop me.

Thirty

We're trying to go home now. We're still trying to find our way home, but sometimes it's hard to know where that is any more. My mother went back to Germany one more time after my father died, just to visit everyone there and see where she grew up. But she was lost. She couldn't recognise anything. Now she wants to find a place in Ireland that she can remember. She says we're going on a trip to find things. She makes a big cake and we pack our bags with sandwiches and rain macs and get up early in the morning for the bus. We travel around the country to see places she went to before she got married, when she came over to Ireland on a pilgrimage, when Ireland was a holy country, full of priests and donkeys with crosses on their backs.

We came to a town where there was a carnival, with lots of people and loudspeakers playing music on the main street. There were vans selling things and a stall where you could throw wooden rings around a bottle of whiskey and win it. You could smell sweet things like candy floss and sometimes a mixture of things like chips and vinegar and diesel from the trucks. We went on the big wheel and I saw my mother and Ciarán getting smaller, waving at us below on the ground. We sat down on a bench outside the town to have the last bit of cake, with the music from the carnival still coming up and down on the wind. Then it's great to see my mother laughing and laughing, because I threw an apple at her and she caught it. And when it was time to move on and she was trying to get up from the bench, we pushed her back down until she was laughing and laughing so much with tears in her eyes. How do we know if she's happy or sad? It was getting late and she started looking for the place she remembered. She wanted to find the house that she stayed in once when she was a pilgrim after the war, coming back from Station Island.

'It must be here,' she said again and again.

We walked for a long time and she kept seeing lots of thing that she remembered, like stone walls and fields full of cows. Sometimes the cows stopped chewing to look at us as if they were surprised to see us in Ireland, so far away from home. It was the summer and we kept walking to keep ahead of the flies. We passed a house with a dog barking. One time, my mother spoke to a man to ask directions and we knew we were on the right road again. We just had to walk around another corner and find a gate where you could see the mountains, my mother said, with the sun going down like holy pictures. She wanted to speak to the woman of the house again where she stayed and the rain was praying the rosary all night. But we never found it. The night came up right behind us. We searched until it got dark and the colour was gone from the land and we could not see a thing any more. You could only smell the hay and the cow dung. It was so dark that you could only see with your nose, my mother said. Maybe she got the wrong road or the wrong mountains in the distance. She said Ireland had changed a bit. Or else it only existed in your imagination.

'Maybe I dreamed it,' she said.

We could see the lights of the next town in the distance. My mother took out a cigarette because she was free to smoke after my father died. We stood on the road and watched her face lighting up with the match. We smelled the new smoke in the clean air and waited. She said she didn't know where to go from here. We were lost, but she laughed and it didn't matter.